THE DELETE™ APPROACH

Designing Errors for Learning and Teaching

THE DELETE™ APPROACH
Designing **Errors** for Learning and Teaching

MICHAEL CHOY

Tech Tree, Singapore

World Scientific

NEW JERSEY · LONDON · SINGAPORE · BEIJING · SHANGHAI · HONG KONG · TAIPEI · CHENNAI · TOKYO

Published by

World Scientific Publishing Co. Pte. Ltd.

5 Toh Tuck Link, Singapore 596224

USA office: 27 Warren Street, Suite 401-402, Hackensack, NJ 07601

UK office: 57 Shelton Street, Covent Garden, London WC2H 9HE

National Library Board, Singapore Cataloguing in Publication Data
Name(s): Choy, Michael, 1971–
Title: The delete approach : designing errors for learning and teaching / Michael Choy.
Description: Singapore : World Scientific Publishing Co. Pte. Ltd., 2024.
Identifier(s): ISBN 978-981-12-7806-8 (hardcover) |
   ISBN 978-981-12-7807-5 (ebook for institutions) |
   ISBN 978-981-12-7808-2 (ebook for individuals)
Subject(s): LCSH: Errors. | Learning. | Cognition.
Classification: DDC 153--dc23

British Library Cataloguing-in-Publication Data
A catalogue record for this book is available from the British Library.

Copyright © 2024 by Michael Choy Seng Kim

All rights reserved.

For any available supplementary material, please visit
https://www.worldscientific.com/worldscibooks/10.1142/13462#t=suppl

Desk Editor: Lai Ann

Typeset by Stallion Press
Email: enquiries@stallionpress.com

Preface

Through errors designed into the experience, learners uncover first principles, the boundaries to how and where rules operate, increase their mindfulness, develop metacognition and competences ... these being characteristics of expertise. The idea is to use errors to laser focus on developing critical competences, leading to expertise.

The parable of ants

Ants are always looking for food. They are social, determined, constantly mindful and alert, knowing when to press on and when to turn back, collecting cues (smell, vibrations, signs of enemy, including humans) so as to make an informed and just-in-time choice. Taking a wrong step or making a wrong turn can be a matter of life and death for the ant ... taking calculated risks is part of life for the ant ... it is always a toss-up between food (life) and death. What is commendable is its acute sense of danger at any point in time ... it is always ready to run, to flee at the first sign of danger. The point for us to learn is how can we, as professionals, adopt the same mindfulness, to switch constantly between risk and safety, between opportunity and flight.

The parable of humans

Humans are always looking for answers and solutions. They are social, determined, sometimes mindful and alert, can be confused and lost at times.

Preface

Typically, when humans realise that they have made an error, they seek to find the correct answer. It is instinctive. We like to use minimal time and energy, to reach our end goal. However, from the learning perspective, it is not desirable because there is a lot we can learn through our errors. At the very basic level, we learn how not to make these errors in the future (hopefully). With us making an error, it also signals that there could be other similar errors out there which we may commit in the future. While in the short term, we should try to cut our losses and find the correct answer or response quickly. However, in the long run, we are better off learning not to make similar errors so that we don't have to take this route again.

More importantly, such errors may be more expensive and carry greater consequences in the future. It is more time-consuming and unproductive if we fail to reflect and learn from our errors. If the reflection is sufficiently deep, we may uncover the first principles that govern the outcomes and that will unearth the true learning of the error-based approach. When we grasp the underpinning principles, these principles supercede the rules that we may follow unthinkingly and allow us to move flexibly and creatively within the space. While rules often restrict us, principles empower us to innovate and establish new ways of doing things.

Of course, there is a limit to how many errors we can commit in our lives. Hence, the better option is to intentionally learn from the errors that others made. This is basis of the DELETE approach. It is about designing errors (especially authentic ones) to help others reflect and prepare for future incidents and situations where such errors may arise. This is especially important in a world that has become more volatile, with shorter response time. Preparation has become even more critical if we seek to do well as an individual, as a business unit, as a family, as a country.

Contents

Preface   v

Introduction   xiii

Part 1 The Reasons for Designing Errors for Learning and Teaching (DELETE)   1

Chapter 1   What Are 'Errors'?   3

Chapter 2   Why Learn from Errors?   13
- a) Research on Error-Based Learning (vs. Errorless Learning) for Novices
- b) Error-Based Learning for Competent Learners
- c) Dreyfus (2004) Skill Acquisition Model
- d) Power to Build Metacognitive Competences

Chapter 3   How Do We Learn?   33
- a) Learning, Atmosphere, Production (LAMP) Model
- b) Three Dimensions of Learning Model (TDLM)
- c) Learner Agency in a VUCA World
- d) Trends in L&D
- e) Nano-Learning Cycle
- f) The Context for Use of Error-Based Approach in Learning and Decision-Making

Contents

Part 2 How DELETE™ (Designing Errors for Learning and Teaching) Works: The Error-Making Process 51

Chapter 4 Competencies and Beyond: Developing Proficiency and Expertise 53
- a) The Nature of Work in the 21st Century
- b) The Nature of Current Instructional Designs
- c) Issues with Predictable Instructional Designs

Chapter 5 Incorporating Variability and Unpredictability in Training to Develop Capabilities 61
- a) Using Errors to Generate Ambiguity and Unpredictability
- b) The Roles of Rules and Boundaries
- c) When Do We Need to Relearn?
- d) How Do We Design the Experience for Rapid Learning or Relearning?
- e) Developing Capabilities Through the DELETE Approach

Chapter 6 Locating the DELETE Approach Within the Curriculum Design Process 73
- a) What Is Curriculum Design?
- b) A Speed Bump for Professionals and Experts to Reflect
- c) Benefits of the DELETE Approach as an Instructional Design Tool

Part 3 The Process of Designing Errors for Learning and Teaching 85

Chapter 7 Examining the DELETE Approach as a Process 87
- a) The Error Process
- b) Points of Interjection and Intervention in the Error-Based Methodology
- c) Phases in Error-Making

Contents

Chapter 8   The Four Parameters in DELETE Approach   99
- a) Type of Errors
- b) Type of Tasks
- c) Engagement Process
- d) Type of Support

Part 4   **The DELETE Process: Designing Error, Task and the Engagement**   **113**

Chapter 9   Designing the Task   115

Chapter 10   Designing the Engagement and Review Process   131

Chapter 11   The DELETE Error Engagement and Experimentation (E^3) Learning Cycle   141
- a) Error Presentation
- b) Reflection and Planning
- c) Task Engagement
- d) Referencing and 'Re-feeding'
- e) Re-experiment

Chapter 12   The Engagement and Review Process: Use Cases   147

Chapter 13   The Seven-Step Process in the DELETE Approach   165

Chapter 14   Preparation and Research: Collate and Analyse Errors   181
- a) Procedural versus Declarative Errors
- b) Domain Types and Levels of Difficulty
- c) Commission versus Omission Errors

Chapter 15   Defining the Types of Errors Using the 3 Cs   193
- a) Selecting the Type of Error Using the 3Cs
- b) Error Selection Matrix
- c) Presenting the Context, Workflow and Error

Contents

Part 5 Developing Competences in Five Critical Areas   203

Chapter 16   Developing Metacognition   209
  i. To Hone Regulatory and Predictive Ability
  ii. To Develop Ability to Evaluate Contexts and Assumptions

Chapter 17   Developing Cognition   223
  i.   To Strengthen Conceptual Understanding and Skillsets in Targeted Areas
  ii. To Develop 'Creative-Critical' Thinking Ability
  iii. To Sharpen Cognitive Adaptability and Flexibility
  iv. To Build Global (Macro) Perspective-Taking Ability

Chapter 18   Developing Emotion   249
  i. To Develop Values and Beliefs
  ii. To Strengthen Psychological Resilience for Unexpected Outcomes

Chapter 19   Developing Psychomotor Skills   259
  i. To Develop Behavioural Responses to Situations and Errors
  ii. To Increase Reflexivity to Errors

Chapter 20   Developing Sociality and Interpersonal Skills   267
  i. To Develop Teamwork Skills Among Team Members
  ii. To Cultivate Collaborative Skills for Individuals

Chapter 21   Holistic Development — Beyond Competency   277
  i.   To Integrate Skillsets Across Domains to Achieve Mastery for the Individual
  ii. To Diagnose Skill Gaps and Non-strengths
  iii. To Prepare the Individual for Future Skill Needs

Contents

Part 6 Selecting and Designing the Errors to Trigger Reflection and Learning   **287**

Chapter 22 Linking Error Design with Learning Outcomes: Metacognition   291

Chapter 23 Linking Error Design with Learning Outcomes: Cognition   297

Chapter 24 Linking Error Design with Learning Outcomes: Emotion   305

Chapter 25 Linking Error Design with Learning Outcomes: Psychomotor   311

Chapter 26 Linking Error Design with Learning Outcomes: Sociality   315

Chapter 27 Linking Error Design with Learning Outcomes: Holistic Development   321

Chapter 28 Refining Errors   329

Part 7 Worked Examples for Students and Adult Learners   **339**

Chapter 29 Designing Errors for Students: Examples   341

Chapter 30 Designing Errors for Adult Learners   379

Chapter 31 Designing Errors Based on Real Life Examples for Purposive Learning   405

Chapter 32 How the DELETE Approach Differs from Other Instructional Designs   415

Chapter 33 Working with AI and Next Steps   419

Contents

References   423

Annex A   *Lesson Design Template for the DELETE Approach*   429

Annex B   *Notes and Models*   433

Index   435

Introduction

Learning occurs when an outcome deviates from expectation ...

Tobler *et al.* (2006)

Errors are seen as a pain for most people. Errors slow work down. They make the people who commit the errors look silly. Most of the time, errors are not welcomed. In fact, they are to be avoided at all cost, especially during assessments and at work.

> **Common Daily Examples**
>
> After a series of intensive interviews to select a suitable candidate for the job, the eventual employee turned out to be highly incompetent and socially inept. This unexpected error led to the entire interview panel to review the hiring and interview process to ensure the error won't happen again. Needless to say, the new hire was fired soon after.
>
> Parents using newspaper articles to teach children of the danger of vices — moral values when taught exist in a vacuum so newspaper articles provide the context for mistakes to be made and values to be adopted.
>
> Six-month-old Josiah puts everything in his mouth to know an object intimately, some are obviously pleasurable, but many are not and may even be dangerous.

Introduction

Not surprisingly, many researchers and educators perceived errors as negative. For example, Skinner (1953) viewed errors as a punishment. He concluded that errors do not contribute to learning. Similarly, Bandura (1986) promoted a guided and error-free learning environment and that 'without informative guidance, much of one's efforts would be expended on costly errors and needless toil' (Bandura, 1986, p. 47).

However, are errors really that useless? Philosophers often waxed lyrical about learning from errors. Even the Bible has sayings about learning from corrections (e.g. Proverbs 12:1).

Whoever loves instruction loves knowledge.

But he who hates correction is stupid.

That is very strong language from King Solomon written more than 3,000 years ago, but isn't it true that one should learn from life lessons and from others? Not many would dispute the point that a person who does not learn from others deserves a strong rebuke.

Errors and Their Impact on Learning

According to Prof. J. Reason (1990) from the University of Cambridge (UK), human error is the single largest cause of failures. More interestingly, training and familiarity with the task do NOT eliminate or reduce errors. In fact, error rates remain stable if the system design is susceptible to error production. What this means is that as long as new situations keep cropping up within the system, the user will continue to make errors. The errors range from slips (e.g. typing wrong letter) to lapses (e.g. remembering something wrongly) to mistakes (e.g. wrong decision due to incorrect reasoning). What the team found was that people make mistakes because of the complexity of the planning and reasoning processes involved and as such, reducing the complexity or making these complexities visible will eliminate some of these processing mistakes.

Introduction

Prof Reason's research also recommends that training should:

- include error scenarios
- promote exploratory trial and error approaches
- emphasise positive side of errors: learning from mistakes

In addition, a separate team of neurobiologists, also from University of Cambridge, UK, conducted experiments on how learning impacted neural activation among brain segments such as orbitofrontal cortex and ventral putamen using magnetic resonance imaging. What was surprising is that activation of the orbitofrontal cortex and ventral putamen occurred when rewards are missing in an unpredictable manner. This means that people learn most vividly when the outcomes are *not* what they expect. Hence, in a typical sales interaction with a congenial customer that brought about a nasty complaint letter would result in greater critical reflection and remembrance than one that ended with a product sale. In other words, predictability can deter learning. Non-predictability (e.g. in the form of errors) can enhance learning as the neural connections are formed or strengthened with such unpredictability.

Learning from errors leverages this concept of adding unpredicted consequence or outcome to make learning sticky.

With this understanding, listed below are three key maxims on error-based learning:

1. *Learning from errors prepares us and our entities for the future.*
2. *Discovering how errors occur reveal the boundaries and the context within which these rules operate and not operate.*
3. *Error-based learning helps us to uncover first principles which moves us from complying to innovating with rules.*

These maxims frame our approach to how we should view errors and the process we undertake to *intentionally* design and facilitate error response in rapid fashion within a safe environment so that we fail fast, fail forward and fail in order to learn. Just like how ants want to fail fast without getting eaten or killed, we want to learn from errors without suffering 'collateral damage' — a safe and secure environment is a critical condition for DELETE, especially where feedback needs to be managed and constructive.

'Errors Define the Boundaries Within Which Rules Operate'

Part 1

The Reasons for Designing Errors for Learning and Teaching (DELETE)

Chapter 1

What Are 'Errors'?

Errors are varied and what is perceived as an error by someone may not necessarily be seen as an error by another. This is to set the context when we examine the different types of errors.

Type 1 Error: Performance-Related Errors

Most people would agree that errors are events when people

- do things contrary to the rules or expectations set either by oneself or by society in general, or
- they omit doing things that are required or expected.

These errors are the result of either performing incorrectly or contrary to the rule who is to say what is right and what is wrong? Does spelling 'right' make it more correct than 'rite'? When does an error become recognised as one? What makes an error an error? Can something that was originally thought to be an error become correct later? If the majority of people think that something is correct, does that mean it is not wrong? There is an element of general acceptance and expectation (including self-acceptance and expectation), which adds a level of subjectivity to the process. The role of experts in determining if an error has occurred is an important one, to add weight to the position to be taken by the general body.

These questions point to the ambiguity and complexity of plans, decisions and actions. We are likely to make decisions and base our actions on our decisions every day of our lives, and most of the time, we hope we make the correct decisions, especially with the major issues. Hence, the question about what makes a process, a decision or an action correct or wrong is important. History has shown that judgments about the correctness of actions and decisions can be swayed and coloured to match the requirements and agenda of the society at that time. Hence, the degree of the error may not be absolute but relative. It depends on a host of different factors including one's self-perception of the correctness of the action and the perception by others involved. The *consequence* or outcome linked to the event is also important as part of the judgment process.

Often, an error occurs because an action or inaction is a deviation from intention, expectation or desirability. Most errors can be clustered according to:

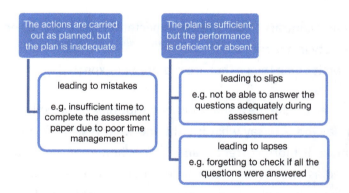

These errors are often committed simply because it is part of human nature. There will always be lapses in concentration, slips in performance or mistakes as a result of poor planning. What is more important is to be aware of these errors before they are made or if they are made, how to *rectify* these errors and avoid making them again. Learning from errors, whether they are our own or from somebody else (which is better), is critical to improving our work performance in the long term. Hence, constantly

What Are 'Errors'?

reviewing and reflecting on our performance is absolutely critical to self-improvement and for rectification of the process. By engaging in constant improvement coupled with a growth mindset (Dweck, 2006), the process can be uplifting and highly empowering.

The empowerment comes with the uncovering of principles that underpin a process. For example, when one understands how cycling is about balancing oneself by propelling forward, that principle that we arrive at through numerous attempts amidst the falling, is both satisfying and empowering. To what extent do we help learners manage their expectations while presenting the rules and boundaries can affect the empowerment process. How can we help learners choose 'correctly', based on what they expect, as they undertake the learning process?

These are important questions which we hope to reflect on at the end of this book. First, let's find out more about errors. What do we know about errors and their roles in facilitating learning?

Listed below are key categories of the general rules and expectations that we have:

Rules and Expectations	Examples
a) Individual expected outcomes based on personal experience (which may be biased or limited)	• Bright skies indicate that it is unlikely to rain • Working hard should lead to better examination results
b) Group (or societal) expectations (based on majority's perceptions and judgments)	• Wedlock pregnancy is generally unacceptable in Asian societies • Giving your seat to the elderly is expected on trains or buses
c) General laws and facts	• Shoplifting if caught will result in legal consequences • Throwing a vase down 10 stories will break it

From the table shown above, we note that errors are 'errors' when there is a reference point or a benchmark which point towards an accepted expectation of 'right'. Anything less or contrary to that benchmark could

Chapter 1

be deemed as wrong or somewhat wrong. If we throw a vase down 10 stories and expect the vase to remain intact upon impact, the eventual result (of the broken vase) will show that we made a clear error. This error occurred because it was contrary to the established law of gravity. Usually, someone young like a 3-year-old child will have some learning to do when it comes to the law of gravity in the context of throwing fragile things. Obviously, throwing vases down 10 stories is somewhat drastic and may be deserving of a good timeout for the 3-year-old child to help him or her register the error!

Imagine the figure above denotes the road with the centre-lane marking. The two lines to the right and left (sides of the road) are the boundaries to which vehicles have to navigate within. Driving outside the boundaries will be dangerous to the driver and the pedestrians.

Similarly, most books and learning designs will guide learners to carry out the correct ways of doing things, i.e. the rules of thinking or behaving. This observance of the rules is analogous to the centre-lane marks guiding the driver. What is not mentioned usually, at least not in detail, are the

An error is a disruptor in the workflow and it may be obvious or hidden from the actor/s to take rectification action to minimise any negative consequence. This disruption is telling because it denotes the boundaries and the underlying contexts that the workflow operates in. As a result, by examining the error and the impact it creates on the workflow, one can learn about the workflow and thereby, gain mastery of the work.

boundaries to which the rule does not apply and that the learner if he ventures beyond the boundaries will be in error.

Hence, errors play an important role in giving clear indications as to the context that the rule applies. Many people often assume wrongly that the rule will apply across different contexts, until they make an error. Then, they will attest that the assumption is incorrect.

One can learn from one's mistakes, but it is wiser to learn from the mistakes of others.

Definition of Type 1 Performance-Related Error

Assuming that we make errors regularly, some of which are non-critical and can be ignored while others may result in severe consequences for us or others, it goes to show that making errors is just part of being human. While we can try to minimise errors, we cannot completely eliminate them simply because of our lack of information or processing power. We do not know everything and even if we do, we cannot do everything. Hence, the potential for errors will always be present. However, it may not be helpful to define errors simply by the consequence of the error as the consequences may be out of our control. For example, the child hurling a vase down 10 stories may end up hurting or killing someone who is walking on the pavement beneath the apartment. Does the death of someone make the error more serious? Technically, it should as the consequence is serious. The intent of the agent in performing the action, i.e. if there is an intention to hurl the vase down to hurt someone is part of the consideration whether an error occurred. An intended action resulting in a consequence that is within expectation may not be considered an error to the actor. On the other hand, an intended action that did not adhere to the expectation (e.g. hurling the vase down to hurt someone and the vase missed the person) could be considered an error to the actor.

Understanding why and how intended and unintended actions result in consequences may then assist educators and ourselves in learning from our errors as the adage goes. For the purpose of the DELETE approach, the assumption is that we are working with logical and rational people with good moral sense so that we can focus on the cognitive and behavioural processes, in order to facilitate learning and improve work performance.

> *In this category of errors, we are defining error-making as an event when a person performs a task or activity which falls short of the intended result, leading to unwanted consequences.*

There are other approaches, such as resilience engineering, which highlight the variability in human performance resulting in successes (results that go according to expectation) and failures (results that are contrary to expectation). Such results are attributed to the efficiency–thoroughness trade-off principle (ETTO principle), which in short refers to whether efficiency (speed) or thoroughness (meticulousness and accuracy) takes priority and so focusing on one will lead to a shortfall in the other.

The Non-Performance Error

In contrast to the situation when the expectations or rules are in the positive (e.g. cross the road when the light is green), the error that arises from non-performance. The outcome is still contrary to expectations and rules (i.e. Do NOT cross the road when the light is red). What this means is that not performing an action is to obey the rule. Hence, going back to the analogy of the centre line of a road with two sides is that this is the space where one should NOT be in. In this flipped situation, the non-performance of the action is important, and can be considered as compiling with the performance expectation. Error-making, as with the earlier definition, is about performing a task or activity leading to an unwanted result when non-performance would have yielded the preferred outcome.

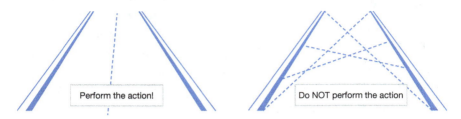

It is important to understand that in both situations (whether performance or non-performance is the rule), there is a *context* to the expectation or rule. For example, when the traffic lights are faulty, showing the red light permanently, then crossing road when the light is red may be justifiable (taking care that there are no oncoming cars, of course). Similarly, even if the light shows green, it may not be a good idea for a pedestrian to cross the road if there is an oncoming ambulance that needs to take a sick person to the hospital and is likely to speed through the lights, with horns blaring. Understanding the context and the location of the boundaries will help users understand when rules or expectations apply and when they do not. Crossing the boundaries will also lead to error which is the second category of error.

Type 2 Error: Boundary-Crossing Errors

Crossing the boundaries may result in error making because the rules do not apply or not in the same way as when the performance is located within the boundaries/context. This understanding is critical to the development of skillsets beyond competency into expertise.

For example, in a true story, a polytechnic student was due to submit his assignments within the week. With his work stored in his laptop, a fire gutted his room which was in the attic of his house. The laptop suffered damage which did not allow him to retrieve the assignment. Thankfully,

Chapter 1

the polytechnic staff, being more experienced, recognised that the assignment submission rule does not apply to him as the boundaries for the rule, which would be typical contexts for students, had been breached. The exemption should apply to him.

However, not all staff (especially the less experienced ones) would recognise the boundaries of rules. Some would insist on applying the standard rule, even when his situation calls for a relook of the context of the rule. In the above-mentioned example, can you imagine the public outcry if the polytechnic staff insisted on the student submitting his assignments despite him suffering from the loss of his property and the failure of his laptop due to the fire?

> "... situational awareness is the feel for the unique contours of the situation she is in ... an intuitive awareness of when to follow the rules and when to break the rules, a feel for the flow of events, a special sensitivity, not necessarily conscious, for how fast to move and what decisions to take that will prevent her from crashing on the rocks ..."
>
> **David Brooks**
> *The New York Times*

The issue is how a staff recognises the rules and their corresponding boundaries. Does experience play a role? I am sure it would. What about clarity with the application of the rules? It would also help. There would be other examples which may be less extreme. For example, should the polytechnic staff extend the submission deadline if a student supplied a letter from his parent that the laptop in which the assignments were stored crashed the night before due to unexplainable reasons? Where are the boundaries to the assignment submission rule? If there is some documentation concerning the boundaries surrounding the rule, it would aid in the implementation of the rule.

In a work environment where contexts and rules change and rapidly evolve, documentation can be difficult as it is a dynamic space. Even if the documentation is extensive with tomes of examples and instructions, would all staff have the time and mental endurance to fully comprehend the content? The answer is likely negative.

What can we do to help learners and staff understand expectations, intent, rules and boundaries, so that they can cope with changing environments and reduce error making? How do we make the rules and boundaries clear and explicit to learners so that they can perform in their assignments and at work? These are areas that educators and management need to look at when attempting to improve learner capabilities.

Ultimately, it would be about going back to first principles and utilising metacognition to check one's thoughts, biases and assumptions when making decisions. Fully grasping the extent of rules and innovating new rules are tasks that experts typically perform. It is in this space of expert performance that we need more practitioners to enter into. Competency is insufficient in a changing environment as competent behaviours are often trained within a structured and standard context. The changes to an environment can lead a staff to unknowingly make errors especially when he or she is not aware that changes have taken place. Then, it becomes risky with a high propensity for errors. In certain circumstances, errors can be life threatening.

Unlike type 1 errors where the performance is not up to par or not according to the stated rules, type 2 errors occur when the issue is outside of the boundaries of the rule, which implies that staff needs to know where the boundaries are and when boundaries are crossed, which may render the rules incoherent, irrelevant and possibly erroneous for one to follow.

Scientists should get used to their experiments failing ...

Prof. David Klenerman
Genome Sequencing Expert
University of Cambridge

Conclusion

This chapter defines errors as performance-related (type 1) and boundary-crossing (type 2) with the latter being more difficult to determine and prevent due to the changing contexts especially in a changing environment. By utilising errors to help learners acquire knowledge of these two types of competencies (how rules operate and where the boundaries are), the assumption is that learners will be more cognisant of when errors may arise due to BOTH types of infringements. By using an error-based learning approach, curriculum designers capitalises on 'failures' to turn a potentially negative situation around to inform future decision-making and behavioural processes in an organised and intentional manner.

Most of us would agree that we should not waste a good mistake and learning from it is a most logical outcome. How to learn from a mistake so that we learn to perform better and at the same time, changing us — impacting our professional identity — will make error design a powerful and transformative tool for us and our learners.

Chapter 2
Why Learn from Errors?

Introduction

In the previous chapter, we learned about what errors mean and why learning from and through errors makes sense. In this chapter, we will dive deeper into why error-based learning can be a powerful and effective means of driving learning, especially to anchor deep understanding and expertise building, for more effective performance in the changing school and work environment.

Learning is as natural as breathing and eating to the typical human being. As a newborn coming into this world, crying and at the same time, picking up new information about the environment and what we can do, learning is about finding ourselves, who we are and what we want to be. The understanding of ourselves, to be a person of worth and to do well in life according to all that we have set out to do is an important and existential need. In short, learning empowers us to be who we want to be. However, learning can also destroy our dreams and character, if we are not careful. It can also destroy our hopes and our values. Learning is an important channel for us to interact with our world, take on new information and skills, shaping and being shaped by our values, beliefs and desires.

Designing errors into our learning process makes us more aware of what can go wrong, sensitises us to underlying assumptions and prompts us to make informed decisions. Preventing errors is a useful motivator as most of us are averse to making errors. When using errors to drive learning, most people have a heightened sense of awareness to question what we

Chapter 2

Sharing by an Experienced Trainer

I had the opportunity to work with a class of 12 adult learners averaging 35 years old, teaching the concepts of training needs analysis. The adult learners were motivated to learn but were weak cognitively. They worked extremely hard with many putting in long hours to complete their assignment. Some worked overnight and then turn up in class the following day.

Despite all the efforts, unfortunately, some really had problems grasping the essence of the concept. Their cognitive ability was low, and the extra effort could not make up for the performance gap. The workshop was also losing momentum due to the difficulties involved.

At this point, I got the class to conduct peer teaching of a few concepts relating to survey, interviews and focus group discussions. However, there was a deviation. The 'experts' have to embed one error in what they are going to present to their listener. The change was remarkable. The learners were quick to point out the error but more importantly, the experts had to determine what constituted an error and to spot it quickly before others did.

The result was amazing. The learners had to pay attention in order to spot the one **error** for individual presentation, resulting in an increase of learners' attention levels. In addition, to embed the error, the experts had to determine what is correct and put the error in a way which makes the spotting more difficult.

Overall, there was significant learning as a result of the errors, which made for a more engaging and constructivist approach to learning. Uncovering the principles underpinning the concepts became the point of discussion, leading to much deeper learning.

hear and see, to reduce the likelihood of committing these errors in the future (especially if you are new to the job). Consciously and intentionally, we take a proactive role in analysing what we learn, so as to do a good job. As a result, the increased learner agency prepares us for the moment when we need to apply the learning in future contexts. Through critical learning, application becomes more informed and deliberate. In other words, one of the critical success factors to apply learning effectively is the degree of cognitive assimilation that has been carried out. Injection of errors facilitates this assimilation of learning, to prime the individual into making the right decisions and avoid making wrong ones in the future.

Learning to enhance our *performance* by not making errors seems straightforward enough. What about learning the *context* in which to perform the tasks? Why is this critical? That is a great question and a useful point for us to examine how contexts impact performance.

With the world becoming a globalised and interconnected entity, it is difficult to determine how world events will unfold, and with that, how our economic landscape cascading to our work environments, will evolve. In short, a more complex and unpredictable global system ensures that the 'norm' does not remain status quo for a long period of time. Increasingly, the term 'VUCA' is now more widely accepted to describe our post-COVID world. 'VUCA' stands for:

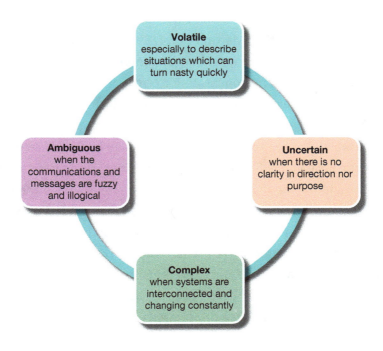

Preparing for 'VUCA' environments may become the new norm. Change is the new constant and as such, typical work rules (or standard operating procedures, i.e. SOPs), are also subject to change. This changing environment results in the 'half-life' of our knowledge and competencies becoming shorter. If our mindset is to learn once (from school), we may shortchange ourselves and risk not being able to adapt to new environments when rules and contexts change. Given that VUCA environments are here to stay, how does error-based learning illuminate the shifts in *BOTH* rules and contexts to facilitate effective performance? Will error-based learning work for everyone? Does it help people learn faster? What is the research for error-based learning?

How Does the Brain Respond to Errors?

This question is an important one as it points to the mechanism for DELETE to effectively impact learning neurologically. Are there cases when error-based learning can hinder rather than facilitate learning? When is the DELETE approach most effective and when does it not quite work?

In an experiment that Martin *et al*. (1996) conducted to measure the level of psychomotor adaptation by the brain, they showed that individuals attempted to compensate for errors in order to achieve the desired outcome. The participants wore prisms, which shifted their visual world by a few degrees, and they were subsequently tasked to throw darts and walk. Due to the visual distortion caused by the visual prisms, the participants had to adjust their movements by a few degrees in order to compensate for the discrepancy. More interestingly, once the visual prism was taken off, the participants continued to respond as if they still had the prism over their eyes! The result was a series of movements made in the opposite direction (e.g. darts were thrown to the right of the bulls-eye instead of at it). In other words, the brain over-compensated. It took a few tries for the brain to adapt back to the natural state before the individuals wore the prism. What this showed was that deviations from the desired outcomes (or errors) can inform the brain to make psychomotor adaptation in order to reduce the deviations. By making the errors obvious and in real time, the brain is able to adjust faster and more accurately. Obviously, the data and implication drawn from this research apply to psychomotor behaviours but it also implies the tendency for the brain to over-compensate when the feedback on the action indicates that a certain behaviour is erroneous.

Errors Must Make Sense to the Brain

There is, however, a caveat to the set of findings by Martin *et al.* (1996). The brain only 'learns' from errors it can make sense of. Hence, if the error has to do with shifting a few degrees to the left of the bullseye, the brain can learn that pattern very quickly. However, if the error is random (e.g. the visual deviation caused by the prism varies), the brain cannot form a pattern consistent with the generated error. Correspondingly, the brain will not be able to adapt accordingly as it cannot make sense of the feedback. The key point to note here is that the errors must make sense to the brain so that the brain can generate its own rationale or 'theory' for adaptation. Otherwise, the errors will be incomprehensible, and adaptation cannot follow. In extreme cases, learned helplessness (Seligman, 1972) creeps in leading to a loss of learner motivation and the individual giving up, simply because the individual does not seem to be able to 'correct the errors' nor exercise any control over the eventual outcomes.

> ... helping the individual to make sense of their errors ... empowers them to improve and perform better.

Sense-Making and Learned Helplessness

Based on his research on animals, Seligman extended the notion of learned helplessness to clinical depression in humans and proposed the theory of learned helplessness as a possible reason for people to become vulnerable to depression and to give up trying.

Learned helplessness is also observed in relationships involving domestic abuse. When people who are abused take on a learned helplessness mentality, where nothing they do can correct nor control the negative outcomes, they often do not tell others, try to get help, or leave the relationships (Ackerman, 2018). They also cannot make sense of what is happening, nor determine what 'errors' they are making except perhaps, it is their 'fate', and they should accept the situation as is, thereby exacerbating the abuse, yielding control to their abusers.

Conversely, research by psychologist Carol Dweck showed that when people can make sense of their errors or failures by attributing them to a lack of effort, they are more able to manage the emotional fallout because of the failure. In 1975, Dweck conducted a study (Dweck, 1975) where she split the participants into two groups:

- Group 1 received intensive training, but still made errors and failed at the tasks. They were told to take responsibility for their failure and attribute it to a lack of effort.
- Group 2 also received intensive training, and they only experienced success. They did not experience any failure nor were they told that they made errors.

Eventually, when both groups experienced failure, the results showed that those in the success-only group showed no improvement in their extreme reactions to failure, while the group that failed before, showed marked improvement in the way they responded to the failure (Ackerman, 2018). By taking on a more positive attributional style where one maintains control over the situation, the individual can be taught to overcome learned helplessness. Psychologists call this attributional style *learned hopefulness.* Learned hopefulness suggests that empowering experiences — ones that provide opportunities to make sense of errors, learn skills and develop a sense of control — can help individuals manage and reduce the debilitating effects of learned helplessness in their professional and personal lives (Zimmerman, 1990).

In short, helping individuals make sense of their errors is important to empower individuals in the learning process. It empowers them to exhibit hope, keep trying to make sense of errors, improve and perform better eventually — to never give up.

When Error-Based Learning Does NOT Make Sense

The need for individuals to make sense of the situation can also be found in research on performance rehabilitation. Whether the learners can make sense of the activities, errors committed, and learn from them is an important factor when deciding between errorless or error-based learning.

According to Ownsworth et al. (2013), the rehabilitation literature shows that people with severe cognitive impairment learn new skills more effectively when errors are avoided during training — *errorless* learning approach — as compared to trial-and-error learning. What happens in trial-and-error learning is that people are encouraged to attempt or guess responses on a task, and they are corrected each time an error is committed, without being provided further feedback on performance. In contrast, errorless involves preventing the person from making errors during the learning phase (i.e. to follow the rules given). From the study, the recommendation was to utilise the errorless approach for teaching task-specific skills to people with severe memory impairment or low cognitive capability. This approach involves modelling each step and having the person practise only correct responses to support habit formation (e.g. rehearsal of the steps to cook rice using a rice cooker). With reduced cognitive (and sense-making) capability, learners need to focus on getting the behaviour right (i.e. following the rules) as the priority. Anything in excess can add to the cognitive load and potentially overwhelm the processing capability of those with cognitive impairment. Once the rules are acquired, the learner can be instructed on the contexts or boundaries to certain rules (e.g. when there is a blackout or when a different type of rice is used).

There is some evidence to suggest that novices, like learners with memory impairment or low capability, are more suited to learning using the errorless approach at the start of the learning process. This approach reduces the cognitive load on the novices and promotes the reinforcement of the basic skillsets and understanding first before they attempt to deepen their competence. However, unlike learners with cognitive impairment, novices with strong cognitive capability but lacking the technical skills or experience, may still undertake error-based learning that is designed to match their level of competency. What this implies is that with sufficient cognitive scaffolding to structure the learning process so that the cognitive demand on novices is manageable, these learners can leverage error-based learning approach to deepen their learning experience. It will still be beneficial for novices when the design is appropriate and learner support is provided.

By the same reasoning, learners who have reached competency or proficiency in the specific skillset possess sufficient cognitive 'credit' by leveraging on their grasp of the key concepts and skillsets as foundational reasoning capability to uncover the first principles and identify potential errors during the error-based learning process. They are also likely to be comfortable with fuzziness and cognitive dissonance if the errors prove complicated and require extensive exploration. Using error-based learning, individuals can deepen their competence by unpacking the rules and boundaries embedded within the topic. Through the process, the competent learners develop stronger metacognitive capability (being aware what they are thinking about) and mindfulness, in addition to being more aware of the contexts in which the skillsets do and do not apply, putting them on the journey to reach expertise.

Building Metacognitive Capability

As mentioned, errorless learning approaches are generally more suitable to helping novices achieve a basic level of competency as errorless learning exerts a lower cognitive load on the learners. To go beyond basic competency, however, most learners need to have a deeper understanding of the context and the limitations of the topic or skill being acquired. Knowing when rules don't apply is as important as knowing when they do. The generalisation of the skill from the training to a novel context (where learners need to determine if the boundaries are breached) is often difficult for these novices due to the errorless learning approach where learners are not given opportunities to explore what the boundaries for themselves. They may be instructed exactly what the boundaries are (e.g. *do x when y happens and x does not apply in these contexts*) but novel situations are such that learners do not know for certain if the novel contexts are within the category of 'these' contexts.

Ownsworth *et al.* (2013) found that the failure to generalise skills after errorless learning has been attributed to an overreliance on the educator to anticipate and prevent learner errors during the learning process, often to drill the learners for performance in assessments. During errorless learning, learners are not encouraged to make errors during the learning process. Often, the educator closely monitors their performance and provides prompts to reduce behaviours resulting in errors. In the long run, learners will need to rely on similar support to achieve error-free performance on a new task as they are not able to self-monitor and correct their performance. Learning is still limited to whatever that was explicitly taught.

Ownsworth *et al.*'s (2013) research highlighted that with error-based learning, where opportunities are designed into the activities for the learners to commit errors, learners become aware of and self-correct these errors through graded prompts and feedback. When learners are encouraged to try or guess at tasks that could lead to an error, an interesting outcome of greater learner inclination to exercise metacognition emerges.

Specifically, through systematic feedback and graded prompts, the learners are given opportunities to practise the following:

- learn to stop, check and self-correct errors regularly
- reflect on the errors made to promote self-awareness and improve future behaviours
- anticipate errors in daily contexts to plan the future strategies based on the requirements.

Over time, the learner is expected to self-internalise a mental algorithm to recognise and correct errors. These self-driven and self-regulation skills can be seen to transfer to other untrained tasks and situations in daily living, including metacognitive skills, the capacity to reflect, monitor and regulate one's own actions. With improved capabilities including metacognitive abilities, the assumption is that the learners recognise and solve the frequent problems that arise in daily situations. In the study, the roles of the educator for both the error-based and errorless approaches are illustrated accordingly (see Fig. 1).

The findings from the study are significant because they show how these different approaches match the needs of learners, who at various stages of skill or knowledge acquisition, will require specific levels of guidance and clarity.

Situational Awareness

In the article 'Situational Awareness and Safety' by Stanton, Chambers, and Piggott (2001), the two types of situational awareness — process and product — were contrasted. In essence, researchers generally define situational awareness as an *appropriate awareness of a situation* (Smith & Hancock, 1995). Three dominant definitions of situational awareness exist:

- an information processing framework (Endsley, 1988), which describes situational awareness as a higher order cognitive processing

Why Learn from Errors?

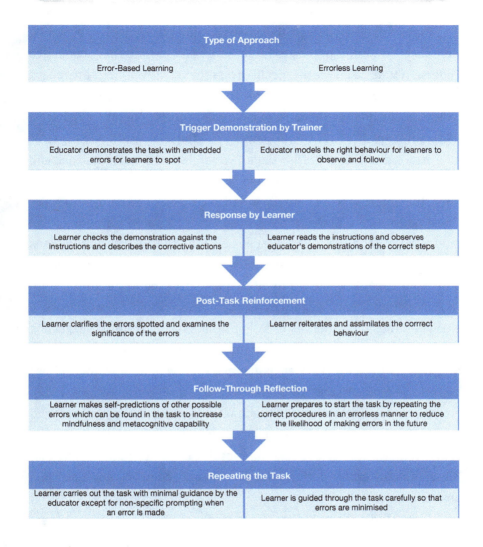

Fig. 1. Comparison Between Error-Based and Errorless Learning Approaches

- an activity approach where situational awareness is a conscious dynamic reflection on the situation (Bedny & Meister, 1999)
- an ecological approach with situational awareness as a dynamic interaction between humans and their environment. It generates momentary knowledge and behaviour (Smith & Hancock, 1995).

These definitions differ in their focus on either the process of acquiring situational awareness or the product of situational awareness. According to Pedersen (1988), all three perspectives on situational awareness are rooted in broader models of human cognitive functioning framed by environmental factors. Based on the research into biological models of human physiology, Pedersen explains that the perceptual system has multiple stages of information processing. The first stage involves detecting relevant signals and targets from a noisy environment and filtering out non-target information. Then, the detected signals are organised into meaningful patterns. Finally, these patterns are understood, sorted into perceptual categories and integrated into the individual's existing beliefs and knowledge. In summary, all three stages require careful attention, driven by the individual's cognitive processing capability, and informed by one's past experiences.

Endsley and her colleagues have in their research with flight controllers, examined the consequences of losing situational awareness, suggesting that individuals who display a lack of situational awareness may need more response time to detect system issues and require more time to diagnose and resolve problems once they have been detected (Endsley & Kiris, 1995).

In another application of situational awareness, Gaba, Howard, and Small (1995) investigated the cognitive processes of anaesthesiologists and contended that situational awareness is a crucial cognitive ability that is essential for expert performance in dynamic, complex, and uncertain environments.

These studies demonstrate the importance of situational awareness in making visible potential errors in the environment and the implication is that expertise is typically the common denominator in many of these 'situationally aware' individuals.

Expertise and Mastery of Craft

Under normal circumstances, this shift from novice to competency and expertise is typically a gradual process, as learners gain experience through

Why Learn from Errors?

work and formal learning, taking up to decades to acquire, but this process can be expedited through increased learner agency when facilitated using error-based learning experiences. Based on what Dreyfus (2004) espoused in his model 'Novice to Expert', there is greater independence and ability to manage fluid and unstructured events as one moves higher up the stages of competence. To develop expertise and mastery of craft, designing scenarios with errors is one possible vehicle where the lack of structure coupled with the volatile and uncertain elements in the scenario can help highly competent workers to operate under those conditions. See the descriptions of the error-based scenarios being used to train workers.

On that note, errors can also be infused into demonstrations to help advanced beginners understand possible pitfalls and difficulties when carrying out tasks. However, compared to error-based scenarios for the proficient

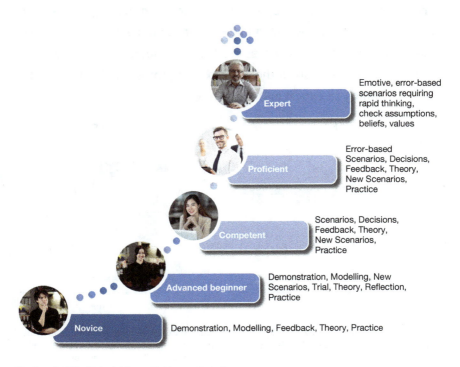

Fig. 2. Dreyfus' Model from Novice to Expert

and expert, the infusion of errors into the training for novice to competent phases are fewer in frequency and involves less critical concepts. The primary purpose of training when it comes to the novices is to get them to be able to perform the basic tasks and avoid critical errors first. As error-based learning requires learners to be able to critically analyse the situation and determine assumptions underpinning errors or even suggest creative solutions, there is a need for these learners to be competent in the tasks before they are trained or taught using more complex error-based learning scenarios.

Hence, if we map the Dreyfus's (2004) model onto this study, we will find that errorless training if targeted at novices will benefit them by equipping them with understanding of the rules of performance. In the case where learners are competent at a task, then error-based learning may move them up the ladder to achieve proficiency and mastery in that activity. As seen from the results of the study by Ownsworth *et al.* (2013), learners gain a level of independence in decision-making and acquire metacognitive capability, which allows them to become more aware of issues and assumptions as well as predict consequences of their actions. All these capabilities add to the toolbox of a professional who is on the way to becoming an expert in that job role.

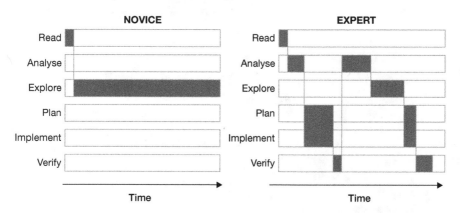

Fig. 3. Different Problem-Solving Activities in Novice and Expert Mathematicians Over Time
Source: Adapted from Schoenfeld, A. H. (1992). Learning to think mathematically: Problem solving, metacognition, and sense making in mathematics. In D. A. Grouws (Ed.), Handbook of research on mathematics teaching and learning: A project of the National Council of Teachers of Mathematics (pp. 334–370). Macmillan Publishing Co, Inc.

Supporting these findings is an earlier study by a Mathematics professor, Alan Schoenfeld (1987), looking at how experts and novices cognitively process information. When faced with the same information, there are distinct differences in the thinking processes adopted by the experts compared to novices. In his study, he examined how his students (who are Mathematics majors) solved problems over time. He noted that 60% of his students would read a problem, start down a solution path and continue going down that path, whether it was productive or not. In contrast, the experts he examined were solving the same problem in a more reflective manner. They iteratively moved among planning, implementing, and evaluating, displaying a metacognitive awareness of the thinking approach they adopted.

Training novices to adopt metacognitive processes (e.g. planning, monitoring how they think, not just trying to think) made a difference in self-directing the way they approached a problem. To train expert problem-solving skills, he would model solving these mathematics questions by voicing aloud his thought processes, often monitoring and adjusting his approach. He would ask his students to do the same, injecting questions to elicit metacognition such as, 'What are you doing now'? 'Why are you trying that approach'?

By first demonstrating the approach and holding the learners to be responsible for thinking about their thinking, Schoenfeld trained the learners to adopt metacognition in their problem-solving approach, making them more circumspect about *how* they were solving the problems. Going forward, in the era of intelligent machines and fake news, the ability to be circumspect and metacognitive would be critical tools in managing reality and artificial intelligence.

"Humans who are limited by slow biological evolution, couldn't compete and would be superseded. The development of full artificial intelligence could spell the end of the human race."

Stephen Hawking
Astrophysicist

Chapter 2

How Experts Make Decisions

In a study conducted by Salant and Spenkuch (2022), both Professors of Managerial Economics and Decision Sciences at the Kellogg School of Management, Northwestern University, on 200 million chess moves by chess players on an online chess platform, they found that players typically consider only a small subset of all possible options. The players pick the first one that they consider good *enough* — meaning, the first move that they believe will produce a win — a strategy that aims for a satisfactory or adequate result, rather than the optimal solution, something that economists call 'satisficing'. Instead of putting maximum exertion towards attaining the ideal outcome, satisficing focuses on putting in effort good enough to get a positive result, as trying for the optimal solution may expend an inordinate amount of energy and resources. As a result, when options are very close in terms of perceived outcomes, players find it difficult to make good 'satisficing' decisions, forcing them to commit errors.

Ownsworth *et al.* (2013) made this point in the study:

You can add as many winning moves as you want … That will not result in more mistakes. If you want to make the problem as hard as possible, you need to add options that are not optimal but are pretty close to being optimal.

What this means is that the learners need a lot of decision-making power when options that are close to being optimal are added to the fray. This forces learners to make difficult decisions when the options are very close to each other in terms of meaning or outcomes, thereby forcing errors on the part of the learners.

In addition, the study also revealed that the time allotted interacted with the skill level of the player to impact the decision-making process. Generally, 'titled' or the world's best players (e.g. Grandmasters) made fewer mistakes than untitled players regardless of how much time they were given to choose moves. However, the difference in performance was smallest when the players had to perform under extreme time pressure, i.e. speed chess that had to be concluded within minutes. With slower matches, untitled players were more likely than titled players to choose a bad move. Hence, the titled players, i.e. the experts, benefit more from having time to think. The point is that, when possible, experts choose not to adopt a 'satisficing' strategy but one which allows them to expend energy (and time) to achieve the most optimal outcome, often requiring considerations about permutations of moves guided by the opponents' playing style.

When applied to the work context, a top-performing staff may not make the right call in a time-sensitive crisis. It seems that the benefits of expertise fade when decisions need to be made in very a short period of time. Hence, it is likely that providing opportunities for learners to think through the issues PRIOR to a crisis may help them avoid adopting the satisficing strategy but one that is considered in advance when time was available for careful thought.

Conclusion

We explored a number of critical concepts underpinning error-based learning. It is important for us to check our own assumptions as we embark on this journey to design and incorporate errors into our learning and assessment processes so that we are aware of the boundaries to the error-based learning paradigm too. With novices, error-based learning can be applied to the acquisition of competency in thinking and performance pertaining to the skill. Here, getting novices to familiarise themselves with the correct processes and outputs while avoiding incorrect processes and outputs. The errors will likely concern what not to do, i.e. performance-related errors.

With the competent and proficient, there is huge upside to moving them into expertise through the exploration of the boundaries to these rules, i.e. boundary-related errors (see Table 1). The need for humans to

Table 1. Characteristics of Learners from Novice to Expert

Stages	Thinking	Behaviour	What Error-Based Learning Does
Expert	Focuses on several critical components and boundaries at the same time; looping back to reflection and trialling of hypotheses, first principles to check outcomes	Innovates, considers alternative means of performing tasks, possibly using new tools developing new frameworks	Helps learners to intentionally search for patterns in the data and uncover first principles; prompts learners to consider assumptions and biases
Proficient	Embraces other means of resolving issues or problems besides those methods taught over time; reconsiders the underlying assumptions and biases to standard work	Encourages self and others to take on new approaches to resolve issues; questions rules	Drives learners to consider other areas or reasons not yet considered; becoming more situationally aware in the process
Competent	Possesses sufficient knowledge to drive performance enhancement and consistency; increases understanding through research and reflection	Performs tasks effectively, honing skills to become more efficient; teaching others	Directs learners to contingencies and potential areas where rules do not apply fully, to deepen their understanding of the limits to the rules
Advanced Beginner	Follows taught thinking patterns	Follows rules, with understanding of when rules may or may not apply	Extends the learning to include boundary exploration, especially to understand when rules do not apply
Novice	Direct, follows rules	Follows rules carefully and not deviate in performing the tasks	When carefully scaffolded, learners can become aware that there are boundaries to the rules

take on this expertise role becomes critical in the years ahead as machines become intelligent and humans need to find the space where machines are not yet able to take on, in order to remain relevant to the society and thus, employable.

As learning designers and educators, we have the responsibility to hone our craft to bring out the character of the skill or concepts to be acquired. The learners will need to experience for themselves what the language and the emotions are when interacting with the topic. Whether it turns out to be bland or flavourful, meaningful or boring, impactful or uneventful, depends largely on the craftsmen — the designer and the teacher. Ultimately, the learning experience is the process that connects the learners with the information. 'Making the lesson come alive' is what most educators are familiar with.

Having deepened the concept of error-based learning, we will now broaden our scope to review what learning means and subsequently, how designing instruction for learning can take place in the Learning and Development (L&D) landscape.

Chapter 3

How Do We Learn?

Typically, this question of learning occupies entire volumes of encyclopaedia, with the research being on-going since time immemorial. How do we learn is a key question to understanding our growth, and with that, the development of our personal and professional identity.

To help us understand the efficacy of error-learning principles, we need to set the foundational framework of learning processes, learner profiles and instructional design principles prior to designing errors for learning. In this chapter, we will look at frameworks on:

a) Learning Process: The *Learning, Atmosphere, Mind and Production* model — to describe how information flow occurs from the environment via our perception (or learning) channels, into mental processing and subsequently output as production deliverables.
b) Learner Profiles: The Illeris' *Three Dimensions of Learning* model — to profile the learner in terms of characteristics involving Cognition, Emotion and Sociality. The levels across these three dimensions provide a useful aggregate on how the learner can interact with different types and degrees of complexity of information.
c) Instructional Design: The *Nano Learning Cycle* — to structure learning sequences and activities in a manner that drives learning in different ways, to achieve various learning outcomes.

While not exhaustive, these three areas of considerations are critical for us to locate the error-based learning approach within the entire learning and development landscape, and to frame learning innovations with sufficient understanding of the theoretical basis and research.

A Learning Framework

Over the years, research into the field of developmental and cognitive psychology has yielded powerful insights into how people learn, with seminal work by psychologist Vygotsky (1978) on the socio-cultural theory of cognitive development highlighting the impact of environmental influences and cognitive scaffolding on learning and cognitive growth, and research by Piaget (1959) on the stages of cognitive growth displayed by children as they mature from infant to adulthood. The extensive research over the past century has enabled the mapping and testing of cognitive models to extract key features of how people process, assimilate and retrieve information. It has also clarified how and why learning difficulties such as dyslexia exist.

The LAMP Model

As a cognitive processing model, the LAMP (Learning, Atmosphere, Mind and Production) Model (Choy, 2002) describes the link across three cognitive processing units (see Fig. 4) as information is tracked and processed from the entry via learning channels (or pipes) to processing (mind) and used by the individual to perform (production). Surrounding these processing units is the environmental attributes (or atmosphere), which affect one's learning and performance.

How Do We Learn?

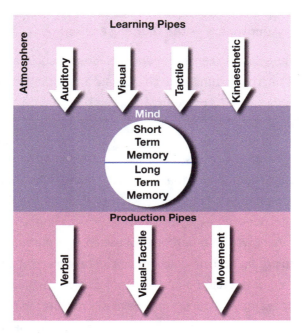

Fig. 4. The LAMP (Learning, Atmosphere, Mind and Production) Model (Choy, 2002)

Learning Pipes	Mind	Production Pipes
Information comes in different forms. We may not receive some types of information as well as others. For example, I may remember the information I see better than I hear. **The preferred ways in which we receive information are known as our <u>learning pipes</u>.** Imagine the learning pipes channelling information into our minds through our eyes, ears, hands and feet. Some pipes are **larger and channel more information** than others.	Information is stored in our minds. It passes through the Learning Pipes before being transferred to the mind for processing. There are techniques to help us remember better. There are many different types of memories. They store information about space, words, numbers and bodily movements. For example, some learners are better at remembering names than multiplication facts.	The way we express ourselves affects the clarity and effectiveness of our message. Generally, we have three types of **production pipes**. The Visual–Tactile producers prefer to write or draw while Verbal producers prefer to talk or sing. Movement producers are best at doing things with their bodies (e.g. sports). When given a choice, choose our strength to ensure that our ideas are communicated correctly and effectively.

Chapter 3

> **Atmosphere — the Learning Environment**
>
> The atmosphere (learning environment) includes the social and physical components such opportunities to collaborate and something as simple as having a sofa to read a book on.

The LAMP model depicts the process of learning in a sequential manner although the reality is that information and skills are acquired in an iterative fashion with it being a cycle rather than a single flow process which the model does not explicitly capture. What is important about the model is that it shows the differences between information perception, processing and production, of which errors can take place at any point but usually observed or detected only at the point of production. What does this mean? For example, a doctor may have misinterpreted the dosage of a particular medicine for a heart ailment when reading the information booklet. As a result, he would have stored the wrong information in his mind. At the appropriate moment, he will then retrieve the wrong information and then instruct the medicine to be dispensed according to the wrong dosage which he had in his mind. While the error was made earlier, during the perception or learning phase, the error can only be detected during the *production* phase. Of course, if he was quizzed about the dosage by the nurse at the point of reading the information booklet, his error could have been detected earlier especially if his description of the dosage is checked by the nurse at that point in time. It is important that we understand how and when errors are generated throughout the entire LAMP process so that we can design errors and tasks to target the specific segments to maximise the learning impact. In other words, designing performance checks (sometimes known as assessments) is an integral part of the learning process and should be intentional, to elicit feedback for the learner.

Case of Jasmine, the 8-Year-Old Girl

There was an 8-year-old girl named Jasmine that I worked with when I was a psychologist with mainstream schools. She had a learning difficulty whereby she could not read letters and words correctly. Despite all the support and interventions provided, her reading ability was still at that of a 5-year-old, making errors reading 'cats', 'dogs' and 'she', for example. As I worked with her, I diagnosed that she possessed a strong ability to sound out letters. Even though Jasmine could not recognise many of the words at first glance, she could take each letter and sound them out individually and then combining them together to make the word. She would then listen to herself read and then comprehend the word. Her primary difficulty was that she often mis-read the letters — 'b' would become 'd' and 'p' would become 'q'. Hence, I got her to use her fingers to mirror the letters and she would memorise the letters based on the shape of her fingers. With practice, it worked marvellously. She managed to reduce the errors from 50% of the time to about 10% or even 5% when she was not tired.

This case goes on to show that understanding how people learn (at the individual level) is critical to personalise learning. More importantly, it empowers individuals to put in the necessary interventions to increase productivity and performance. For Jasmine, the 'finger' intervention has worked to increase her confidence and gave her a new avenue to access print and read on her own. One day when I was working with her, she smiled shyly at me and said softly, 'I passed my English'. It was the first time in her life she had ever passed a class test. I beamed, 'Well done, Jasmine! I know you can do it'. Deep in my heart, I realise that empowering people to learn can change their lives and it became my personal and professional calling from then on. I enjoy seeing people learn better.

Chapter 3

Teasing apart the perception, processing and production segments and determining the learning needs of individuals can be critical even for learners without any learning difficulties. Knowing your largest learning pipes (auditory, visual, tactile or kinaesthetic) and your most preferred production pipes (verbal, visual–tactile or movement) can make or break your career. It can also determine the things you want to do in life, based on your strengths.

Finally, the atmosphere during which perception, processing and production occur can impact the effectiveness of the entire process. If the doctor described in the earlier paragraph required a quiet environment to learn but the reading of the information booklet was conducted along the busy corridor of the Accident and Emergency ward, his ability to capture the information would have been affected.

In the same manner, the likelihood of errors during production can be accentuated if a person works better in the evening but is forced to perform in the morning. The person's ability may not be at optimum level and hence, there is a stronger likelihood of errors occurring then. Have you observed some staff at 8.30 a.m. and they looked like they just woke up? Their eyelids are barely peeled back, and they have problems articulating a full sentence. However, when you engage them at 10 p.m. at night, they come alive and can throw up new ideas faster than you can jot them down.

Likewise, if a student learns better in a collaborative environment but during the busy run-up to the year-end examination, he has no choice but to study alone, his learning effectiveness may also be affected, resulting in possible errors and misinterpretation. In summary, both the physical and social atmospheres are important factors when considering learning processes for the individual.

Having looked at the perception and production processes in some detail, we will further examine how learning is perceived and processed by the Mind based on the nature of the information and skillsets in the next part.

How Do We Know When Learning Has Taken Place?

The earlier segment on the LAMP model describes the processes in which perception, processing and production occur in conjunction to result in concept and skill acquisition. However, it does not tell us when and if learning has truly taken place. How do we recognise learning and to what extent has someone learned something? These are questions which require further examination. With our understanding of the processes as described in the LAMP model, we will now delve into the Learning and Mind processes ('L' and 'M' segments of the LAMP model) and the assumption is that improved learning and processing results in enhanced performance (or production).

Three Dimensions of Learning (TDLM)

Often, adult learners learn on the job in the workplace through apprenticeship or straightforward requests for help from colleagues. Learning is also often just in time and contextualised to the job tasks at hand. Students pick up new skills from their teachers, tutors and classmates. They also acquire just-in-time skills and knowledge to undertake assessments and examinations. The nature of learning and knowledge is complex and highly intertwined with the context that learning and work performance take place in.

As such, learning is perceived as embedded in a social context. According to Salomon and Perkins (1998, p. 2), *"individual learning is rarely truly individual: it almost always entails some social mediation, even if not immediately apparent"*.

It is also clear, as mentioned in the earlier paragraph on the LAMP model, that Individual and social learning complement each other. Illeris (2002) has integrated the various components found in the literature on learning into one conceptual framework.

Chapter 3

The Three Dimensions of Learning Model (Illeris, 2002) describes interaction of three dimensions interacting to produce effective learning in the individual:

- cognition (knowledge, understanding, skills)
- emotion (incentives, motivational factors)
- sociality (learning and working environment)

The three dimensions interact with each other with the learner striving to acquire both emotional stability and cognitive competence while at the same time interacting with the sociality element of the environment. This could refer to the physical or the human aspect of interaction (corresponding to the 'Atmosphere' in the LAMP model).

More specifically, Illeris defines the three dimensions:

1. Cognition
   Learning involves the acquisition of content and skills. It involves giving meaning to facts, events and experiences.
2. Emotion
   Learning is an emotional or psychodynamic process, i.e. it affects one's psychological state as evidenced by changes to one's feelings, emotions, attitudes and motivations.
3. Sociality
   Learning is a social interactional process between the individual and surroundings. For example, the community of practice is an important source of information especially for the novice learner.

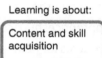

Learning is about:
- Content and skill acquisition
- Emotional changes
- Social interactions

The implications of learning seemed to be far-reaching, given that some researchers and scholars (e.g. Lave and Wenger (1991) have interpreted the learning process in terms of the creation of a new social self. A learner reinvents himself or herself based on new engagements with the learning

How Do We Learn?

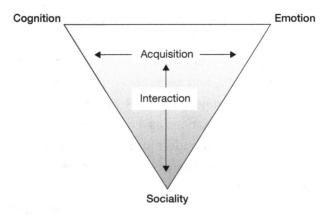

Fig. 5. The Three Dimensions of Learning

community, also known as a community of practice or the Sociality dimension. By being part of the community (such as a class or an online forum group), the learner establishes an identity for himself or herself and as a result, engages in a learning process that is authentic and situated. The recognition that the community assigns to the learner becomes motivating and satisfying. It is akin to being accepted by others in the community. While information processing is individual, occurring in our minds, the learning process is often social, and the feedback provided by peers, or our trainers can facilitate the learning. Social learning often results in positive outcomes such as better work or examination performance. This in turn drives up motivation levels.

As a result, the learner endeavours to acquire cognitive knowledge and skills to achieve higher levels of incentives and motivations (emotion). For example, my 12-year-old son prefers to learn with his peers around him. They may not be directly interacting with him but just being with people motivates him. Realising this preference, we put him in student care centres and learning centres, to provide the social atmosphere that he needs.

The Modern Learner in a VUCA World

Translating Illeris' TDLM into what we observe in our current society, the modern learner, according to Bersin by Deloitte (2014), is an overwhelmed, distracted and impatient creature of habit who engages with the internet more than 27 times a day and unlocks the mobile phone at least nine times every hour. Sociality is likely to be engaged online, with social media and social learning predominating. It is also a possibility that the modern learner may engage with bots (e.g. WoeBot, ChatGPT) in conversations as if conversing with a human. The conversational pedagogy that underpins the exchange is not unlike the dialogic engagement between humans and could even be more learning-focused. That makes technology an alternative sociality partner for learners in the near future. The modern learner also possesses a strong sense of utility, needing to make use of every minute in one's life and living life to the fullest although the extent of mindfulness and purpose may not be clear. Motivation may be driven by life's purpose rather than to earn the top dollar.

In the post-COVID-19 era, remote or hybrid work arrangement has become the norm. There is more flexibility and less work structure for the average worker. The employee is untethered, living and working in multiple locations, dialling in through video calls for team meetings, with some employees preferring to work from home or anywhere that is convenient and affordable, without needing to make unproductive and long daily journeys from one's home to the office and back. Learning and engagements are on-demand when the need arises. ChatGPT, YouTube and Google have become the world's greatest just-in-time teacher, empowering staff to perform tasks, often with little human coaching. When needed, employees come together for collaborative work activities or they seek advice from experts either in their organisation or from the sector. The social learning space has become impromptu but critical for picking up work skills and advice, especially after the pandemic. Learning is no longer confined to only classrooms and trainers. It is useful to note that the half-life of professional skills has halved from 5 years to 2.5 years and may drop even further in the future. Moving on from one's job may just be the only option left if one wishes to upgrade rapidly.

How Do We Learn?

Corroborating Deloitte's report, a research team (Barrero, Bloom, & Davis, 2021) studying work from home arrangements, polled more than 900 employees who recently left their jobs and found that inflexible work arrangements were the number 1 reason people quit, with about 39% of respondents citing the 'ability to work from home more' as their top priority.

Likewise, a similar survey of 2,050 workers conducted by OwlLabs (2021), a video conferencing platform, showed one in three people who worked remotely during the pandemic said they would quit if they weren't able to continue working from home.

'It's a perfect storm', Professor Nicholas Bloom, an economics professor from Stanford University, remarked, 'You have executives pushing for a return to the office, employees wanting to work from home and a tight labour market'. Further to that, Bloom expected employers who resisted offering work from home arrangements to relent soon and allow their staff the option for flexible work arrangements indefinitely. In a corresponding survey of 30,519 staff from organisations of different sizes, 18.5–30.2% of the respondents reflected that employers were granting work arrangement flexibility. Additionally, a survey of 13,507 full-time employees showed

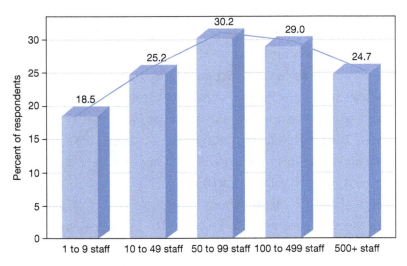

Fig. 6. Post-COVID Work-From-Home Plans by Firm Size
Source: Adapted from OwlLabs (Sept 2021). State of remote work. Retrieved on 3 Jan 2023 from: https:// owllabs.com/state-of-remote-work/2021/.

that 49.5 % preferred working two days from home and three days at the workplace.

These data point to the shift of employers' and employees' perspectives to how and where work should be conducted. Reducing commute hours to improve productivity and performing personal errands is key reason for employees to prefer flexible work arrangements while savings in rent would be one major reason for employers to allow employees to work from home. These expectations are not likely to be temporary and can impact how workers build their work capability over time. On the work front, flexible work arrangements have provided a more diverse range of options for workers to find appropriate matches with their own needs. This represents an increase in agency for workers to find their own space and time needed to grow professionally amid the changing work contexts and constraints. In tandem with these changing expectations and work arrangements, the growth in digital channels for learning has resulted in a boon for learners to pick up skills rapidly. These trends will accentuate the differences between the digital 'haves' and 'have-nots' or the digital natives and immigrants. Those who are able to exercise learner agency in leveraging these tools for learning will be able to grow faster and effectively, to grasp the opportunities, which are presenting themselves in this Volatile, Uncertain, Complex, Ambiguous (VUCA) world.

This is where Kellenberg, Schmidt, and Werner's (2017) research showing that successful lifelong learning for the adult learner is about the confluence of three factors: self-determination, self-regulation and (self)-reflection. They highlight the integration of these three factors in a triarch model as important for driving self-improvement and capability development, beyond mindless activities in a busy life. Through these three factors, learners are empowered with increased agency in a VUCA world by simply asking, 'Why I am doing what I am doing?' How can I improve myself and add value to my life?

> *"The best teachers teach themselves."*
> **David Brooks**
> *The New York Times*

What else can or should I learn? These are great questions and point toward a self-determining, self-regulating and self-reflective.

Trends in Learning and Development (L&D)

The exponential growth in L&D tools over the past decade has been nothing short of amazing. According to Marr (2022), the market for online learning services and e-learning is forecast to reach $50 billion with annual growth of 15% between 2020 and 2025. A study by IBM into its own remote learning initiatives found that learners were able to engage in more content, at one-third of the cost to the company, resulting in $200 million cost savings. The shift to micro-learning and online learning, especially facilitated by the explosive growth of Massive Open Online Courses (MOOCs) such as Udemy, Coursera, EdX is a phenomenon that has been observed for a long time now except that the pandemic in 2020 and 2021 has expedited the need for online learning when in-person learning was not possible. What educators proclaimed as impossible became possible by virtue of need. The learning experienced was not perfect but it was manageable and provided the means of learners globally to continue their education.

For some workers, the online courses made it possible to switch to new job roles, given that the pandemic made some jobs redundant. For example, retail staff who had no customers picked up digital marketing skills to promote their companies' products and services, thereby ensuring their continual employment.

While online learning is a veritable means of learning, there are other important factors which determine how an adult learner learns. According to HR News (2022), the five trends observed in learning and development are:

1. Learning and development need to be purpose-driven
2. Online training is the future
3. On-demand learning will be the norm

4. Learning will become more social
5. Cross-skilling is part of the list of desired goals

These practices such as purpose-driven learning, on-demand learning, social learning, cross-skilling are tagged on with online learning creating multiple permutations of engagement for the learners, often leading to a myriad of options which can be both confusing and enticing to different types of learners. Hence, adaptive learning underpinned by Artificial Intelligence (AI) is often touted as one means of meeting these needs. The possibility of intelligent agents (e.g. ChatGPT by Open.ai) taking on questions by learners is real and can be implemented once the technology is carefully harnessed, underpinned by ethical principles, for benefits to human users.

In a similar vein, Bernard Marr (2022) in his article on Forbes.com noted the following trends:

- Remote learning
- Lifelong learning (subscription services)
- Immersive learning technology — Augmented Reality and Virtual Reality
- AI and automation in the classroom
- Nano-learning

While trends such as AI, AR and VR have been in the news for some time now, nano-learning describes a new EdTech concept where learners can undertake ultra-bite-sized lessons exactly when and where they need these lessons. With this approach, it did not matter if learners did not memorise what they learned because learners could simply re-learn it as the nano-sized information is easily accessible.

Nano-Learning Cycle

In their presentation at a UNESCO conference, Choy *et al*. (2021) illustrated how using chatbots for learning can help adult learners achieve short bursts of effective learning for work. In a pilot study with more than 1,200 learners, both quantitative (achieving 4.6 out of 5.0 Likert rating scale for a range of seven indicators) and qualitative data showed that nano-learning cycles matched the needs of adult learners, especially when they need to learn when working. The injection of the emotive element was also instrumental in driving the learning process:

> FWL: Feeling stressfree and have enough time to take a break when I wish too
>
> WM: ... the interaction with Amy (the bot) — it is fun.

The level of comprehensibility increased with the focus on the content underpinned by direct conversations with the learners. Through conversations, the learners engaged in 'WhatsApp-like' engagements, which reduced the anxiety for the learners while keeping their focus on the content. The key is in keeping the dialogic flow tight with some meaningful bantering and a lot more clarifications and quizzing within the short nano-learning cycle. Crafting identifiable personas for the chatbots was the key to facilitating the flow of the conversations, increasing the resonance that learners had with the chatbots:

> CCC: It's fun and easy to understand and [content was] more integrated
>
> NMA: ... everything from this chatbot (was good). Better way to understand.

What is a Nano Learning™ Loop?

Nestled within a conversational cycle, short Nano Learning™ Loops designed to last about 5 minutes each are critical to maintaining the flow of the conversation while driving learning and giving feedback to the learners.

The dialogic exchange ensures that the flow of the conversation is intentional and benefits the learners engaged in the conversation. Compared to typical chats for leisure or relationship building, chatbots for learning are designed to help learners achieve learning outcomes.

Chapter 3

Fig. 7. Relationship Between Conversational Cycle and Nano Learning™ Loops Framework

The Context for the Use of Error-Based Approach in Facilitating Learning and Decision Making

In this chapter, we have covered several critical learning models and concepts, namely:

Table 2. Summary of Models in Relation to Error-Based Learning

	Models and Concepts	Learning	Implications for Error-Based Approach
1	LAMP (Learning, Atmosphere, Mind and Production) Model	Relates to how learning and production are different even though they are linked	Error-Based Approach (EBL) is production-driven as learners are asked to resolve issues, spot and/or correct errors. Learning may or may not have been completed before the EBL activity. Learning will be layered on to past learning as EBL uncovers learners' understanding of the concepts.
2	TDLM (Three Dimensions of Learning Model)	Illustrates the learning needs of the adult learner	Errors can be designed to address the cognitive, emotional and social domains, creating a holistic approach to learning.
3	Learner agency in a VUCA (Volatile, Uncertain, Complex, Ambiguous) world	Where changing work arrangements and online learning provide learners with options to learn and do things differently from the past	The VUCA work and learning environments point to the need for learners to remain adaptable and responsive in their thinking and coping mechanisms. EBL equips learners with the metacognitive capability to manage volatility and the creativity to change.
4	Trends in Learning and Development	Point to just-in-time capability building through tech-enabled learning at the workplace	With tech-enabled learning, EBL can be implemented in a scalable and personalised manner. The impact of EBL is measurable and the refinements to the EBL triggers are data-driven.
5	Nano-Learning	Matches the way learners want to learn quickly in rapid and nano-sized learning cycles	EBL instances will need to be crafted to fit within nano-learning cycles where learning is layered on spirally with each cycle.

How Do We Learn?

Within our understanding of the learning processes in relation to the LAMP model and the TDLM dimensions, we can pinpoint how specially designed errors will impact learning for the individual, in a targeted manner. For example, under the TDLM, errors can be custom designed to achieve certain outcomes (e.g. pre-empting leadership errors within the social domain). As such, it is critical that the EBL approach takes reference from the various learning models and processes to ensure that the benefits are real and anchored to current learning frameworks.

Since errors can be attributed to any one of the Learning, Atmosphere, Mind and Production segments, it may be useful to integrate the LAMP model with the TDLM for a more comprehensive framework when looking at learning through EBL.

Specifically, the three TDLM dimensions (Cognition, Emotion and Sociality) are useful in detailing the skill and concept acquisition process for the Learning, Atmosphere and Mind segments. We can add Performance enhancement to the framework to include errors which are production in nature (due to the lack of practice or familiarity).

The approach to honing decision-making is to provide problems with options that are close to the most optimal solution. These problems would be most difficult for those who are proficient in the domain to resolve. Incorporating slight errors into the options would require subtlety and good design skill, on top of strong subject matter expertise. It won't be easy to design these error-based learning experiences though. The first step is to acknowledge the need for these error-infused problems for decision-making exercises. Following which, the design process will take over.

In summary, the EBL approach addresses skill and knowledge gaps in four critical areas as listed in Table 2. These areas are collated from both the LAMP and TDLM models. The next chapter is devoted to describing, with illustrations, how the design of the errors for learning and teaching, also known as the DELETE approach, will address these critical areas in order to improve learning and performance.

Part 2

How DELETE™ (Designing Errors for Learning and Teaching) Works: The Error-Making Process

Part 2

Introduction

In the previous segment, we covered the roles of errors in facilitating learning, especially for learners upgrading from novice to experts and how people learn. In typical learning design fashion, training activities are usually structured and sequenced to achieve learning outcomes. The assumption is that there are correct processes and behaviours, which the learners will acquire during training. In reality, school and work situations are far more complex and unpredictable compared to learning scenarios. As such, it is unclear if these design principles will prepare our learners sufficiently for a chaotic world, given that the emphasis is to do what is set as correct rather than learn to work with unconnected pieces of information, which requires independent thinking and reflection.

This chapter will explore the impact of designed errors to trigger reflection and questioning of assumptions in a targeted manner. The 'Designing Errors for Learning and Teaching' **(DELETE™)** approach advocates the careful design of errors to make explicit the boundaries to which the concepts are not applicable. Through critical reflection, learners are forced to examine their learning and assumptions especially when contexts are uncertain and current rules and Standard Operating Procedures (SOPs) may not apply. This is to allow prevailing assumptions to surface and be examined, leading to greater mindfulness and metacognition at work.

Chapter 4

Competencies and Beyond: Developing Proficiency and Expertise

The Nature of Work in the 21st Century

In the current context of work, especially with rapid technological advancements and globalisation, it will be naive to consider any type or category of work as permanent or long term. Major developments in automation and communication have transformed work practices all over the world to the extent that fields previously considered as safe and unchanging such as medical or educational services are being reshaped to reflect market pressure and societal expectations. Workers, whether blue- or white-collared, must adapt at a very fast pace, to cope with the transformations at the workplace, to avoid being relegated as backward and redundant. This rapid transformation of work is even more apparent to the personnel in the Armed Forces. For example, the US Navy launched the first unmanned fighter plane, capable of delivering warheads, from an aircraft carrier, in the mid-2010s, while drone technology proved incisive and game-changing during the Ukraine war, leading to the rise of asymmetric warfare where a smaller player can still win by using precise and less expensive tools to target the opponent's weak points or critical structure. Elsewhere, there are developments on invisibility cloaks, communication jamming mechanisms and bio-terrorism among others, all of which have serious implications on war and peace operations, especially in light of how the war in Ukraine has upended many previously held assumptions concerning rule of law and warfare. The Volatile, Uncertain, Complex, Ambiguous (VUCA) world is real, and we need to respond to these changes pre-emptively rather than retroactively, if we were to leverage the tools and capabilities to achieve better outcomes.

It is interesting to note that many Continuing Education and Training (CET) researchers (e.g. Billet, 2004; Dreyfus, 2004; Illeris, 2008) recognise that training is critical to helping workers acquire key competencies for work. However, they also advocate the use of work and work environments to promote the development of capabilities or competences. According to Jørgensen (1999, p. 4),

> *Competences... the person can apply this professional knowledge — and more than that, apply it in relation to the requirements inherent in a situation which perhaps in addition is uncertain and unpredictable.*

In effect, competences encapsulate more than basic competencies, which are usually viewed as specific skill sets needed to complete tasks. Hence, the understanding is that all the competencies one possesses do not add up to one's competence to get the job the done well. The literature on learning at and for work revolves around a number of areas of which individual disposition and competences, interactional competencies and workplace policies and affordances are relevant to our discussion. See Fig. 8.

The three areas depicted in Fig. 8 also suggest that focusing on developing a worker's competencies (or skill sets) is only part of the development process. There are other non-skill related competences (e.g. innovation, values and adaptive behaviours), which allow the worker to manage non-standard issues and make the correct decisions accordingly, over the longer term, within the context of work.

The Nature of Current Instructional Designs

Interestingly, while advancements in technology and psychological interventions to enhance human performance have been progressing

Competencies and Beyond: Developing Proficiency and Expertise

Fig. 8. Three of the Key Areas Considered Important in CET Training and Work Performance

at a fast pace, developments in CET instructional designs, especially in local contexts, have lagged somewhat behind. The CET sector in Asia is still relatively embedded in traditional pedagogy, where accumulation of facts and competencies seems sufficient and the reproduction of required behaviours a success indicator celebrated with the award of certificates and qualifications.

One of the issues associated with instructional design and to some extent, learning design work involves the assumption that learning is about facilitating learners to learn the right way of doing the right things. In fact, this focus on learning right processes and right concepts or skill sets underpins most instructional design theories. It is common to see instructivist designs which provide a demonstration at the start followed by learner practice to guide learners to imitate the correct behaviour correctly. Subsequently, there may be debriefs to alert learners to possible areas of difficulties and blind spots. Other designs that are more constructivist in nature may allow learners to experience the issues first hand before they acquire the theoretical underpinning afterwards. For both general design approaches, the focus is mostly about directing the learner towards achieving the learning outcomes or objectives.

> There is a story about a surgeon commenting to a medical student, "I can teach you in ten minutes how to take out an appendix but it will take me four years to teach you what to do if something goes wrong."

The assumption is that once the learners have achieved the learning objectives, the learners are deemed to be competent and can perform the job role. That assumption, in my opinion, needs to be questioned, especially in the current context of changing work environments and emerging challenges, which present wicked problems for the person in the workplace. The use of learning outcomes in training may be useful when inducting or training the novice worker but once the worker has gained sufficient experience in the job and is able to manage the basic skill sets, training by objectives appears to be less effective (Illeris, 2008). More importantly, the assumption that we should train workers to do the right things and in the right ways is based on a myopic view of what work is. In reality, the judgement call of 'correctness' is based on the situation at hand. Hence, what is correct in a certain situation can be extremely inappropriate in another.

Ultimately, the competences involved in a job centre round making the right decisions for the right situation. It involves having the right frame of mind and belief system to make difficult decisions and the psychological resilience to stick with them. Hence, while competency training may suffice for the novice, it may not provide sufficient development for the worker who is going beyond completing the tasks into performing the job.

In addition, getting the task performed correctly sometimes does not contribute to learning. It merely reinforces the 'correct' behaviour

Competencies and Beyond: Developing Proficiency and Expertise

or performance. When learners focus on perfecting the right behaviours in class, it may possibly shackle learners to a whole list of SOPs and 'best practices', which in turn, may hinder the development of thinking processes and competences for effective work performance later.

As mentioned in an earlier chapter, when a

Assumptions Behind Current Instructional Designs

1. There are right ways to do the task.
2. There are right tasks to do.
3. The contexts remain essentially similar over time.
4. SOPs are crafted to allow efficiency.
5. Following best practices will ensure optimum work performance.
6. Learners are expected to adhere to the learning design and achieve the learning outcomes set.

novice progresses towards being an expert in a particular field, he or she will begin to exhibit stronger skill acquisition capabilities, a higher level of independence, transformations in mindset and an innovative ability, which are superior to the novice or the competent worker Dreyfus (2004). Hart (1986) put forward other attributes that characterise an expert, which include effectiveness (solving problems with an acceptable rate of success), efficiency (solving problems quickly) and awareness of limitations (willing to say when they cannot solve a problem). A key feature of how novices move into competent and eventually expert status is the ability to work independently due to an acute sense of what getting the job done well entails. Much of this sensing involves an ability to streamline work based on his perceived understanding of the context and the required actions to resolve the issues. Sometimes, it appears to be intuitive. However, the ability to recognise relevant information comes with years of experience in reading situations correctly and accurately. While it appears that training in general can develop the novice into a competent worker, a certain degree of variedness and unpredictability at work is generally required to facilitate the development of the expert. To a large extent, an expert is expected to organise knowledge effectively, have superior recall of information and have improved abilities to abstract knowledge to *new* situations, compared to lay people (Feltovitch, Prietula, & Ericsson, 2006). Tetlock's (2005) study, based on several hundred political experts, showed that the single most powerful predictor of forecasting skill had little to do with *what* experts think, and more to do with *how* they think. Hence, understanding how one thinks may expedite the development of expertise for the competent worker.

Issues with Predictable Instructional Designs

Brain research conducted by Prof. Tobler *et al*. (2006) from Cambridge University, UK, indicates that people learn most vividly when the outcomes are not in line with their own expectations. The MRI scans show that segments of the brain seem to be most alert when expected rewards are **not** given. In other words, non-predictability can enhance learning as the neural connections are formed or strengthened with such unpredictability.

> The data suggest that people learn most vividly when the outcomes are not in line with their own expectations.

However, the issue with most learning design is that learning is generally predictable and well-structured, with clear learning outcomes and possibly assessment requirements. For novices, structured learning aids them to develop their own mental framework of learning. On the other hand, workers who are already competent in performing the tasks will require a level of variability in the design to help them attend to critical concepts. If training becomes too predictable, these experienced workers may subsequently develop a sense of 'been there, done that' and tune out for the rest of the entire programme. Training the competent to become experts then requires a different set of assumptions and learning approaches.

Richard Sennet (2008) in his book, *The Craftsman*, describes how the development of craftsmanship is an arduous process whereby the craftsman develops skills of imagination, to create and do a job well for its own sake.

> *... first, that all skills, even the most abstract, begin as bodily practices; second, that technical understanding develops through the powers of imagination... resistance and ambiguity can be instructive experiences; to work well, every craftsman has to learn from these experiences rather than fight them.*
>
> Sennett
> (2008, p. 10)

According to Sennett (2008), it will be the resistance and ambiguity that forces the craftsman to acquire new skill sets, to innovate and imagine and finally develop expertise. In this regard, the question of how these resistances and ambiguities can be incorporated into learning experiences for expertise to be cultivated and developed needs to be addressed.

Chapter 5
Incorporating Variability and Unpredictability in Training to Develop Capabilities

Introduction

Our present-day work landscape with its high level of variability and uncertainty requires educators to review how we design training and if traditional instructional approaches still work. We do need to take a hard look at what else we need to do to prepare our workforce for future work. Listed subsequently are the arguments for a serious review of current instructional designs:

- Work is evolving rapidly with new job roles (e.g. AI trainer and YouTuber) emerging every few months. The unpredictability of work presents new challenges, especially for those in frontline work (e.g. nurses and retail staff) and ICT sectors as new technological advancements and changes in equipment and procedures continue to swarm these sectors incessantly.
- The nature of current instructional designs is geared towards achieving predetermined learning outcomes, which in itself is based on the assumption that there is fixed list of items to do in a certain manner. However, with rapidly changing work contexts, we must question this assumption. Instructional designs which are overly predictable with little room for variability (e.g. to drill SOPs into learners) may actually be detrimental to developing expertise such as innovation and problem-solving skills.

- Development of workers from competent to expert requires the presentation of variability and ambiguity to allow workers to develop competences from competencies.

Hence, what will constitute a possible alternative to the current instructional designs that are available to us? If we are advocating a learning design that does not provide specific right answers but answers that are dependent on the context and situation, will our learners be receptive?

To incorporate ambiguity in a deliberate and measured manner, the learning design should include a set of design rules to free up space to question prior learning and propose new ways of doing things within different contexts. New learning is generated when learners make their own connections with the learning materials in ways which they have not experienced before, bringing a new sense of mindfulness and empowerment about how work can be carried out differently and more effectively.

Using Errors to Generate Ambiguity and Unpredictability

Reason (1990) found human error to be the single largest cause of failures at work. What the team found was that people make errors because of the complexity of the planning and reasoning processes involved in performing tasks and if the complexity can be reduced or if these complexities are made visible, some of these processing errors can be eliminated. What the findings imply is that if a reverse engineering approach is taken, these errors can be used as triggers for learners to reflect on their planning and reasoning processes and determine the contexts in which the errors are made. The presentation of unexpected errors will introduce ambiguity and unpredictability in the learning process, especially for experienced workers in particular fields and should present instructive moments for professional development. Hence, the crux of this approach lies in the design of the errors to take the learners out of the learning comfort zone so that they question long-held assumptions and beliefs, to move further along the novice-expert spectrum to become craftsmen in their own fields of work.

Prof Reason's research also recommends that training should:

- include error scenarios
- promote exploratory trial and error approaches
- emphasise positive side of errors such as learning from mistakes

More interestingly, Reason's (1990) research findings indicate that training and familiarity with the task do NOT eliminate or reduce errors. In fact, error rates remain stable if the system design is susceptible to error production. What this means is that as long as new situations keep cropping up within the system, the user will continue to make errors. The errors range from slips (e.g. typing a wrong letter) to lapses (e.g. remembering something wrongly) to mistakes (e.g. wrong decision due to incorrect reasoning). The above findings seem to corroborate with the hypothesis that competency training, which focuses on making tasks familiar, does not equip workers with the competence to manage new situations in a productive manner. In effect, when contexts change, the right way of doing things may not be relevant or right anymore, something that is highly critical to advanced professional development of workers.

The Roles of Rules and Boundaries

a) Following Rules

Learning often entails the acquisition of concepts and procedures, then performing the tasks or activities according to these rules, as closely as possible to the standard. These operating rules guide how one behaves in an acceptable manner based on shared agreement within the industry. These operating rules indicate what to do and what NOT to do (e.g. 10 commandments, school rules, math question — a different approach, e.g.

diagrams vs. formula, standard operating procedures to work a machine). You need to be clear that there are To-Do rules and Not-To-Do rules that should be followed carefully in typical learning paradigms. Learners are deemed as competent when they can perform these tasks according to the measurable standards.

Not-To-Do rules (akin to non-performance of tasks) are similar to To-Do rules in that they are just phrased negatively. They are also part of the defining boundaries surrounding the To-Do rules. The purpose of rules is to guide users in following them and the nature of rules is to be clear with as little ambiguity as possible. It is important not to mix the Not-To-Do rules (e.g. Do not cross the road when the light is red) with boundaries because these rules have their corresponding boundaries. Breaking these rules will entail consequences (i.e. accidents may occur if one crosses the road when the light is red). These not-to-do rules may have the corresponding To-Do rule (e.g. 'Cross the road safely when the light is green').

There are 'rules' that are declarative (vs. procedural) in nature. These conceptual 'rules' provide knowledge for you to navigate within and to base decisions off them. Hence, the purpose of these declarative 'rules' could be for labelling (e.g. World War Two ended in 1945), thereby providing shared understanding, building on evidence and knowledge underpinned by logic.

b) Observing the Contextual Boundaries

Besides the rules, what is often not focused on, are the contextual boundaries within which the rules operate. These attached contexts, whether socio-economic, cultural, spiritual, psychological, emotional or other areas, are extremely important to determine whether you applied the rules appropriately, within the context.

If you understand rules, SOPs or algorithms, they are guidelines to which you can follow without too much consideration because someone has done the thinking for you. However, all rules operate within the boundaries because there are NO rules which can operate everywhere under all circumstances. As such, specifying the contextual boundaries becomes important if you want to know the extent to which the rules operate. As mentioned earlier, issues arise when we follow the To-Do and Not-To-Do rules without understanding the boundaries of these rules.

c) The Nature of Contexts

Compared to rules, contexts are more difficult to ascertain and describe. According to the earlier example of road crossing, even if the light may be green, a possible boundary of the rule is when a car is speeding towards the pedestrian crossing. In this case, with the speeding car approaching, the contextual boundary has changed and even if the light is green, do NOT cross the road.

What this example shows us is that contexts are multi-faceted, often implicit and impossible to fully describe due to the innumerable permutations. In current terms, contexts can be described as 'VUCA', which implies that they can shift and often, unknown to the observers of the rules. The key is to constantly evaluate the state of the rules and the contextual boundaries of application. What this means is that establishing the contexts is insufficient, it is equally important to determine the boundaries of the contexts so that you do not cross the boundaries where the rules do not operate within, resulting in errors.

d) Who Knows the Contextual Boundaries?

The person who uses the rules most often is likely to know where the boundaries lie. However, this is not always true as it depends on whether the person constantly reflects on the status of the rule and if contexts have shifted. It takes someone with metacognitive awareness to uncover any changes to the rule and contexts. In short, the person with an expertise mindset, constantly pondering over issues and observation of the outcomes from following the rules will likely know where the boundaries are. Even this is not guaranteed as complacency and negative transfer may hinder new reflections and learning, resulting in errors, sometimes basic ones.

Chapter 5

> **Rules and Contextual Boundaries: An Example**
>
> A case in point about how changing contextual boundaries can lead to errors is illustrated in the following fictitious example:
>
> A new HR staff involved in selecting potential candidates overseas had just assessed the applicants on a knowledge test. He was met with his country counterpart and was handed a handwritten list of applicant names along with their index numbers. The names were carefully kept, to be used later for marking and checking of identities. A thumb drive with the same list of names was also handed over to the HR staff to expedite processing.
>
> The test papers, the handwritten name list and the thumb drive were handed over to the analysis unit for scoring and results processing. The candidates were informed of the test outcomes after three months.
>
> This was when a query was raised concerning the absence of two candidates from the test, based on the released results. Upon checking, the horrific error was discovered. Spend a minute to guess what that error was. Give it a try. Turn to the next page to find out.

When Do We Need to Relearn?

This is an important question especially in our current world where knowledge can become obsolete within months in certain cases. If we are not careful, our past knowledge (and competency) can lead us to commit serious errors when there are changes to rules and/or contexts. Psychologists term this as 'negative transfer'. This is relatively common when we transfer our past learning to contexts which have changed with or without us realising the change. See the example in the grey box, which illustrates the importance of knowing the contextual boundaries when following the rules.

Rules and Contextual Boundaries: An Example (cont'd)

Well, what guesses did you make? How did the error arise?

To put it simply, the analysis unit did not realise that the sequence of names in the handwritten list did not correspond with the sequence of names in the list found in the thumb drive and when the results of the ability test were assigned based solely on (the wrong) index numbers in the list in the thumb drive rather than the handwritten list, the candidates were given each other's results. This also led to the two absent candidates being given a score and the two candidates present at the test being marked as absent. As a result, the wrong candidates were hired for the job despite careful screening!

How does this example of miscommunication underpinned by the lack of checking procedures during the analysis phase relate to the principles of rules and contexts? What are the rules, context and its boundaries?

Rules:
- Check the sequence of names in both the given list and the list in the thumb drive (or sent over emails) to ensure that they are the same, with the same index numbers.
- Confirm with the testing staff that the list of names is the same as those tested, with the same index numbers.
- Check the names and the index numbers of the candidates after processing of results.
- *New* rule: names of candidates should be submitted a week prior to the test and cannot be changed subsequently at the test venue.

Context: The overseas contexts present other challenges especially when name lists can change at the last minute, new candidates added by the country counterpart and communication can be hampered due language barrier.

(*Continued*)

(*Continued*)

Contextual Boundaries: The rules apply if:
- the candidates' assigned index numbers do not deviate from the original list
- throughout the process of testing, analysing and generation of results, the names of the candidates and their assigned index numbers remain unchanged, e.g. name variants should not be entertained.

While this story appears esoteric, it is not uncommon to hear of people making errors when using data spreadsheets, especially in the copying and pasting of data. Many of these errors occur when users did not realise that the datapoints between the old list (e.g. Rows 1–20) and new list (now Rows 1–19) are not the same, leading to wrong assignment of data (especially in research). More importantly, what are the first principles that we can glean from this lesson?

Hence, relearning is needed when rules and/or contexts are changed. It helps us to reboot our system so that we are mindful how we ought to behave and what we need to expect in terms of outcomes when guided by the rules within the changed contexts. At the start, it may not be easy and we may still commit errors but with careful and intentional re-wiring of our behaviour, we would be able to manage the process. Hence, pre-emptive relearning is critical in the light of upcoming changes. These changes may be as simple as buying a new mobile phone (e.g. a foldable version) to something more serious and complex as using a new software to process financial data, for submission to auditors. This leads us to the next question:

Incorporating Variability and Unpredictability

How Do We Design the Experience for Rapid Learning or Relearning?

The key is to determine the rules that learners need to acquire together with the contexts. Once the learners are familiar with the rules and contexts, SWITCH the rules and/or contexts to help establish new behaviours. In the well-known story about Goliath, the giant, and the shepherd boy, David, it was a case of the changing the context from traditional warfare of hand-to-hand combat and using the sword, shield and helmet to the use of 'missile warfare' where more contemporary weapons of sling and stones are used. Goliath failed to realise the change in context and with that the rules of engagement had changed, leading to his demise.

When designing errors for learning, the clarity to what these rules are and the contexts they operate in can be difficult to ascertain. Often, expertise is needed to make these rules explicit. Even then, there is a limit to what one knows. Hence, to manage expectations, determining the level of fuzziness to the learning task and contexts may be useful. However, the learning outcomes need to be clear and these are usually articulated in relation to the rules and contexts set. We will discuss the specific details to the designing (DELETE) process in the next chapter. It suffices at this point, to say that the focus is on designing the experience for the learners to uncover the rules AND contexts for themselves. Often, it implies the need for the learners to consider the *first principles*, which often underpin the rules. Active discussion and analysis of the rules at hand can be a useful exercise for learners to deepen their understanding and subsequent application of the rules, especially within the right context. See inset for the story about interpreting data (rule) within the right context.

In varying the rules and contexts for the learners to experience *progressively*, there is heightened awareness that the issues are not straightforward and warrant metacognition, i.e. thinking about their assumptions and thinking. Over time, the learner's metacognitive capability can be activated quickly (hopefully!) when the situation arises.

Chapter 5

Varying the Context: An Example

In his book, *How Not to Be Wrong*, American mathematician Jordan Ellenberg shares a compelling tale of how the American forces during World War 2 used numbers to determine the best way to reinforce the armour on their war planes, so that they can survive the rain of bullets and flak from enemy guns.

To obtain some data for decision making, the Airforce analysed all the planes that returned from their combat missions and discovered that the planes had the most number of bullet holes in the wings, the tail and fuselage (see Fig. 9).

Given that the weight of the planes is critical to ensure manoeuvrability and speed, the armour could not be strengthened across the entire plane. If you were part of the team, where would you add the armour? See the next page for the continuation of the story.

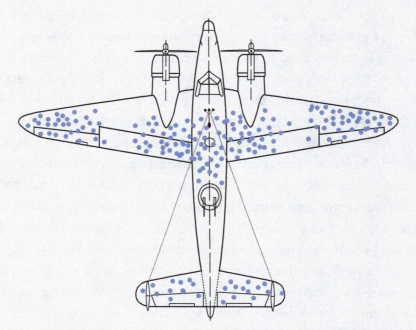

Fig. 9. Showing Which Parts of the Plane that Suffered the Most Bullet Holes (Credit: McGeddon/CC-BY-SA-4.0)

Developing Capabilities Through the DELETE Approach

You are probably getting a sense of how error-based learning works by now, where the errors help you (and your learners) to focus on critical concepts in the topic. The answers are not shown at the start and learners need to uncover the concepts, often through critical reflection and discussion.

In many of these constructivist learning experiences (where learners uncover and mentally construct the concepts themselves), it is common to find that the outcomes include mindsets related to innovation, curiosity

---

Varying the Context: An Example

Well, if you decided to add armour to the parts of the plane with the most bullet holes, you are not alone. After discussing, the Air Force command, based on the data, decided to add armour to cover the parts with the most bullet holes. They wanted maximum efficiency to determine *how much* armour to be added so they referred the case to Abraham Wald, a brilliant statistician of his time.

However, upon reviewing the data, Wald sent the request back to them and replied to them quite differently from what was requested. The Airforce was asked to relook WHERE they should add the armour instead of how much to add.

He explained that the context should NOT be of the planes that returned to base since these planes survived the shooting despite the bullet holes. The context to be considered should be those planes that suffered hits to the engines and hence, did NOT survive the return trip. The reinforcement of armour should be based on the second context, not the first, and the data belonging to the second context were NOT part of the original database!

Finally, the decision was made to put the extra armour where the bullet holes were not present, i.e. on the engines, giving the American airplanes the extra protection that they needed.

This story by Ellen illustrates not just why data are important but also the context in which the data are interpreted is also critical.

and a constant drive to improve processes. These mindsets augur well for the current and future economies and work landscape where VUCA characteristics will be the norm.

Developing Expertise in Children and Adults

It is a misnomer that expertise can only be found in adults due to the experience expected. The counter argument is that children and youth can gain some level of expertise too, especially if they have spent significant amount of time working through specific rules and concepts, experimenting with the applications of these rules within different contexts.

For example, some children and youth have mastered specific skills (e.g. playing musical instruments, sports, academic concepts), at their level of competence, with sufficient grasp of the concept to expertly play or perform that piece of work. Hence, designing errors for these young learners to develop capabilities is possible and can be useful to fast track their growth, and move them into expertise. For these young learners, the learning instances will need to be constrained to specific contexts that they understand, due to their limited perspectives of the world (although having said that, many young people are already quite attuned to the events of the world, due to exposure to TikTok, YouTube and the like).

In the next few chapters, you will review how these learning experiences involving errors can be designed and developed to drive capability development, in short, the DELETE approach.

Chapter 6

Locating the DELETE Approach Within the Curriculum Design Process

Thus far, the chapters have laid the foundation with the exposition on what learning means, defining error-based learning and the learner profiles that will benefit from the approach.

Taking a step back, this chapter will look at design at the curriculum level, which is a more macro perspective than at the modular or activity level. The emphasis is on constructive alignment across modules and activities with the incorporation of the DELETE approach as an instructional design tool to achieve curriculum outcomes. In short, curriculum designers need to consider other key issues such as strategic intent of the curriculum, the learner and the expected graduate profile.

Difference Between Curriculum Design and Instructional Design

While the terms 'curriculum design' and 'instructional design' are often used interchangeably in the literature, they do have different meanings and foci. Curriculum design takes on a wider perspective pertaining to standards development, educational goals and achievements, some of which require several years of engagement for the learners to achieve. The intended journey that the learner goes through and graduates with are areas that the curriculum designer needs to address.

With instructional design, the focus is about the specific learning instances and experiences crafted within lessons and modules. Instructional design takes a narrower perspective and focuses on course materials, methods and objectives and courseware (e.g. lesson plans, learner guides) is often a key deliverable of the instructional design process. Hence, the DELETE approach falls within the category of an instructional design theory, to review how learning can be recrafted for a different and more effective learning experience for the various learner profiles, to achieve higher order outcomes.

How Does the DELETE Approach Impact Curriculum Design?

In curriculum design, there are several elements which are critical for consideration:

a) Curriculum models
b) Learner and graduate profile
c) Assessment scope

These three areas are part of the overall curriculum structure (see Fig. 10), which determines how the various modules within the curriculum ought to be designed and aligned. We will examine briefly how the DELETE approach can impact the above-mentioned areas to produce a more effective learning experience for the learners.

a) *Curriculum Model*

Depending on the curriculum model decided by the curriculum designer and stakeholders, the DELETE approach can be aligned to the model accordingly. See Table 3 for alignment details.

In the context of curriculum models, the design of errors should be aligned with the characteristics of selected curriculum model for the

Locating the DELETE Approach Within the Curriculum Design Process

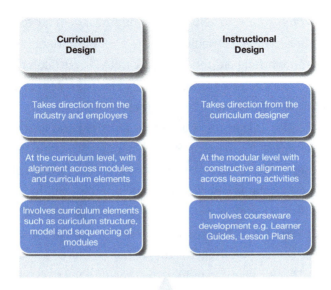

Fig. 10. Differences Between Curriculum and Instructional Design

Table 3. Four Curriculum Models and Error-Based Learning

Type of Curriculum Model	Outcome of Model	Purpose of DELETE Errors	Examples of DELETE Errors
Syllabus	Learning to know	To examine learner's declarative and process knowledge	Correcting the wrong labels attached to the parts of the flower; nurse corrects the wrong functions attached to the different parts of the brain
Product	Learning to reach an end point	To review the competence of the learner	Identifying a wrongly dissected plant part in biology class; asking a waiter to relay a table that is laid out wrongly
Process	Learning how to do or think	To develop cognitive ability, observational skills, identification of errors and problem-solving skills	Stating the points in an observation when the wrong catalyst or chemical is poured in Chemistry class; spotting the points when the retail assistant did not adhere to SOP during her interaction with the customer
Praxis	Learning one's beliefs, values and mindsets	To check values, beliefs and mindsets	Stating if there is anything wrong with the mind set or values of a character in the story (e.g. *Lord of the Flies*); working out the issues in a miscommunication between two staff and assigning the blame accordingly based on assumptions and values

programme. For example, to help achieve the curriculum outcomes, which are based on the selected curriculum model, the appropriate type of errors needs to be thoughtfully crafted. By using DELETE, curriculum designers will find these errors to be extremely useful to help learners to acquire the necessary competence. What does this mean?

The implication is that there are more tools at hand for the designer to achieve the required curriculum goals. For example, using the designed error as the trigger event, the facilitator will be able to, through questioning and probing, guide the learners to discover and develop for themselves useful life skills involving questioning assumptions and metacognitive awareness of their own thinking patterns. If the learners are trained to perform a critical job role (e.g. senior management or key personnel), then the DELETE approach can reduce the time needed to train these staff to undertake the required tasks by focusing directly on critical skillsets, bypassing the less relevant or easier parts of the tasks. Such learning activities can push learners to consider areas not commonly discussed (e.g. assumptions or sensitive topics) so as to develop resilience and preparedness for future crises. Inevitably, the curriculum designers need to set the right expectations for downstream instructional design by setting the parameters accordingly. These parameters will include the curriculum models (e.g. product curriculum which may mean a focus on cognitive and psychomotor skillsets), the accompanying DELETE approach (e.g. to increase psychomotor reflexivity to errors) to achieve the expected graduate profiles (e.g. a more nimble and macro-issue thinker).

b) *Learner and Graduate Profile*
To fully benefit from the DELETE approach, the expected profile of learners is someone who reflects, possesses a good level of cognitive and communication skills, unpacks concepts and joins the dots to formulate learning. In other words, a certain degree of learning autonomy is needed by the learners to leverage error-based learning instances, which may be fuzzy at the start. With sufficient unpacking, the errors designed into the

experiences should provide useful triggers and focus for the learners to make sense of the underlying concepts and the contextual boundaries. While the facilitators and trainers can attempt to unpack the learning for the learners, the essence of the learning is best served by oneself, channelled through reflective tools amid a constructivist pedagogical frame.

In the same vein, the graduate profile, is dependent on the individual learners being able to adequately process the information and learning to fully benefit from the experience. Having said that, the DELETE experience should prepare the 'graduate' learner for situations beyond the norm and where thinking needs to be extended into the adjoining contexts. What this means is that the learners should be able to question assumptions, cite associated concepts, uncover first principles when reviewing issues and be self-aware, especially of one's own biases and preconceived notions of the issue. Graduates are likely to be able to pre-empt issues or at least not be caught unaware when issues arise. The caveat is that it takes years of honing to develop this pre-empting metacognitive capability so the DELETE approach is to set the stage for the individual learner to progress further along on this self-development journey.

c) *Expanding the Assessment Scope*

One way in which the DELETE approach is used effectively is to stage the unveiling of the error (in bite sizes) to draw the candidates into the space where they think of possible outcomes based on what they know of the scenario, which then prepares them for contingencies and the corresponding preventive measures.

For example, a typical scenario that I put trainee assessors through is to forewarn them that the video that they are going to watch shows an assessor who despite her compassion, committed a lapse in judgement when she conducted her assessment.

This sets the learners up to expect issues and to pre-empt these issues where possible. Next, I would ask the learners to watch the entire video in parts, stopping at specific moments, before the onset of the error, after the error was committed and finally, at the presentation of the final outcome due to the decisions made by the characters.

It almost never fails to amaze me at the *number of possible errors* that the learners would bring up and all of these would be possible, some highly plausible ones. There were also minor errors brought up, some of which would escape the attention of the other learners. Through the moments when the learners brainstormed the issues, debated the merits of the issues brought up, without my commenting whether it was the error in the video, the learners made huge discoveries about:

a) themselves, especially their own pedagogical beliefs
b) how their beliefs *differed* from other seemingly like-minded professionals
c) their understanding of the concepts being discussed
d) the underlying first principles, in this case, about what constitute competency-based assessment

The richness of the discussion and the passion shown by the learners when they debated what constituted errors made the DELETE sessions highly emotionally charged, with some learners insisting that their points were valid. One reason for the emotive engagement lies in the triggering of the learners' professional identity. Many of these learners might have been performing the tasks in the manner shown for a long time and to have them reconsider their approach or even to be labelled as incorrect was a wake-up call for some of them. The magical moment was when their fellow classmates proceeded to explain the first principles in detail with some showing that 'Eureka' moment when they finally realised the principles governing the behaviour they have been exhibiting or defending for some time.

Often, the eventual revelation of the error that they were supposed to identify paled in importance compared to the process they undertook to uncover their underlying assumptions and beliefs. By getting the learners to foretell the error, the learners actually uncovered a lot more other areas which could *NEVER* have been achieved through the typical 'show and tell' approach, i.e. show the error and telling the learners how to avoid committing the error. The learners demonstrated agency in driving what they thought were the rules and the contextual boundaries related to the rules.

From the perspective of performance assessment, the demonstration of the knowledge and performance can be made with the gradual unfolding of the scenarios as candidates respond to the changes in context. In the account given earlier, the issue was that the assessor allowed the candidate who had started the assessment to defer due to the recent death of her brother. She was not in the right psychological state to take the assessment. However, as the candidate had started the assessment proper (including the Written Test), it was not fair to other candidates for her to be able to defer her assessment while they could not (under other circumstances). Even though it sounds cruel, the candidate should be given a 'fail' result based on assessment procedures. She would also have to undertake the entire assessment again. The underlying first principle here is that the assessor should have confirmed with the candidates that they were fit and proper to undertake the assessment BEFORE the assessment started. Once the assessment has started, it would have to be completed.

Designing errors into assessments can facilitate the uncovering of candidates' professional beliefs and values, the capability of candidates to respond to unpredictable situations and determine metacognitive capabilities. The challenge is always the lack of consistent or standard answers since there would be too many possible answers (e.g. how you would respond to the candidate's sharing that her brother passed away the previous week). Hence, the quality of the assessors is critical to ensure that the assessment is valid and reliable, with the focus on getting candidates to demonstrate what it takes to perform the job role.

The value of error-based learning is thinking beyond the question and context, to uncovering first principles and other boundaries governing the rules in the case.

A Speed Bump for Learners to Slow Down and Reflect

The irony of what I label as *'the Expert Syndrome'* is that because the expert knows so much and is so skilful that he becomes oblivious to certain assumptions and contexts being irrelevant or are no longer applicable. For example, when a computer broke down and refused to boot up, an IT professional spent a few days taking apart the entire desktop computer and replaced the components in the hardware, including the motherboard, the graphics card, RAM. After replacing the components and attempting to turn on the computer for the umpteenth time, he finally realised that the issue was really the humble spring in the reset button (found in the casing) that was faulty. It was a classic case of missing the forest for the trees and while uncommon, professionals and experts do tend to have certain preconceived notions and bias which then get them into a certain mode of thinking which blinkers them from certain blind spots. Using error-based learning helps unpack these biases to remind professionals to constantly review their assumptions, in the event that the rules and the contexts have changed.

Benefits of the DELETE Approach as an Instructional Design Tool

Wrapping up, this chapter describes the curriculum design considerations when adopting DELETE as a possible tool to craft learning instances, to deepen learning, beyond the typical competencies, into metacognitive capabilities and beliefs.

Locating the DELETE Approach Within the Curriculum Design Process

As such, there are specific benefits of using DELETE approach over other more typical approaches such as correcting the learner's errors and giving feedback when that happens. The list of benefits from the *Designer's* point of view includes:

- The correct level of analysis can be targeted to deepen learning for the learner.
- The design of the learning can be more precise without the need to wait for the learner to make the mistake and create the 'teachable' moment.
- The learner's understanding can be checked in the middle of the process, e.g. at the third step of the solution.
- The time taken to check understanding is shortened since the initial stages of the solution are already crafted and the learner can be directed to the problematic step.
- The support for the learner can be increased according to the learning needs of the learner, e.g. providing hints.
- The learner may find it easier to experience success and gain self-confidence in managing these questions.
- The learner may find it more motivating to identify errors than to start from scratch to solve a problem.
- The atypical errors can be highlighted to learners to help establish the boundaries for certain rules or assumptions, e.g. the breaking down of certain physical laws at light speed.
- Differentiated curriculum, in the form of having the same problem but providing different degrees of support (e.g. extent of correct answer given) to students of varying ability, can be carried out easily.
- The activity can facilitate the learners to discover underlying first principles when working through the problems on their own. Generally, when learners actively seek to understand the issues and concepts, their learning becomes sticky and deeper.

Chapter 6

The reasons stated earlier are for designers to consider DELETE as one of the approaches in learning design. Likewise, *learners* benefit from the DELETE approach as it provides opportunities for them to deepen their learning:

- through the design of novel contexts and errors, which may occur in real life or workplace
- by adopting an experiential approach to working through the issues
- by pitching the tasks at different levels of Bloom's Taxonomy, e.g. analysis, synthesis, evaluation
- by making learning social when the learners work in teams
- in making learning satisfying and motivating
- as they build associations and cognitive networks among key concepts — what to do and what not to do
- by learning the boundaries of the scope or task (for both 'to-do' and 'not-to-do' rules)
- by targeting difficult concepts in the task so that learners focus on what are crucial and difficult
- by focusing on critical and/or common errors in contingency training, e.g. fire-fighting or disaster management
- by allowing the learners to propose alternative solutions, which may be more elegant or creative than the original
- by facilitating the uncovering of first principles through self-discovery and reflection
- by increasing the learner's metacognitive capability as one questions underlying assumptions and way of thinking

> *Personally, I am always ready to learn, although I do not always like to be taught.*
> Winston Churchill

Learning is highly personal because no one can do the learning for you. The way we learn will vary and utilising errors to deepen reflection is one method that could uncover bias and professional beliefs for the individual learner. It would require the facilitator or teacher to be equipped with a broader set of instructional skills to implement error-based learning. For example, the debriefing session needs to be carefully constructed and learner-driven to derive maximal benefits from errors designed into the learning.

By agreeing that the error-based learning approach can and should be incorporated as part of the curriculum design, learning designers can now follow through on aligning and crafting the specific lesson activities and materials to include the tasks and outcomes structured on the DELETE process.

Part 3

The Process of Designing Errors for Learning and Teaching

Chapter 7
Examining the DELETE Approach as a Process

In this segment, we will dive into the error design process. There are a number of steps involved in DELETE, but we will start with the end outcome for the learner in mind. Before we do that, let's recap the key concepts we discussed over the past few chapters:

- the Learning, Atmosphere, Mind and Production model
- the Three Dimensions of Learning Model
- the nano-learning cycles to drive nuggetised learning packages
- the roles of rules and contexts
- the DELETE approach as one of the instructional design approaches within curriculum design
- the benefits of the DELETE approach

These concepts are useful in laying the foundation of what learning is, and the corresponding outcomes that arise from learning. As learning is multi-faceted, learners require diverse experiences and engagements to achieve different outcomes and goals. However, it is not sufficient to expose learners (whether school students or adult learners) to a range of learning instances haphazardly. The approach needs to be intentional, and the learning goals aligned with the process of making learning happen. On this note, DELETE is about intentional design to achieve key outcomes — some of which can be

> ... it is about starting somewhere and with learning, the process is as important as the goal.

difficult to measure (e.g. metacognition) or can take a long time to develop. However, it is about starting somewhere and with learning, the process is as important as the goal.

How People Make Errors: The Error Process

In this chapter, we will focus on how the mental functions involving cognition, emotion, sociality and psychomotor processing will affect the quality of production outcomes. Underpinning the mental functions is the metacognitive capability of the Mind. This refers to one's ability to monitor and evaluate the quality of thinking. A common example is when someone snaps out of daydreaming, in realisation that he is not focusing on his work.

> *Metacognition ... involves the conscious, often intentional monitoring and evaluation of our own mental processes and behaviors ... metacognition serves to correct the wandering mind, suppressing spontaneous thoughts and bringing attention back to more "worthwhile" tasks.*
>
> Fox and Christoff (2014)

Finally, the Atmosphere (or learning environment) comprising the socio-psychological elements affects the level of performance of the Mind, by being either distractors or important inputs for mental processing.

Refer to Fig. 11, which depicts the metacognitive regulation and the performance processes of the (Mind) and the socio-psychological environment (Atmosphere) feeding inputs into the Mind.

These processes occur concurrently and they interact to facilitate the production of outcomes, i.e. performance. The Mind and Atmosphere are components playing critical roles in the pre-error, error and post-error phases. We will examine further how these components as briefly described above behave during the entire error-making process.

At the same time, the socio-psychological environment cannot be ignored. These four elements will also be used actively to facilitate learning

Examining the DELETE Approach as a Process

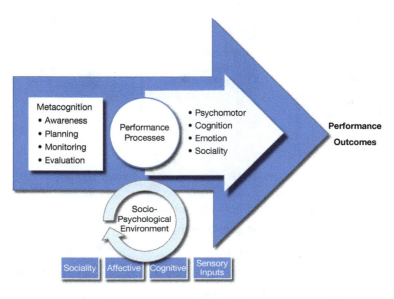

Fig. 11. Metacognitive Regulation, the Performance Processes of the (Mind) and the Socio-Psychological Environment (Atmosphere)

in the DELETE approach, for example tapping on sociality or the 'others' elements (e.g. peers making mistakes) to drive error creation and resolution. If your teammates vent their frustration on you during the group discussion or role play, that adds to the negative Affective environment, fuelling the pressure and stress reflective of authentic work environments. Cognitive processing refers to the information that is being fed into our learning pipes (perception) and the information may be convoluted, confusing or even downright erroneous, while sensory inputs refer to environmental distractors such as noise, light and room layout.

The Error Process

To better understand and address error-making, it's helpful to break down the error process into three distinct phases: Pre-Error, Error and Post-Error (see Fig. 12). This approach allows us to closely examine each phase and the corresponding training necessary to acquire mastery of the skills required to manage and reduce errors. By taking a phased approach to error analysis

Chapter 7

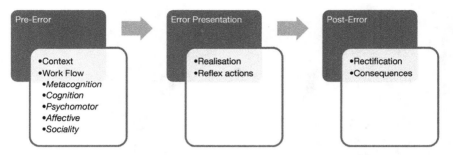

Fig. 12. Pre-error Presentation, Error Presentation and Post-error Presentation

and design, we can more effectively address each phase and develop strategies to minimise the likelihood of errors occurring.

These three phases describe what we do prior to, during and after the error occurrence.

> *"The fool wanders, a wise man travels."*
>
> **Thomas Fuller**

There is also the *learning phase,* which follows subsequently. We will examine the learning phase in the second half of this chapter, but let's take a closer look at the error process.

At the *pre-error* phase, the individual may not be paying much attention to the environment around him or to what he was doing. He probably was on 'automatic' mode, especially if he was performing routine work. The workflow may stem from what he was used to doing or what he has planned to do.

During the *error* phase, the facilitator will inject an error into the workflow, which may result in a sudden (or gradual) realisation on the part of the learner that he was making an error. This realisation may take a while or may not even happen until the consequences are clear (e.g. an accident).

Once the error has been committed, in the *post-error* phase, the person will carry out rectification to resolve the issue and reduce the impact of the error. In some situations, the realisation may result in a reflex response (both verbal and psychomotor). Some people may 'freeze' in a non-responsive state as part of the 'flight or fight' response when adrenaline levels increase. This is then followed by a trained response (if there is one).

Some errors can be rectified, while the effects of others are irreversible. As a result, the person has to suffer the consequence of the error. If the error is not fatal, a phase of reflection ensures that learning occurs so that the person reduces the likelihood of committing the same error again.

Example: Driving Home

The workflow would stem from what he was used to doing (e.g. driving at 80 km/h on the highway with the music blaring away). While he may not be paying full attention to the driving process, he is mindful of the cars around him and the state of his own car. He sensed some 'heaviness' in the car but felt that it was nothing serious. He resolved to take it to the mechanics first thing on Monday. He increased the speed slightly to 90 km/h in order to reach home faster in the hope that the car can remain problem-free for the next 20 minutes. Then, strangely, dark smoke pervaded the car. At that point, he realised something was very wrong and gave out a loud shout in the car. He immediately, on reflex, hit the brakes to stop the car. However, he forgot he was on the highway. His braking action resulted in the car crashing into him from behind. His car jerked forwards, throwing him forward, causing whiplash to his neck. Despite the injury, he managed to control the car to keep it within his traffic lane and avoiding the central divider. With the smoke still bellowing from his engine, he switched off his engine and unbuckled his seat belt. As his car screeched to a halt, he tumbled out of his car and crawled along the central divider to about 10 m away before collapsing on the grass verge.

In summary, the events unfolded as follows:

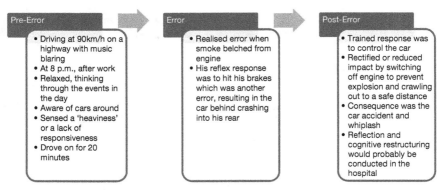

Fig. 13. Example of the Pre, Error and Post-error Presentations

This example is hypothetical and is used to illustrate how the three phases of pre-error, error and post-error can be mapped onto an accident as such. There are less serious errors that are reversible and so, have less serious implications. There are also other errors which are irreversible, but the consequences can be mitigated (e.g. apologising over a dinner treat).

To what extent can carefully designed learning mitigate errors and the consequences of those errors? At the pre-error stage, can learners develop a sense of monitoring or awareness to prevent errors? At the error stage, can learners recondition their awareness and realisation faster to identify reasons for the error or situation? Finally, at the post-error stage, can one's reflex actions be re-conditioned along with their trained responses to ensure the impact of the errors is minimised and rectification of errors can be carried out in a logical and resource-effective manner. Again, prior training using errors may aid in the correct selection of rectification strategies. Some term this as scenario planning and training. With error-based learning, the targeted learner response is more specific to the scenarios and closely linked to the consequences.

The Points of Interjection and Intervention in the Error-Based Learning Methodology

These are two points in the entire process of error-making, which require the designer and/or the facilitator to interfere with the flow of events. The first interference is the *point of interjection* and that is

Two Points of Active Design
1. Point of Interjection of Error
2. Point of Intervention of Task

when the error is inserted into the workflow. It could be a make-believe error, or a real error and the learner must deal with the error then. The second interference is the *point of intervention,* which is when the learners carry out the learning tasks. This could range from learners pausing the error rectification process to begin reflecting or innovate to overcome the circumstances.

The diagram below depicts how these two points fit into the **Error-Making** and **Learning** Processes:

Fig. 14. Error-Making Process and the Learning Process

Designing errors can target the pre-error phase, the error phase and the rectification phase. The point is that people can learn to be mindful and vigilant before the error occurs, realise quickly when an error is committed and rectify responsibly and logically after an error is discovered.

Determining the points in which interjections of errors and interventions of learner task and support ought to be made to train people in predicting, preventing, evaluating and rectifying errors is part of the error and task design process. This identification of the points of interjections and intervention is important and needs further examination. Naturally, appropriate timing provides authenticity of the errors for learning to be maximised. For example, allowing the erroneous behaviour to drag on for too long without the appropriate intervention to support the learner would be disastrous from the learning perspective. The learners may end up demotivated or even worse, demoralised due to the failure to extricate themselves from the situation. The opportunity to resolve the error themselves and thereby empowering them with the confidence to face similar errors and situations in the future is part of the learning and growth process. We should empower the learners with autonomy to navigate their way out of these situations and develop their capability to manage future events, which may not be similar in nature but similar in sequence and impact. It may be useful to emphasise that the DELETE approach is constructive and targets building not destroying of learners' confidence, professional and personal growth.

Chapter 7

Error-Making: Setting Context

The DELETE approach is not just an exercise in error prevention or avoidance but also for learners to be *aware* of possible errors, promoting a conscious effort to plan for contingencies while at the same time, incurring the least risk and resources. If we can use the model to analyse how and when learners make errors during their workflow, we can potentially help our learners gain mastery of the skillsets.

Table 4 gives a more granular perspective to how error design works. It frames the pre-error, error presentation and post-error making with the key factors and the learning and reflection activities in the DELETE approach to train metacognitive regulation and performance processes across the five phases in error-making. The various environmental conditions are imposed on the individual to develop the individual's capability. Generally, the tougher the environmental and instructional stresses, the greater the learner capability needed to manage the DELETE activity and the competency of the educator in designing and facilitating the activity effectively.

The Phases in Error-Making

The table describes the roles of the learning designer to effect the changes to metacognitive regulation, performance processes and the learning design and approaches across the three phases. What is important is to map these changes in relation to how we want the learners to respond and learn from their responses. In effect, the DELETE approach leverages the error as the focal point for learning by intentionally facilitating the learner to think, act and feel in a certain way. This implies that the learning designer needs to skillfully craft the experience using different features of the DELETE approach. This transition from pre to post error presentation is critical as there is an element of learner prediction, which facilitates the buildup of learner's awareness of errors in typical work circumstances.

Table 4. Processes involved in the Pre-, Error and Post-Error Presentations

Phase Factors	Description	Pre-Error			Post-Error		Learning
		Context	Workflow	Error Presentation	Rectification	Consequences	Reflection and Planning
Metacognitive Regulation* i. Awareness ii. Planning iii. Monitoring iv. Evaluation	To ensure superior performance, our mind monitors and evaluates what we think and do (i.e. metacognition — 'thinking about thinking'). With that comes awareness of the surroundings, one's thinking processes and the overarching planning needed to achieve one's goals. Errors occur when the level of awareness is low, e.g. assuming the situation is 'normal' and so adopts a relaxed state, leading to misevaluation and wrong decisions.	Train perceptual/ sensory modalities to pick up useful pre-emptive cues from the environment	Train planning behaviour	Train monitoring and evaluation behaviour	Train re-planning ability based on realignment with original goals	Evaluate best- and worst-case consequences	Link back to metacognitive processes
Performance Processes[ii] v. Psychomotor vi. Cognition vii. Emotion viii. Sociality	Usually in the limelight, our performance processes involve all our capabilities especially psychomotor and cognitive. What is often overlooked are our emotional state (e.g. being calm) and sociality capability (e.g. teamwork). In a crisis, any of these processes, if not functioning well, can hinder performance.	Train perceptual/ sensory modalities to pick up useful environmental cognitive, affective, social information	Train competence in performing tasks	• Re-condition reflex responses to more constructive ones • Train ability to stop workflow • Develop finer evaluation capabilities • Positivise affective states during crisis	• Train recovery processes • Train capability to seek new inputs, to ask relevant questions	Train psychological resilience and affect	Train reflection processes Incorporation into experience

(Continued)

Table 4. (Continued)

Phase Factors	Description	Pre-Error			Post-Error		Learning
		Context	Workflow	Error Presentation	Rectification	Consequences	Reflection and Planning
Learning Design and Approaches	Based on the requirements for each phase of the error-making process, the learning design can target specific learning behaviours to help learners gain mastery, both in metacognitive regulation and performance processes.	Decision on when to insert: a) Errors b) Tasks Train insertion of cognitive disruptors and triggers to break own Frame of Mind	To train awareness, real-time cognitive tracking: a) Follow actions till error occurs b) Ask learners to articulate plans and expectations	Design and present Multiple Error Scenarios Track cognitive evaluation of problems, errors Train emotional control by upping affective levels, e.g. panicky teammates, peers and experts give wrong inputs	Provide options for decision-making through conditional branching and inputs from experts and peers Train rapid reflective practice through the 4 lenses	Develop cognitive and psychological resilience through positive psychology conditioning	Train reflective practice using Brookfield's four Lenses/ Reflective Questions for Learners Critical Incident Questionnaire
Examples	These examples should be sequenced together to form a full learning activity within the pre-error, error and post-error framework. In so doing, the impact and learning will be full and authentic.	Incorporate contextual cues to facilitate and distract learners from the issues at hand based on requirements of authentic work environments	Changing roles, e.g. Machine Gun shooter to 0.5 inch gun shooter OR Recently promoted manager adopting past practices of following orders only OR Conducting the same chemistry experiment in Artic — what outcomes are expected?	Tracking how long it takes before learner stops following erroneous behaviour Present different types of information ix. Learner clicks on those he finds useful x. He clicks on questions which he wants answers to	Present options for learners to select and backtrack if necessary Capturing of actions with learners articulating the reasons for actions	Consequences to be realistic with crying and screaming (e.g. deaths of teammates or platoon mates) Reconditioning of mental and psychological states through positive self-talk and encouragement	Learner practises using the four lenses after the exercise or activity to reflect on all the issues related to decisions and errors.

*Livingston, J. (1997). Metacognition: An Overview. Retrieved on 9 Mar 2015 from: www.gse.buffalo.edu/fas/shuell/cep564/metacog.htm.
#Drawing from Illeris' work on learning models.

Apparently, the mere contiguity between a stimulus and reward is insufficient for an increase in pleasantness of that stimulus. Rather, learning depends crucially on the presence of an error in the prediction of an appetitive outcome.

Tobler et al. (2006, p. 12)

What Tobler *et al.* (2006) meant was simply that errors can facilitate learning, especially when learners develop that predictive ability to plan new behaviours. Their goal is to attain desired outcomes and avoid errors or punitive consequences. Learning designers can adopt the DELETE Approach by INTENTIONALLY embedding different types of errors at the required level, stage and degree based on an instructional design (e.g. the Experiential Learning Model or Gagne's Nine Events of Instruction).

From the table, you may wonder how we decide on the type of error, task or support that we need to create or provide so that we bring about the learning outcome. You may also wonder if there is a systematic process to design the process for each category of learning outcome. These are good questions. Let's find out.

Chapter 8
The Four Parameters in DELETE Approach

The DELETE approach attempts to coordinate the various parameters in the learning design collectively to bring about an experience for the learners. The parameters that we need to carefully design in the DELETE Approach are:

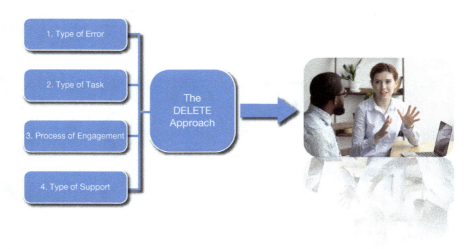

Fig. 15.   The 4 Parameters in the DELETE Approach

Brief Description of the 4 Parameters

There could be other parameters that we may need to consider downstream but for now, these four parameters are likely what we need to focus on, to bring about the DELETE experience for the learner. Getting them right needs a good grasp of how these parameters INTERACT with each other. Remember that the permutations based on these four parameters are already massive and so, it would be commendable if we can master a few of these combinations to achieve the learning outcomes that we want. Let's have a go at this.

- *Parameter 1: Type of Errors*

As we have expounded on, the DELETE approach has the effect of using mistakes of others to clearly illustrate what the rules for application are. For example, see the following erroneous statement,

> "... there are potentially negative effects of making errors — they may demotivate and increase stress and anxiety ... To reduce these negative effects and to maximise the positive ones, it is necessary to explicitly integrate the problem of errors into the training process and to develop strategies of error management."
>
> **Frese and Altmann**
> (1989, p. 79)

Wesley looked up and perceived a friendly-looking being with wings glided* across the heavens.

* refers to a grammatically incorrect statement or solution

Now, for a learner who has no concept of perception words such as 'look', 'taste', 'see' and 'smell' will also not understand the effect perception words have on tenses of the observed action.

Hence, the statement ought to read:

Wesley looked up and perceived a friendly-looking being with wings glide (or gliding) across the heavens.

The error found in the earlier statement stems from not observing a prevailing rule (in this case, a grammatical rule).

In terms of error-based learning, it would constitute a performance (or procedural) error. In this case, the learner did not apply the grammatical rule correctly. By collating errors for a particular concept, skill or value, we can analyse the errors to determine the profile of the topic and surface the difficult concepts. Hence, a particular topic (e.g. fractions) may have several difficult concepts based on the errors made by learners.

There are other types of errors which will be further elaborated in later chapters, knowledge (or declarative) errors being the other category besides procedural errors. In addition, if we consider the domains (from Bloom's Taxonomy) that the errors or tasks are found in, we can also see how these error categories can be useful. The domains include:

- Metacognition
- Cognition
- Psychomotor
- Emotion
- Social (in the more recent versions of Bloom's Taxonomy)

In this regard, categorising the errors based on Bloom's Taxonomy facilitates the design of the task. For example, an error in the psychomotor domain is likely to comprise a task that requires movement and possibly demonstration. Hence, carrying a chemistry experiment based on instructions is primarily a psychomotor activity with the error possibly being the selection and mixing of wrong chemicals together. For the adult learner, a psychomotor error could be not stopping in time at the traffic lights when the light has already turned red. Do note, however, there is also the context that could turn what is seen as incorrect in most situations to a correct behaviour. In the example above, if the driver moves on, past the traffic junction even when the light has turned red so that the ambulance behind it can pass, may be exhibiting the correct behaviour. Hence, errors can also arise due to the mismatch with the context rather than just the incorrect implementation of the Standard Operating Procedure (SOP) or rule.

By first identifying the type (and level) of errors to be crafted into the learning experience, we can pinpoint the precise performance we want the learner to attain (e.g. from identify to rectify and prevent the error). The learner performance (or non-performance) will then drive the reflection and learning, especially if the learner does not pick up the error or performs the task incorrectly.

- *Parameter 2: Type of Tasks*

Correspondingly, the tasks are designed as a follow-up to the error analysis by the learner. Like the errors, these tasks are to be selected and pitched at the right level. For learners who are not yet skilled in the topic, asking them to *recall* the facts about the concept may be sufficient (e.g. cite the 'Grammar Perception Rule'). After reviewing the error, the learner is told to cite the rule that is violated here (which is the Perception Rule). If the learners attempt to transfer the rule to the context of the error and correct the error, that is wonderful but, in this example, the task is pitched at the recall level, so the learner who does not attempt to correct the error using the rule is not wrong.

Hence, the task must be designed to match the learner's level of proficiency. Through this example, you may see how flexible the DELETE approach is. Similarly, if the learners encountering the error are highly skilled, the task designed for them may require them to evaluate how the error was made and how to avoid making such errors in the future. Pitched at the evaluation level (on Bloom's Taxonomy), the learners perform a more complex and cognitively demanding task compared to the first case where the task required the learners to only recall a related fact.

To make the design of the DELETE approach versatile, you as the designer have the option of setting several tasks, pitched at different levels to match learner proficiency and profile. In this way, the same error can be used for different learner groups, by designing tasks at varying levels of difficulty, granting the teacher or trainer the autonomy to make the decision during the process of learner engagement, as to which task/s the learner needs to perform.

The Four Parameters in DELETE Approach

With the possibility of varying levels of difficulties, a branching design can be adopted where learners can be channelled into differentiated learning pathways based on their responses — the better performers taking on more difficult tasks and the weaker performers taking on simpler tasks, thereby generating success for a spectrum of learners with varying abilities.

Therefore, the errors need to be accompanied by tasks so that the learners will be put through a sequence of activities, also termed as the engagement process. Learning designers typically select a learning approach or theory to structure the process. In an earlier chapter, we briefly discussed the nano-learning cycle as one of the instructional design theories. There are other theories, and we will examine a couple of theories in a later chapter.

- *Parameter 3: Engagement Process*

The way in which the engagement process is determined depends on whether you as the learning designer want to use the error as:

- a 'trigger' or stimulus for reflection and learning of the concept OR
- an application after one has learned the theory

Both approaches are possible, depending on the learner profile (i.e. novice or competent; cognitively strong or weak) and learning outcome (i.e. higher levels on Bloom's Taxonomy such as analysis, creation or lower levels such as recall and comprehension).

Shown on the next page is an example of an experiential learning approach underpinning the engagement process. The process starts with a cognitive or physical trigger (e.g. role play a defender trying to fend off a cyberattack where errors made allowed the attack to succeed) to stimulate learner interest from the onset. This, in turn, drives the engagement process, and the eventual acquisition of the skill or knowledge (e.g. cybersecurity features and protection concepts) to prevent future attacks.

Chapter 8

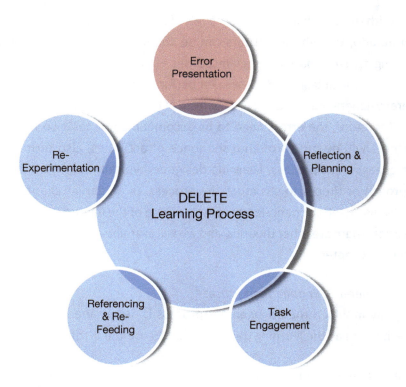

Fig. 16.   The Learning Process in DELETE Approach

Specifically, the engagement process based on a modified experiential learning approach could look like this:

Drawing from work by David Kolb on Experiential Learning Cycle, the Error Engagement and Experimentation (3Es) Cycle (see Fig. 16) provides a structured process for learning because the learners need to construct the knowledge for themselves through individual or peer reflection. The initial experience generated at the Error Presentation (EP) stage is critical as the experience would have galvanised the learner to first reflect about why the activity resulted in a certain consequence and to find out more about the theoretical concepts behind it.

As a result, the initial activity provides a strong impetus for the learner to learn. The stronger the experience (whether positive or negative), the stronger the motivation the learner has to learn. To clarify, the error can be presented in any form or format, besides in text on paper. Video recordings, story format, role-play, pictorial slideshow, comics, verbal exposition and drawings are possibilities. Having a variety of presentation styles will increase the motivation of learners to the task and bring a level of richness to the context of the error. We have created video clips of an actor screaming at the camera (to present a first-person perspective) and the learner viewing the video clip needs to respond to the character in the emotively charged scenario. It was a memorable albeit hair-raising experience for the learner, to say the least.

As Keith and Frese (2008) would emphasise, the active exploration by learners to determine the nature and type of errors is critical to allow for active construction of their own understanding of the issues at hand. Hence, when presenting the errors to the learners, there are several approaches possible. However, these should not be about telling the learners how to resolve the error. It could be an explicit presentation of the errors and contexts OR designing the activity such that the learners are encouraged to make as many errors as possible. The latter approach being a lot more fluid and dynamic, leading to unpredictable learning results but nonetheless, can be extremely effective and impactful as Keith and Frese's (2008) study shows.

Besides the E^3 experiential approach, other theories such as Gagne's Nine Events of Instruction and Romiskowski's Psychomotor Theory can also be useful. However, I am of the opinion that the E^3 Approach (based on Experiential Learning Theory) is suitable to structure the DELETE approach as the learners learn to reflect and construct their own learning, leading to deeper and more effective learning. However, having said that, there is no reason why educators cannot use other instructional design theories for the DELETE approach as long as the learners are still able to engage with the error and achieve the learning outcomes.

The learner experience is the focus here, as learners navigate their way through the process. With some fuzziness and a potential lack of clarity during the learning process, designers may wish to put into the process different types and levels of learner support. This leads us to Parameter 4 — the type of learner support that we can provide.

- *Parameter 4: Type of Support*

Seemingly less important, support has been found to be a key driver to nudge learners and users to move forward in their quest to achieve specific outcomes, especially in the digital arena (think online games, social media challenges and physical fitness challenges on apps). Over the years, I have also found that classes that have a strong sense of camaraderie generally can push each other on to complete their course, especially those that require discipline over a period of time. The journey can be arduous and mentally exhausting, so journeying alone can be a difficult and painful trudge.

To be clear, the type of learner support can range from social (e.g. from peers or facilitators), cognitive (e.g. cues on areas to focus on or additional resources) and psychological (e.g. motivators such as points on leaderboard and chatbot personas cheering the learner on). Having a range of support matched to the needs of the learners is critical. For example, the more senior learners may benefit from social support where they learn in bite-sized formats while the digitally savvy generation may prefer challenges which award points and recognition on their social media accounts.

Table 5 Illustrates the type and degree of support that learning designers can provide throughout the process of engagement. Giving a good motivating start to the learning may not be a bad idea and likewise, providing recognition in the form of certificates and social media points will draw potential learners to the course, which is a win–win for the learner and the course owner.

You may have also noticed that the following table also shows negative learner support. This is intentional as part of a possible learning design if resilience and mental fortitude are required developmental milestones. For personnel involved in work environments where stress, time pressure and conflicting information are prevalent (e.g. hospitals, armed forces

Table 5. Degree of Support

Levels	Degree of Support	Examples of Cognitive, Psychological and Social Support
3	Highly Positive	Focused questioning Options for selection Collaborative learning Certificates and social media rewards
2		Hint; Additional resources or simplified information pack
1		Positive Encouragement; paired tutoring
0	Neutral	No inputs given; timed response
−1		Discouragement
−2		Distractions with non-related issues
−3	Highly Negative	Intentional side-tracking Confusing information given

and certain financial markets), this form of training equips learners to differentiate truth from half-truths and build a level of mindfulness and mental clarity despite the on-going external chaos. To qualify, the negative learner support options are not common and should be used carefully, with learners being informed prior to the learning engagement and given the option to withdraw from the process at any point in time.

By varying the degree and type of support, learner independence and resilience can be built up in an intentional and structured manner. Hence, if the support is to be positive, collaborative learning structures in the form of teamwork or coaching can take place. On the other hand, for negative degrees of support, distractors can be used to confuse learners in a manner that forces them to be clear on their decision-making process and the subsequent actions to be performed. This form of distraction can build metacognition and self-evaluative behaviour in learners operating in challenging workplace affordances.

Chapter 8

Types of Cases

As mentioned earlier, with at least four parameters in the DELETE approach, the number of possible designs is enormous. Hence, a proposed solution deemed as an error in certain cases may not be perceived as errors in others, especially in problems with ill-defined solutions. Winston Churchill, in the story on the right, does not seem to think that not washing hands after visiting the toilet is an error, thereby setting up an interesting discourse on how subjective and norm-based the practice of handwashing is. It also points out how errors are highly dependent on the context and under different situations, something acceptable (e.g. not washing hands after using the toilet in Harrow) can become unacceptable (e.g. not washing hands in Eton).

> A young man after seeing Churchill leave the bathroom without washing his hands, said: *"At Eton, they taught us to wash our hands after using the toilet."*
>
> Churchill: *"At Harrow, they taught us not to piss on our hands."*

Is Prevention Better than Cure?

This adage is worth us spending some time examining in terms of the assumptions behind it. Often, we are persuaded to avoid mistakes because of the consequences which we are expected to bear. Naturally, no one wants to, nor should they aspire to make mistakes, especially ones which they already know and have experienced. It is part of the growth process that we learn through mistakes, both our own and others. Having said that, because making *some* mistakes does facilitate our growth, is it also correct to say that preventing mistakes may result in us learning and growing less?

It is also common knowledge that providing ourselves with the necessary exposure to events and roles helps us mature to handle new tasks and activities better. For example, being a parent allows the person to empathise with other parents how parenthood can be a thankless yet emotionally rewarding role. Embedded in that activity are obviously all the responsibilities associated with child caring. More importantly, there are numerous mistakes made which dot the experience and these mistakes could be defining moments which pivot us towards better (or worse) parents.

Brookfield (1995) termed these as critical incidents, of which when reflected on and taken seriously, can be springboards to great learning and growth. On this note, going back to our earlier question, 'Is the adage "Prevention is better than cure" still applicable or correct'?

Dissecting this further, there are mistakes which we HAVE to make due to us trying new ventures and experiences. There are also mistakes that can be avoided but are committed because of us not paying sufficient attention or not thinking through. These are 'silly' mistakes (e.g. missing a step while coming down a flight of stairs).

It will be the former mistakes that are valuable as they provide us with new experiences and enable us to see new perspectives and consequences, especially if we took time to reflect and learn from these mistakes. These mistakes which allow us to check our assumptions and take us up another level of maturity and development are the ones we want to make often, to facilitate our growth. These mistakes can be great learning moments for us but the emphasis is that we need to reflect after making the mistakes so that we can learn, make our conclusions, as well as bear the consequences. On this note, prevention (as in not even attempting new experiences) may not be better than cure because avoidance cannot grant us new learning.

The Error Message

It is true that sometimes getting the error message on our computers can be really irritating because we cannot seem to get a piece of software to work. These error messages may range from the generic (e.g. no response) to the specific in nature. It will be the latter which gives us (or our IT helpdesk) more cues as to how to resolve the issue. Likewise, the error message we craft for ourselves after making an error is important. What do we tell our brain after making an error? Do we reprimand ourselves as 'silly', 'stupid' or do we encourage ourselves in a constructive manner with 'remember to save your work on the computer every 10 minutes'? By being constructive, we can programme our cognitive wiring to respond positively and target the behaviour directly for improvement. In the same way, using errors for learning is meant to be constructive and meaningful as the outcome is for learning and growth, not about being negative or risk avoidance. This spirit of error-based learning must be clear in order that the process of designing errors is located within the right context, with the appropriate objectives, coupled with constructive feedback.

Conclusion

In this chapter, we examined the impact of the DELETE approach and how by being intentional and structured, designers leverage errors and learning tasks to target specific skill areas for capability development. Usually used after the learners have acquired some competency in the concept, DELETE allows learners to check their own assumptions and relearn if their assumptions are wrong. For educators, using DELETE to focus on key errors will facilitate learner revisions before assessments, especially in areas which learners are prone to making mistakes — errors which are common and sometimes with unclear boundaries.

By splitting the error-making process into three phases: pre-error, error presentation and post-error, one can target specific cognitive and behavioural processes by designing errors for learning. An example of a pre-error process may be 'awareness' and the learner may have low levels of awareness and so, have difficulties picking up environmental cues. This results in delays when it comes to realising a particular situation has deteriorated. By designing errors that target 'awareness', the learner becomes more attuned to environmental cues and hence, develops his or her metacognitive regulation capability. Likewise, for post-error capability,

The Four Parameters in DELETE Approach

activities such as error rectification training can be designed to help learners to cope better with errors especially in time-sensitive situations such as transportation or financial sectors.

The design of the DELETE learning activity involves careful tweaking of the four parameters to ensure constructive alignment. By varying the levels across the four parameters, the designer can provide a differentiated curriculum for learners with a wide range of abilities to achieve competence, either in his or her job or in school. To recap, the four parameters are:

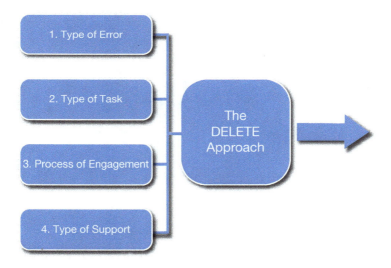

It will be useful to discuss the specificity of design for the four parameters in greater detail but at this point, as part of the overview, it is sufficient to note that the design of the DELETE learning activity should be outcome-driven with the focus on helping learners achieve a measurable learning outcome. The way in which we achieve this is by varying the four parameters listed above.

The next few chapters will describe the ***process*** of designing the DELETE learning activity at the various selected points of intervention in the error-based methodology, of which how the four parameters are constructed for effective learning will also be discussed.

Part 4

The DELETE Process: Designing Error, Task and the Engagement

Chapter 9

Designing the Task

To continue with the earlier brief discussion on task design, this chapter is dedicated to the art of designing tasks which are appropriate, motivating and aligned with the designed error and more importantly, with the learning outcomes.

Most educators when using errors to rectify mistakes focus on what is wrong and is to be corrected. While this is logical and practical in most work scenarios, a lot more can be extracted from error identification, rectification and evaluation to deepen the learning. It DOESN'T need to be just error correction. As described in the earlier chapter on designing errors, the ensuing task could be about identifying reasons for errors, adding new information to the problem 'to make the error correct' or even predicting the errors which are yet to be made but are highly likely, given the tendencies of the learner or scenario under consideration.

A key functionality of the error-based learning approach is to allow learners to examine the contexts in which the error is made in order to avoid future incidences of these errors. Notably, the metacognitive skills such as predicting when the errors are emerging and being adaptable when the contexts change (as with dynamic errors) are key skill sets to be developed through error-based learning. As such, solving errors is only one aspect of the engagement process. The other key aspect is to heighten and strengthen the metacognitive awareness of the learners.

Hence, to state it simply, the designer needs to be clear what the error and task are designed to achieve (i.e. learning outcomes) and how to measure the effectiveness of the ERROR and TASK. It is likely that BOTH the engagement **PROCESS** and the quality of the resultant **PRODUCT** should figure in the overall evaluation matrix.

The Process

The educator should at certain points in time, monitor the thought processes of the learner in arriving at certain conclusions and check those in order to heighten metacognitive processes. If the learner can articulate his or her thoughts aloud during the process, *how* the learner thinks can be tracked and facilitated. Designing discussion questions which allow for peer feedback may be useful here so that the process of thinking through is facilitated to develop metacognitive awareness.

The Product

The product of the task will be one of the indicators to both the learners and the educators on the amount of learning that has taken place through the task. There may or may not be one correct product or outcome. Some tasks may lead to multiple products or outcomes (e.g. evaluation of the reasons for making the error) and so the value is in the strengthening of the reasoning process to produce those outcomes. For example, helping learners to formulate their ethical viewpoints about 'grey' issues may be one DELETE activity in which multiple products is acceptable.

It is useful to keep in mind the focus on both the thinking process and the product from the task in the ensuing discussion.

Locating the Task Design in the DELETE Approach

Going back to the flowchart on designing the DELETE activity, the design of the task follows the error design process. Hence, the tasks (see Fig. 17) should be a natural extension of the error design in that the task will bring out the requirements expected of the learner after encountering the error.

Designing the Task

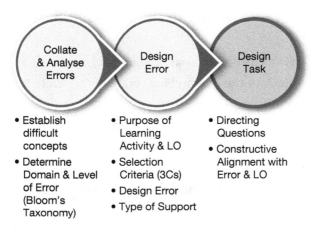

Fig. 17. Task Design and Errors

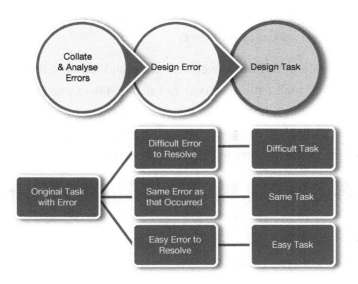

Fig. 18. Task and Error Designs

Pitching at the Right Level

Based on Bloom's Taxonomy, the task designed can be more difficult, at the same level of difficulty or simpler than the original task where the error was made. Figure 18 shows the possible permutations in the design of the error and the task.

Chapter 9

Examples of Tasks *Linked to the Levels in Bloom's Taxonomy*

- Learners spot mistakes (analysis, application)
- Learners articulate the overarching rationale/principle to the correct answer (analysis)
- Learners review and suggest the contextual contributions and assumptions to the error (analysis)
- Learners propose answers to the error (synthesis)
- Learners propose an encompassing reason behind a series of mistakes across different contexts (meta-analysis)
- Learners suggest other possible mistakes that can be made based on the pattern of errors (meta-synthesis)
- Learners build an overarching theory or model based on studies of a family of errors (meta-synthesis)

Taking reference from the error-making and learning processes (see Fig. 19), we will realise these tasks do not all target the same set of skills and by extension, they address different phases in the error-making process. Again, this diversity in design allows for targeted training of skillsets which contributes to the mastery of the skillsets required for the craft.

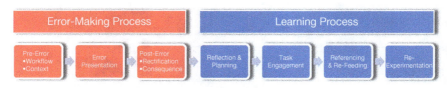

Fig. 19. Error-Making Process and Learning Process

We start with the metacognitive skills which predominantly figure in the pre-error phase but having said that, this skillset underpins performance for subsequent decision-making and monitoring processes in the error and post-error phases because these processes depend on the quality of inputs generated through metacognitive 'awareness' and 'planning' functions. Listed on the following page are some examples of the *tasks* associated with the development of metacognitive skills:

A) Metacognitive

Task	Targeted Skill (Learning Outcome)	Targeted Phase
1. Describe relevant environmental and social cues that may affect subsequent outcomes.	To Develop Ability to Evaluate Contexts and Assumptions	Context
2. Predict issues and recommend plans of action according to the evolving environmental conditions.	To Hone Metacognitive and Predictive Ability	Workflow
3. Analyse the next step to be taken in line with the original thought process.	To Develop Ability to Evaluate Contexts & Assumptions	Workflow
4. Highlight the critical elements in the environment or situation as it evolves.	To Develop Ability to Evaluate Contexts and Assumptions	Context
5. Determine the final choice after checking personal biases and contextual constraints.	To Hone Metacognitive and Predictive Ability	Workflow

Listed below are some of the tasks pegged to the more familiar levels in the Bloom's Taxonomy (denoting cognitive difficulty), targeted skills and the phase in the error-making process that the targeted skill sits within:

B) Cognitive

Task	Level	Targeted Skill (Learning Outcome)	Targeted Phase
1. Recall the theory or concept involved.	Knowledge	To Strengthen Conceptual Understanding and Skillsets in Targeted Problematic Areas	Workflow and Rectification

(Continued)

(*Continued*)

Task	Level	Targeted Skill (Learning Outcome)	Targeted Phase
2. Cite reasons how the identified error arose.	Comprehension	To Strengthen Conceptual Understanding and Skillsets in Targeted Problematic Areas	Workflow and Rectification
3. State the factors which contributed to the error.	Comprehension	To Strengthen Conceptual Understanding and Skillsets in Targeted Problematic Areas	Workflow and Rectification
4. Determine if there is an error found in the question/answer presented.	Analysis	To Develop 'Creative-Critical' Thinking Ability	Error Presentation
5. Identify the context and factors that contributed to the error.	Analysis	To Strengthen Conceptual Understanding and Skillsets in Targeted Problematic Areas	Context
6. Cite other errors which can be made besides the one identified.	Analysis	To Strengthen Conceptual Understanding and Skillsets in Targeted Problematic Areas	Error Presentation
7. Identify the reasons for the errors.	Analysis	To Strengthen Conceptual Understanding and Skillsets in Targeted Problematic Areas	Error Presentation

Designing the Task

(*Continued*)

Task	Level	Targeted Skill (Learning Outcome)	Targeted Phase
8. Identify the error, if any.	Analysis	To Strengthen Conceptual Understanding and Skillsets in Targeted Problematic Areas	Error Presentation
9. Suggest the contexts in which the error may not be wrong.	Application	To Develop 'Creative-Critical' Thinking Ability	Context
10. Add other information to make right the 'error'.	Application	To Develop 'Creative-Critical' Thinking Ability	Context and Consequence
11. Rectify the errors.	Synthesis	To Sharpen Cognitive Adaptability and Flexibility	Rectification
12. Propose other solutions.	Synthesis	To Sharpen Cognitive Adaptability and Flexibility	Rectification
13. Replicate the process prior to making of error.	Synthesis	To Sharpen Cognitive Adaptability and Flexibility	Workflow
14. Complete the solution.	Synthesis	To Sharpen Cognitive Adaptability and Flexibility	Workflow
15. Evaluate the assumptions which underpin the onset of the error and the rectification response.	Evaluation	To Develop 'Creative-Critical' Thinking Ability	Context and Rectification

(*Continued*)

(*Continued*)

Task	Level	Targeted Skill (Learning Outcome)	Targeted Phase
16. Evaluate the worked solution.	Evaluation	To Develop 'Creative-Critical' Thinking Ability	Workflow and Consequence
17. Provide justification/s as the error unfolds in a dynamic case.	Evaluation	To Develop 'Creative-Critical' Thinking Ability	Error and Consequence
18. Evaluate the soundness of rectification options and recommend other options.	Evaluation Synthesis	To Build Global (Macro) Perspective-Taking Ability	Workflow, Rectification, Consequence

These sample tasks belong to the cognitive domain and comprise many of what learners need to do at work or in school. A scan of these tasks reveals recalling of the concepts, problem-solving competencies and evaluation skills among others — ranging from the straightforward to the complex. They can challenge operational staff who take instructions from their supervisors to managers and senior management who need to plan strategically for the organisation.

Similarly, but not in isolation, are the outcomes in the affective domain. These affective outcomes primarily refer to one's values and beliefs, across the different levels. At the higher levels, the learners embrace and internalise the values in a deeply involved manner, often manifested as passion.

C) Emotion/Affective

Task	Level	Targeted Skill (Learning Outcome)	Targeted Phase
1. Examine the values which underpin the erroneous response.	Respond	To Develop Values and Beliefs	Rectification
2. Defend the values and beliefs set out in the workflow.	Value	To Develop Values and Beliefs	Workflow
3. Provide alternative perspectives to the beliefs which govern the workflow.	Value	To Develop Values and Beliefs	Workflow
4. Determine the beliefs which underpin the individual's decision-making process during the rectification phase.	Value	To Develop Values and Beliefs	Rectification
5. Suggest how one's values differs from or are similar to the organisation's values.	Organise	To Develop Values and Beliefs	Workflow and Rectification
6. State other values which are associated with the workflow shown in the case.	Organise	To Develop Values and Beliefs	Workflow
7. Recommend ways to build the psychological resilience of the individual and team to respond appropriately during crisis.	Internalise	To Strengthen Psychological Resilience for Unexpected Outcomes	Consequence
8. Verify the individual's action as consistent with his or her own values.	Internalise	To Develop Values and Beliefs	Error and Rectification

In the psychomotor domain, learners move from imitation to perfecting and finally, naturalising these movements as one becomes an expert in these skills. The list of possible tasks reflects the transition from simple to complex levels of psychomotor skills.

D) Psychomotor

Task	Level	Targeted Skill (Learning Outcome)	Targeted Phase
1. Identify psychomotor erroneous responses.	Imitate	To Develop Behavioural Responses to Situations and Errors	Error
2. Match prescribed psychomotor workflow to assigned contexts.	Imitate	To Develop Behavioural Responses to Situations and Errors	Workflow
3. Implement modified behavioural workflow to anomalous contexts.	Manipulate	To Develop Behavioural Responses to Situations and Errors	Workflow
4. Complete unstructured behavioural workflow in atypical contexts.	Perfect	To Develop Behavioural Responses to Situations and Errors	Workflow
5. Increase the speed of reflexes to situations.	Perfect	To Increase Reflexivity to Errors	Workflow
6. Show consequences of psychomotor responses if left unchecked.	Articulate	To Develop Behavioural Responses to Situations and Errors	Consequence

Designing the Task

(*Continued*)

Task	Level	Targeted Skill (Learning Outcome)	Targeted Phase
7. Evaluate psychomotor responses to error.	Articulate	To Develop Behavioural Responses to Situations and Errors	Rectification
8. Rectify behavioural responses to situation.	Articulate	To Develop Behavioural Responses to Situations and Errors	Rectification
9. Refine behavioural workflow to novel situations.	Naturalise	To Develop Behavioural Responses to Situations and Errors	Workflow

In the sociality domain, the task gets more complicated as other people are involved. These could range from conflict management to collaborative skills and workflow among the team members.

E) Sociality

Task	Targeted Skill (Learning Outcome)	Targeted Phase
1. Recommend ways to build mutual understanding among team members during workflow.	To Develop Teamwork Skills Among Team Members	Workflow
2. Establish rectification workflow among team members to minimise impact of error.	To Develop Teamwork Skills Among Team Members	Error and Rectification
3. Build collaborative and teamwork skills.	To Cultivate Collaborative Skills for Individuals	Workflow and Rectification
4. Develop negotiation and conflict management skills.	To Cultivate Collaborative Skills for Individuals	Rectification
5. Strengthen team spirit to share responsibility and consequences.	To Develop Teamwork Skills Among Team Members	Consequence

Finally, when viewed in a holistic manner, these tasks often integrate the different skills to formulate a natural and authentic set of tasks performed in the workplace or school. For example, a project requiring members from three teams to come together to discuss the issues and problem solve led to a serious outburst and conflict among the teams. Get the learners to suggest what possible errors the team members made, from the sociality, cognitive and affective domains, resulting in the conflict. This example would likely resemble item 3 in the table below.

F) Holistic Development

Task	Targeted Skill (Learning Outcome)	Targeted Phase
1. Resolve the errors using contextual cues prior to error presentation with high time and social pressure from stakeholders.	To Integrate Skillsets Across Domains (Metacognitive, Cognitive and Affective) to Achieve Mastery for the Individual	Context, Rectification
2. Reverse error rectification (end to beginning) to establish reasons for the issues and critical junctures.	To Integrate Skillsets Across Domains (Metacognitive & Cognitive) to Achieve Mastery for the Individual	Context, Error and Rectification
3. Identify contextual cues, plan workflow, spot errors and rectify errors when presented with a partial construction of issues in a dynamically evolving environment.	To Diagnose Skill Gaps, Potential Errors and Non-strengths	Context, Workflow, Error, Rectification, Consequence Reflection

Designing the Task

(Continued)

Task	Targeted Skill (Learning Outcome)	Targeted Phase
4. Manage a novel error-embedded situation outside of the typical job role, with severe consequences for wrong decisions.	To Prepare the Individual for Future Skill Needs	Context, Workflow, Error, Rectification, Consequence Reflection

Given that there are many possible permutations of errors and the contexts they occur in which a learner may encounter in his or her professional career, it becomes pertinent that the learner adopts an enquiring, open and reflective mind to question assumptions and mindsets. Designing the error and task to target specific capability development is critical to the success of using carefully designed errors to drive learning.

Additional Options in the Design of the Error and Task

1. The Nature of Error and Task

While it seems common, we should remember that the error does not necessarily have to be cognitive in nature (e.g. case) but it can be psychomotor (e.g. a wrongly fixed engine) and social or affective (e.g. a video demonstration of someone displaying poor leadership or emotive skills). These examples can be set within the contexts of the workplace, school and family. More importantly, the error and the task should correspond to real-world issues and responses so that the learner can attempt to apply to their own situations easily.

2. Using Stories to Present Errors

The contexts in the stories are critical to allow learners to identify with the situation and to draw from their prior experience. With stories, there

Chapter 9

is likely to be greater motivation for the learners to attempt the question, in the hope that there will be learning which can aid them in their current work. The crafting of the story to connect with the learner, especially culturally or professionally will impact the eventual application of learning to the learner's work context. Hence, having as many hooks as possible, based on the targeted learner profile is important. The challenge is when the learner profile is not clear or if the number of learners is expected to be huge (e.g. e-learning courses) that matching learner profile is a problem.

In addition, the disadvantage to using stories to paint the context is that with highly specific contexts, learners may not see the relevance to the problem or learning. The learners may dump down the approach and reduce the significance of the learning. Furthermore, the level of interest among learners may dip as a result, resulting in a spiralling downwards of the approach.

The other risk is that the story is quite esoteric, resulting in a highly specific context that the learners cannot identify with. As such, the error can become over-specific, resulting in reduced application of learning. For example, Facebook invitation to friends for a party ... resulted in the police turning up to disperse the thousands of guests who turned up 'self-invited'. While this story can provide the context for the error of putting out invitations on Facebook carelessly, most readers will find the story amusing and silly and are unlikely to consider themselves potential culprits of this error. Hence, using a story to showcase errors is a useful technique but the story must be something that the learners in general can relate to meaningfully.

3. Engaging Emotions for Affective Learning
While the DELETE approach is primarily a cognitive process which involves deep reflection and problem-solving abilities, it does not preclude the emotional faculty. Hence, it is possible that the DELETE problem could be to watch video clips (e.g. on explosion involving fire cracker factory) showing errors in order to elicit positive (e.g. love, compassion) and negative (e.g.

fear, anger) emotions. The elicitation of strong emotions within the learner may drive the self-reflection and learning process since the intensity of the incident is a means to engage the learner in questioning basic assumptions and belief systems. Especially if strong emotions are involved, the teacher or trainer should be mindful that learners cannot switch out of the emotional state immediately after the DELETE session. It is important for the learners to be given time and if necessary, careful explanations to help the learners re-establish normalcy again.

4. Increasing Motivation
By varying the degree of difficulty, the learner is presented with errors that are pitched at the appropriate level for success. The primary purpose is to ensure initial success and to build perseverance through work.

To add to the repertoire of motivational techniques, the following strategies can be attempted:

- Competitive team approach — let the students form teams of three learners each to compete on the speed, accuracy and rationale for error detection
- Spot the number of mistakes chart — plot the number of errors which a learner can spot and correct for a month with a corresponding reward or recognition
- Allow the learners make the errors for others to solve — Setters mark the errors corrected
- Solve work-relevant errors — e.g. pose errors that doctors, salespersons or lawyers make and allow learners to correct them — emphasise the danger of such errors.

It is important to set the relevant context in order for learners to be interested in a particular topic. The learners must see the value of their learning in the real world. Hence, groups of learners solving cross-disciplinary errors with real-life application should be encouraged.

5. *Developing Social Communication Skills*

By working in small groups, the learners learn to communicate their errors confidently and accept comments willingly, even if they disagree with them. Part of working together is the ability to accept feedback and build on ideas by others. Being amiable and supportive are important characteristics, along with critical thinking skills, leadership and determination. Remember that learner support through groupwork is one of the four parameters in the DELETE approach.

Conclusion

Designing meaningful tasks is important to ensure the success of the DELETE process since the error on its own will not bring about the learning. It will be the task to draw the lesson out of the error and the facilitator who will have to guide the process so that the learning is substantial and appropriate. Depending on the outcomes expected from the activity, the task should always differ accordingly. Usually, besides the nature of the courseware, the learner profile comes first in determining the design of the error.

To translate the above-mentioned list of targeted skills and tasks into actual learning activities and resources, we need to integrate them into the engagement process involving error presentation, reflection, referencing and re-feeding and re-experimentation. In other words, having designed a strong error and the accompanying task is not sufficient.

To drive the learning forward, the learners should be engaged through a structured reflection (e.g. using questions), referencing and re-feeding (to provide time for the learners to internalise the content) and for further experimentation to get formative feedback, which is what the next chapter is about.

Chapter 10
Designing the Engagement and Review Process

To take the concept of designing errors to stimulate learning further, this chapter will deep dive into the parameters that designers should consider when mapping out the learning engagement process. Upon completing the error-making process, the learners move into the learning engagement process. One assumption of the learning engagement process is that the right fit between the learner profile (e.g. motivation or cognitive ability) and error characteristics will maximise learning effectiveness. What the engagement process entails is also described in detail.

All men make mistakes, but only wise men learn from their mistakes.
                                                        Winston Churchill

Cognitive scientist James Reason (1990) states in his book *Human Error* that in order to reduce error rates, we must acknowledge human behaviour in system design whereby designers should:

- allow user to explore via ***experimentation***
- provide tools for users to perform experiments/test hypotheses without having to do them in high-risk irreversible work situations
- provide feedback to increase error observability
- provide symbolic cues and confidence measures

These measures centre round empowering users with the autonomy to explore, experiment and extract key principles and threshold concepts when learning. Similarly, Prof. David Klenerman, renowned geneticist, University of Cambridge, commented,

> Schools could 'demystify' the scientific process by giving students much more open-ended practicals, where the focus would be on the process of designing and executing experiments rather than obtaining successful results from them.

The shift from informing learners to learners finding out for themselves what they need to learn, with sufficient scaffolding, creates the space to generate new findings and boundaries governing these findings. Designing and reviewing the engagement process can be part of this effort to make errors an instrumental design feature in the learning process. What is also important for us to remember is that not all learners will be able to manage their learning with constantly changing variables or problems. A certain level of competency, coupled with cognitive agility will be necessary for learners to benefit from this form of learning design.

Getting the Right Fit with Learner Profile and Error Characteristics

— *Parameters for Consideration*

There is no fixed rule to determining design approaches although there are four useful factors we should take into consideration:

- The level of learner *motivation and competency*
  — if both learner motivation and competency are low, allowing the learner to achieve some initial success is important before setting more challenging errors to resolve. Typically, learner motivation may also be influenced by learner competency and capability as most learners want to engage in learning only when they are *confident* that they can manage the learning.

- The *context*
  — in which the original errors were found (e.g. in comprehension passages, problem sums, science experiments, work situations) and whether the designed errors should be located in a similar context or not
  — If the error is located in a different context (e.g. determining the growth rate of a plant instead of the speed of a car), the error will assess if the learner is able to transfer or contextualise the concept to this new context. It is also a test of the learner's grasp of the concept.

- The amount of *time* available
  — for learner to work through the errors will determine the degree of cognitive agility required
  — time is critical for the learner to reflect and explore different means of engaging with the concept
  — if time is not an issue, the learner may be asked to resolve two or more similar errors in the same exercise to increase reflectivity and sensitivity to errors developing as one works through the exercise.

- Consider the pre-error and post-error activities
  — so that the DELETE learning activity is part of an *overall flow of learning activities* designed to enhance learner experience
  — Some pre-reading on the topic may help ease the learner into the topic while post-DELETE activities such as structured questions or related stories to reinforce learning can also sustain the interest in the topic.

To recapitulate, the entire DELETE process includes both the error-making process and the learning process. The former includes the error presentation segment, while the latter requires the learner to undergo the learning process which includes reflection and task engagement. See the following page for the recap of the two processes.

Chapter 10

These four factors (as listed above) will contribute to the overall success of the DELETE approach if the fit with learner profile and the error characteristics are appropriate. Once we have clarity on the learner motivation, time allotted, the context of the error and the pre/post-error activities, the conduct of the DELETE activity can proceed in an informed manner.

The Learning Process

As depicted in an earlier chapter, the DELETE Error Presentation, Engagement and Experimentation (E^3) Learning Cycle has the following stages (as shown in the diagram below):

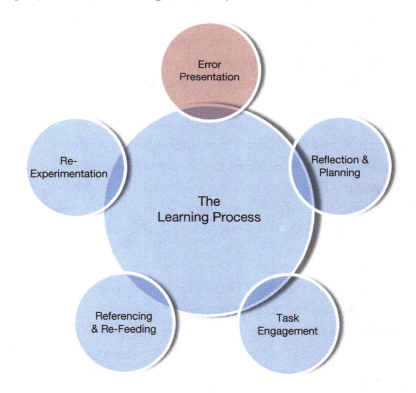

Designing the Engagement and Review Process

The strength of the learning process in DELETE lies in the protected time for learners to reflect and re-feed. With sufficient opportunities to critically reflect on the error and subsequently, to review the learning based on one's learning style, it places the mind in an optimal position for learning and assimilation. The re-experimentation will force the mind to apply the concepts or skills learned in a slightly modified environment, thereby allowing for transfer of learning.

Specifically, the sub-tasks expected of learners for each of the five stages are listed below.

As a learner, one would expect issues such as the types of errors, types of tasks and degree of support to emerge as key issues during the DELETE process. For weak learners, the errors and/or tasks asked for may be simpler and shorter. The support may be from the classmates and the trainer. On the flip side, the more capable learner will experience more difficult errors and/or tasks with less support (or possibly negative support) from classmates or trainer. Much of the information will come from self-directed learning and critical reflection.

Summary: The DELETE Experience

The DELETE Experience constitutes a reflective and learning process whereby the learner encounters the **error** and performs the required task, framed by the engagement process and support. Generally, the error can

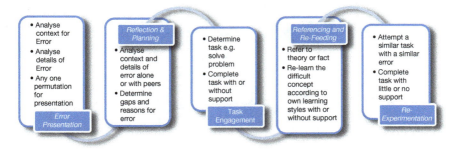

Fig. 20. Sub-Tasks Across the Five Stages in Error Presentation Process

Chapter 10

be presented either *fully*, *partially* or *not at all*. It can also be presented in *static* (i.e. no further additional information) or *dynamic* (i.e. situation is still unfolding) formats. These considerations will be discussed in a later chapter. It suffices to know that the presentation of the error, tasks, rectification measures and context can be varied. Depending on the competence that is being targeted, the appropriate permutation is designed to bring about the desired competence. Below is one example of how DELETE is used to develop learners' competence in identifying contextual cues to avoid wrong application of concepts or skill sets in the future.

Example: Resolving Conflicts with Team Members

To give an example of how an error is partially presented in a dynamic manner, we can design the presentation of the issue to comprise four 7-minute video clips beginning with the manager presenting the issue (to resolve conflicts of a male staff with a female subordinate) and meeting the female staff at a cafe to discuss solutions. The error that was made by

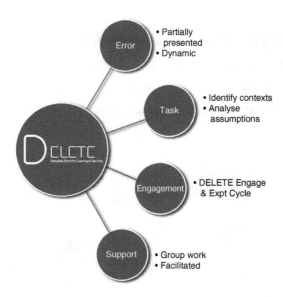

Fig. 21.   Types of Error, Task, Engagement and Support

136

Designing the Engagement and Review Process

the male staff is described in detail by the manager. She thought he was trying to pressure her to date him and sent an email to senior management to complain of sexual harassment by the male staff. Following which, video clips on the female subordinate and two other workers articulating the issue individually will be shown to the learners at different points of the discussion so that the learners only hear a different side to the issue each time. Naturally, these perspectives are subjective and only showcase part of the issue, capturing the 'dynamic' change of events as the issue unfolds.

The learners are **tasked**, after the presentation of *each* video clip, to reflect and identify the *contexts* that contributed to the error and to analyse the *assumptions* made which resulted in the error. The advantage of this partially presented (dynamic) error is that learners are presented with a range of ambiguities which allows the learners to give a corresponding range of responses on the contexts and assumptions. Learners are expected to also change their mind after receiving more information about the error from the later video clips. What is important is that the learners determine the contextual issues which led to the error and reflect on how these contextual issues and assumptions may be applicable to their own work. In effect, this design facilitates the development of cognitive abilities to review contexts, assumptions and beliefs and to question standard ways of doing things within the boundaries of the issue.

Finally, learners are tasked to state the *first principles* governing the interaction between male and female colleagues and how managers ought to resolve these issues expediently and decisively. Obviously, the context will differ across organisations and carrying out this exercise, to clarify boundaries and rules, will be useful and critical, for the safety of staff and stakeholders.

A point to note is that learner support can be adjusted to match the learner profiles (e.g. years of experience and cognitive ability) so that the engagement process is not overwhelming but beneficial. If necessary, the facilitator can take on small-group coaching to handhold the learners who face difficulties.

Chapter 10

As you may decipher from this example, the incorporation of some ambiguity and unpredictability can cause confusion to some learners. It is at the discretion of the learning designers to review the level of ambiguity (e.g. by presenting the error fully in a static manner) required. However, if ambiguity and unpredictability can be injected into the DELETE experience, learners are likely to engage in issues which are not straightforward and can dynamically change as the learners' reason through the issues. There are no clearly right answers and few clearly wrong answers. Instead, there will be multiple responses, depending on the case

> Part of my work in the past required me to travel to China, Indonesia, Malaysia and Vietnam. As such, I am particularly attuned to cultural norms and expectations. I recall one trip which was amusing when we think about it now, but it wasn't so funny then. Well, the incident happened at the end of the working trip. My colleague and I were on our way to the airport, after concluding a successful business trip. We were driven to the airport and accompanied by the official. It was early summer then and there were impromptu fruit stalls set up along the road where farmers were selling large winter melons. As it was a relatively long journey, we made small talk with the official, just to keep the conversation going. It was going well. After passing a number of these fruit stalls, my junior colleague remarked, 'Those melons look huge. They must be very sweet'. Wow. That innocuous remark caught me by surprise and alarm bells started ringing in mind. I was hoping the official didn't notice her remark. Unfortunately, the official did. She promptly stopped the car without even asking us and before we realised, she had bought five bags full of huge melons! Bearing in mind that we each had several pieces of luggage and laptops with us, the additional weight was not something I particularly wanted. We tried to reject the official's kind gesture but because she had already bought the melons, there was nothing we could do except graciously accept them. I took a quick glance at my colleague. She looked at me sheepishly. I had to help carry those melons up the plane!

Designing the Engagement and Review Process

This story points out the fact that there are boundaries which the practitioner (i.e. me) will know. The rules do not indicate that we should not comment on melons when on the way to the airport although it would have helped us a lot then. There are probably too many other possible contexts which cannot be covered by rules. What is more important is that her error has helped define the boundary in inter-cultural behaviour: Do not make positive comments on objects or foods especially those which can be bought. Neutral ones will be more acceptable. Another case in point, a senior officer commented enthusiastically on how tasty a dessert was. No guesses there but that same dessert was served for the next five days when the officer was there! He must have regretted saying it! Remember that there are boundaries to the rules. These boundaries are crossed when the compliments are perceived as 'requests' which culturally, the host is obliged to accede to!

presented. In fact, the learners are encouraged to think creatively and critically at the same time (or what I term as 'creatical' thinking). Through sufficient exposure to the DELETE approach, awareness of competences such as mindfulness, metacognitive ability and innovativeness are further heightened. They will also be more aware of where the boundaries are, as guided by the error presented.

In the next chapter, we will go on to examine how to extract maximum learning benefit from the error presentation. The learning task, reflection process, theory-building and re-experimentation segments will be discussed further. It is critical to also note that the error presentation with the rectifications and consequences are only triggers to drive the learning. The next process involving how the individual picks up the necessary information or skills to complete the learning cycle needs to be carefully crafted so that the DELETE process is not aborted midway before learning is completed. It is a deliberate attempt to emphasise that the learning does not stop when the problem is solved (at the rectification segment), but that further consideration and reflection are needed to pre-empt or prepare for future occurrences of similar issues. Better still if the workflow is now refined based on the learning process so that the system is further strengthened to reduce errors and address old assumptions.

Chapter 11

The DELETE Error Engagement and Experimentation (E³) Learning Cycle

In this segment, we will describe the five stages in the DELETE Error Engagement and Experimentation (E³) Learning Cycle in greater detail.

1. Error Presentation

See the earlier chapters on information about pre-error, error presentation and post-error stages, to understand the error design process. In the presentation of the error/s, learners may experience error/s which are presented:

- Fully or Partially (which implies that the learners may not know the full picture of what happened and may be tasked with uncovering the error and/or first principles)
- Dynamically or Statically (which implies that the error may be presented over a series of vignettes or video clips, layering on more information over time)

The error presentation is the process when learners analyse the specific aspects of the error and the context surrounding or leading to the error. Hence, to ensure relevance to the learners, the error ought to be designed and presented in line with the learning outcomes (aligned with the level and domain in Bloom's Taxonomy). Going forward, when enabled by AI, the presentation of error in a branching manner can make this process a highly dynamic and responsive approach.

2. Reflection and Planning

A key part of learning involves close monitoring and reflection of the action taken by learners. Often, learners carry out certain reflection processes such as:

- analyse context and details of error alone or with peers
- determine gaps and reasons for error

Once the error has been presented (even partially), the learners ought to start reasoning what they need to do in response, based on the task. Here, they engage in a reflection on the error to determine the contexts and rules, to uncover the cause of error and possible rectifications. However, at this stage, the reflection carried should not be confused with the subsequent task. That will be the next stage. This stage of reflection and planning is simply to provide time and opportunity for the learners to engage with the error. If there are prior experiences with similar errors, this is when the learners can elicit these experiences to engage with the task more effectively.

However, it is also important that learners adopt a careful stance on using past experiences since many experiences can interfere with the learning especially if the errors seem to be similar with one's past experiences but in actual fact, they are quite different in nature. Being able to locate the error within one's own experience and context of work and organisation should be the emphasis for this stage. Thinking through, empathising with, and allowing for some dissociation from the case may be useful for the learner since the element of taking a step back can help the learner engage better with the case later. Based on experience, getting the learners to reflect rather than jump right into the case has the effect of getting the learners to think more laterally and creatively since many also consider assumptions and less obvious issues when there is time to reflect and rethink.

The downside to reflection sometimes is that negative transfer can take place as a result of the learner's own experience which may not be associated with the case or task at hand. Negative transfer takes place when one's experience exhibits similarity to the case presented, but the reality is that they are both quite different in nature. Hence, when the learner attempts to elicit the same frame of reference, it can really confuse the learner.

One common example is when a driver who is used to left-wheel drive goes to another country with cars that utilise right-wheel drive. The beginning first hours can be disorientating as the driver looks at the wrong side for on-coming cars or to turn into a side road. Negative transfer can be a huge deterrence to effective learning especially when one's experience is extremely strong (e.g. driving automaticity) and it confuses the learners significantly. As such, it is important that if the facilitator is aware of possible negative transfer, some warning could be given beforehand. However, if the error was designed to intentionally take into account the possible negative transfer, then it will be an extremely powerful learning experience later on, as learners struggle with applying their own experience to the case, in an ineffective manner. Just like drivers driving on the wrong side of the road, they will pick up the cues very fast.

3. Task Engagement

In the previous chapter on task engagement, we explored different outcomes that drive the task engagement process. For example, learners may be required to

- determine task, e.g. solve problem (as described in detail in an earlier chapter)
- complete task with or without support

Chapter 11

In relation to the Error Presentation and Engagement Process, the task is pivotal to having the learners continue the learning process. They need to see the relevance of the error and the task to their own learning experience. Hence, the more related they see the error to their own work or to the questions they encounter, the more likely they will engage with the error activity. Motivational theories (e.g. Self-Determination Theory) will apply to this stage of engagement with the learners. Preferably, the learners will identify with the error to want to continue the learning process. Over time, they may treat this activity as 'fun' and intrinsically want to carry on with the task. Often, during task engagements, learners may require further assistance in the form of more instruction or coaching. The next stage, Referencing and Re-feeding provides learners with the necessary information to understand how to carry out the task more effectively. The learning becomes concretised at that stage.

4. Referencing and 'Re-feeding'

As its name implies, there is a repetition of a process which in this case refers to the self-review of information. Upon reading or being taught a concept, the learner can review the concept through his or her own preferred learning style. It is critical that the learner is aware and understands his or her preferred learning style so that maximal learning can occur. Listed

Auditory	Tactile
• Listen to explanations • Read text aloud to self • Make voice recordings of notes using phone	• Write keywords • Draw diagrams • Make short notes • Type key points as Notes on mobile phone

Visual	Kinaesthetic
• Highlight keywords • Look at diagrams • Draw concept maps • Take pictures with mobile phone	• Discuss with others • Teach yourself • Use Hand Actions • Take pictures of Hand Actions with phone

below are some examples of how the four different types of learners can 're-feed' themselves.

Usually, the time allotted for 're-feeding' lasts about 5–10 minutes and this is intentionally kept short so that the mind is actively engaged during this period. The learners can refer to reference sources (whether texts, video clips or experts) for information on the concept embedded in the error. On this note, it is important to keep the referencing segment short so that boredom does not set in. Once the time is up, the trainer moves ahead to continue with the next step which in the DELETE Engagement and Experimentation cycle has to do with re-experimentation. The brevity of the 're-feeding' process also implies that the concepts learned are bite-sized for easy assimilation. Hence, allowing learners to 're-feed' every 20–30 minutes is advisable to allow the mind to refresh and 'save' the learning in the long-term memory. If the learners still have significant issues with carrying out the task, the educator can adjust the level of support provided so that the learners can attain a level of achievement at the re-experimentation stage. The re-experimentation process ought to be rewarding as learners are most likely able to succeed with the amount of help given during the task and the referencing stages.

5. Re-experiment

At this stage, the learners have a second attempt at the activity, to attempt to achieve success regardless of what happened earlier with the task. Here, learners should:

- attempt a similar task with a similar error
- complete task with little or no support

The first point about attempting a similar task with a similar error suggests reinforcing the learning that preceded the re-experimentation process, while the second point is to assess the competence of the learner performing the task independently. By pulling together the entire learning process at the end for the individual learners to attempt the task with little or no support, it signals to the learners that they must be responsible for their own learning. Here, the learning cycle ends, for this particular cycle. Of course, learners can continue with the learning process by attempting other similar errors and then learning from them.

Chapter 12

The Engagement and Review Process: Use Cases

In this chapter, we will look at several case studies to anchor our understanding of the DELETE Error Presentation, Engagement and Experimentation (E^3) Learning Cycle. Let's look at the first case.

Case 1: Bank Officers Managing Loan Transactions

Objective: **To Develop Ability to Evaluate Contexts and Assumptions** — to identify contextual cues and assumptions to review current workflows and the boundaries to these workflows.

Context: Bank staff processing applications for home loans need to acquire the competencies to complete the loan transaction and at the same time, comply with the strict bank regulations concerning home loans. Here are details of the learning design (see Table 6):

Food for Thought

Errors can come from anywhere, but some errors are life changing. For example, a surgeon removing the wrong kidney or **amputating the wrong limb**, would have devastating consequences.

Medicine is not the only field where basic errors due to left-right confusion determine life or death: it was postulated that **a steersman turning the ship right instead of left** contributed to the sinking of the Titanic.

Chapter 12

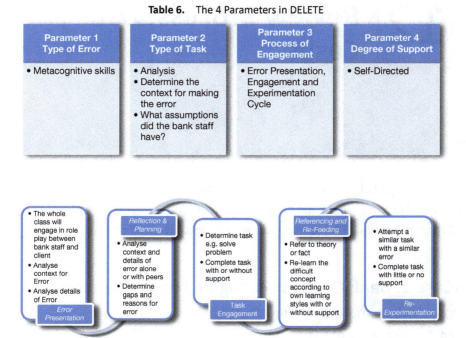

Table 6. The 4 Parameters in DELETE

Parameter 1 Type of Error	Parameter 2 Type of Task	Parameter 3 Process of Engagement	Parameter 4 Degree of Support
• Metacognitive skills	• Analysis • Determine the context for making the error • What assumptions did the bank staff have?	• Error Presentation, Engagement and Experimentation Cycle	• Self-Directed

Fig. 22. The DELETE E³ Learning Cycle

The error is designed into the key processing steps when the staff must work with the client to determine the type of home loan required. Hence, it is an application error because the SOPs were not adhered to despite being made clear to the learners. However, there are several assumptions and contextual issues contributing to the error being committed (see Fig. 22).

Stage 1: Error Presentation

a) Context and Workflow

The context is that there is a long queue for services in the bank and the noise level has risen markedly due to the customers getting impatient. The workflow is that the customers get a queue number, and they wait for their number to be flashed on the screen. There are several instances that the customers left without waiting for their turn. Hence, precious time is wasted in waiting for these absent customers.

b) Error Presentation

All the learners carry out a 'mass' role play following instructions in a manual which embeds the error of not asking the right questions (to arrive at the right type of home loan). This manual is given to the learners at the start of the exercise. The learners have a few minutes to read the manual and try out the instructions with the 'client'. When ready, the role play begins with the bank officers asking questions about the client's credit status. Some of the errors are embedded in the script. The bank officers are not told which part of the script is erroneous, so the officers are expected to carry out the role play according to the script. Subsequently, the clients call up the bank to complain that there were errors in the product specification being sold to them. The loan details were not in accordance with what the bank officers mentioned. Also, based on the customer's income, the loan amounts were in excess and were in violation of the regulations set by the banking and finance regulator.

c) Rectification

To rectify the error, the bank officers called up the customers individually to explain the error and offered to provide additional freebies to appease the customers. They also requested that the customers keep the incidents to themselves if they wish to keep the freebies. Finally, the errors were rectified but they were logged in the bank's financial transactional record as changes rather than as errors.

Role play ends here.

Stage 2: Reflection and Planning

Following the role play with the client, the learners are asked to critically reflect on the interaction and plan how to determine the error and the context in which the error was made either through targeted questions or confirming with reference sources.

Stage 3: Task Engagement

The learners will then carry out the task assigned.

In this case, the bank staff is required to analyse the context in which the error was made and the assumptions that he or she had. In other words, what were the environmental and cognitive factors that contributed to the error being made? Was the client in a rush to complete the transaction and key questions were left out as a result? Could a product-specific checklist assist in the client engagement process? Was the bank staff trained to prioritise questions to target key areas for background checks? Was there pressure for the staff to sell a few bank loans each day?

At a deeper level, were there assumptions that the bank staff had which were not substantiated and hence, untrue at the point of interaction with the client? Did the bank staff assume that the client will disclose key information (e.g. bankruptcy record or credit card default history) at the first session of discussion? Did the staff assume that all clients are rational and logical? To what extent should these assumptions be re-examined to increase fidelity of such client engagement sessions?

At this stage, if the learners are confused or stuck or getting off track from the primary areas for discussion and learning, the facilitator can pose questions for the learners to reflect and work out the answer themselves. Here, the level of support is only at the critical questioning level to empower the learners with the right mindset and cognitive reasoning processes. There are strong grounds not to provide the learners with the standard answers so as to build reasoning power and adaptability especially when meeting different types of clients. What was the issue with logging the errors as changes rather than mistakes? Were there attempts to cover up the mistakes?

Stage 4: Referencing and Re-feeding

With the reflection and task engagement stages, the learners are given the time and space to reflect and arrive at their own conclusions. However, note that there are no 'correct' answers provided thus far. There may be some support in terms of peer advice or targeted questioning to drive thinking, the textbook answers have not yet been given. Depending on the type of learners and the learning outcomes set, the learners may be given some form of reference sources (e.g. expert explanation or texts) to anchor the learning. At this stage, the learners are expected to compare their initial reflection process and the answers they arrived at with the expert viewpoints (or the 'correct answer'). There may be further debates or discussion at this point to allow for further assimilation of the key concepts. To further internalise the concepts, learners are given some time (3–5 minutes) to 're-feed' themselves based on their own learning preferences (e.g. auditory, visual, tactile and kinaesthetic).

In the case of the bank officer, the correct series of questions to ask the client is provided and the officer compares the correct series with the initial incorrect series of questions (errors) to determine if he or she was right in the analytical process.

Stage 5: Re-experimentation

This stage is known as the re-experimentation if we consider the error presentation process as allowing the learners to have the first go at experimentation. In this re-experimentation stage, the learners will attempt to carry out the transaction again, this time in the correct manner and with the appropriate cognitive mindsets.

Debrief

Finally, there is a debriefing by the facilitator to draw the entire role play together as a learning activity. What is key in this DELETE activity is that the error is made clear to all so that there is no confusion, and the correct series of steps is communicated in detail again. Here, the learners are encouraged to analyse:

- their presumptions, hunches and mindsets
- other possible errors that may arise as a result
- their metacognitive processes (or thinking patterns) by asking
  a. 'What (are we thinking about now)?
  b. Now What? (Are we satisfied with our thinking process and if not, what can we do)?

Returning to the learning outcome, the DELETE activity allows targeted learning of key questions, which need to be asked to ensure comprehensive background checks in compliance with the regulations set by financial authorities and aligned with the bank's own SOP requirements. Hence, without compromising quality, DELETE reinforces the metacognitive processes of bank staff to review their assumptions of client behaviour and how they should engage clients to more effectively serve them and complete the transaction in a timely manner.

Case 2: Bank Officer Mis-Selling Products

Objective: Sharpening Cognitive Adaptability and Flexibility — to cope with a constantly changing wicked problem and error

This example will showcase how a similar context (Bank Officer with Client applying for a home loan) can be modified to achieve a different outcome. Here, the objective is to sharpen cognitive ability to work more effectively with clients who have difficulties making up their minds in selecting the type of home loan or those clients who tend to offer contradictory information. The error is that the bank officer ended up mis-selling the financial product. Listed on the following page are the parameters to the activity (see Table 7):

The Engagement and Review Process

Table 7. The Four Parameters in the DELETE Approach

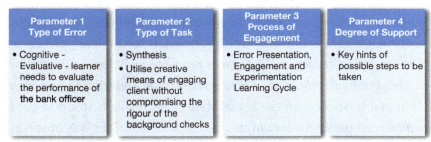

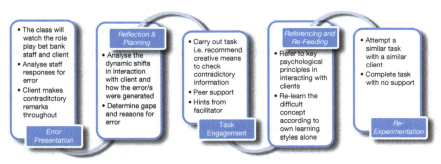

Fig. 23. The DELETE E³ Learning Cycle

Based on the above description of the error, the 'client' is expected to dynamically alter the contexts and the error as the bank officer grapples with the issues and background checks. In this case, the alignment between the error and the task must be tight as the learning outcome is that the learner is able to understand the dynamic issues involved in the interactions with clients who provide contradictory information and then creatively develop new means of engaging these types of clients, beyond those reflected in the SOPs. Hence, based on the observation of how the bank officer is managing the dynamic shifts in client behaviour and responses, the learner will need to make recommendations, some possibly quite creative, on how best to work with such clients in the future.

Stage 1: Error Presentation

The learners observe a role play between the bank officer and the client. The client presents contradictory information to the bank officer as the conversation continues. The errors presented will focus on how the client led the bank officer on 'a wild goose chase' and tried to present a picture that is better than the actual state of his financial status to get a much-needed personal loan. In this case, the bank officer was observed to be led along and did not take control of the discussion and background checks. As a result, some of the mandatory questions were asked, but the answers given did not seem to have addressed the question although some information was given. Due to the need to chase sales targets, the bank officer allowed the loan request to go through based on information that was not entirely true without questioning or checking further.

Stage 2: Reflection and Planning

Time is provided for learners to reflect on how they would approach this process in the workplace. Some of the key questions that the learner needs to consider are:

- What would they do if a client proves uncertain or difficult?
- What assumptions did the observed bank officer have, pertaining to such clients?
- Why did the bank officer allow the client to lead the conversation and not try to inject key questions or follow the sequence of questions in the checklist provided by the bank?
- What would be key skillsets that the bank officer needs to acquire to prevent future occurrences?

Stage 3: Task Engagement

The bank officer has to consider different means of engaging such clients especially if these clients utilise flattery or engage in 'name throwing' (i.e.

list famous personalities as their close acquaintances). At what point in the conversation will the bank officer have to be firm or adopt some of these more innovative client engagement strategies? At this stage, the learner needs to propose key strategies to engage such clients and provide the reasons to support their answer.

Make recommendations based on either their own experience or from literature. Facilitator may provide hints or brief answers to questions from learners to guide them along.

Stage 4: Referencing and Re-feeding

The facilitator will introduce key concepts such as Game Theory and psychological principles in interactions such as non-verbal body language. Learners will engage in discussion to further adapt the application of these concepts to the case observed. They should then list how they will attempt to address the needs of clients who present an inaccurate picture of their financial status based on the principles presented. Further to this, the learners can take a few minutes to 're-feed' the information by self-teaching, jotting down key points or drawing mind maps to retain the information learned.

Stage 5: Re-experimentation

The learner now engages in a role play with a different client but with a similar style of presenting information in haphazard and sometimes contradictory manner. Where possible, the role play should be video recorded to allow the learner to review the video clip for self-improvements. Learners are also expected to experiment with creative and novel ways to reduce the contradiction presented by the client and to get at the actual situation underneath the façade. Peer support in terms of comments and input can facilitate the learner to learn from the role play.

Chapter 12

Debrief

Learners review the success level of their recommendations and make changes to the process, if necessary. Facilitator debriefs the learners, comments on what happens in real-life situations and provides further advice on how best to manage learners who expect the staff to pander to. More importantly, the consideration about the assumptions and mindsets ought to have been dealt with in the earlier phases so that the bank staff can focus on getting the clients to be truthful and complete the transaction or loan with the correct mindsets.

For this case, the learners are encouraged to analyse:

- their presumptions, hunches and mindsets
- their metacognitive processes (or thinking patterns) by asking:
  - So What (are the consequences and is this really important)?
  - In What Ways? (Are the weaknesses or the strengths in our thinking hindering or facilitating performance)?

Case 3: Students Reading the Compass Wrongly

Objective: Developing Creatical (Creative and Critical) Thinking Ability — to add missing information to the problem for creative solutioning process.

Geography students when asked to provide the compass bearing of *point A* with reference from a particular position on the map (see Fig. 24). One of the typical errors that learners make is that they read the compass

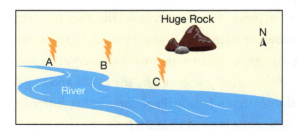

Fig. 24. The Map in the Learning Activity

156

The Engagement and Review Process

Table 8. The Four Parameters in the DELETE Approach

Parameter 1 Type of Error	Parameter 2 Type of Task	Parameter 3 Process of Engagement	Parameter 4 Degree of Support
• Psychomotor- precision in reading a compass	• Application • Add the necessary information in order to successfully read the compass	• Error Presentation, Engagement and Experimentation(E^3) Learning Cycle	• Call a friend

from the South point rather than North point. Hence, the difficult concept for the learners is to begin compass reading by referencing from the North Pole.

The error (see Table 8) is designed to check the way students read the compass to determine the bearing of a location from a particular position. Hence, it has to do with a procedure and is a psychomotor error. Based on an incomplete map, which shows the possible locations of the entity, the learners will have to add more information to the case to complete the case.

In this case, the learners are tasked to indicate where the reader is standing in relation to the entity being observed. The only information will be the erroneous compass reading and the possible locations of the entity.

Stage 1: Error Presentation

A recent thunderstorm resulted in a house being struck by lightning (point A), about 10 km from where Abbey (☺) was staying. She determined that it was about 80° bearing from her house. She made a mistake. Can you identify where her house was, what the common mistake was and suggest how to avoid making the same mistake?

Stage 2: Reflection and Planning

Firstly, learners are expected to understand the question and try to elicit prior experience for answers. They need to respond to questions such as 'How did Abbey make the mistake?' and 'What are the underlying competencies required to read a compass accurately?'

Stage 3: Task Engagement

Based on the level of support, the learners can 'call' or ask one friend (social support) to discuss the problem. Here, the learners are to determine what the common mistake is. They are to reflect on what the correct location of Abbey's house is and how they can correct Abbey on her mistake. More importantly, at this stage, learners are expected to creatively analyse the mistake and provide possible rationale for the proposed mistake made. Learners need to justify why they think a particular mistake is common, whether based on their own experience or by logic. They will also need to indicate the location of Abbey's house based on the erroneous reading and the location of the other items (e.g. rock, river) on the map.

Stage 4: Referencing and Re-feeding

Common errors that learners make are shared at this point with examples such as reading from the opposite direction on the compass (instead of clockwise, it will be anticlockwise) and not using the actual North (as indicated by the arrow on the map) but the vertical line (parallel to the paper) as the North instead. Learners can then compare their answers with the common errors shared here by the facilitators. Given that the activity is to develop 'creatical ability' of learners, it is vital to allow for some creative license, especially for answers which may not be one of the common errors shared but still logical on all counts.

Learners are given time to assimilate the information based on their own learning styles, whether to write the points down or self-teach or draw mind maps.

Stage 5: Re-experimentation

A new problem and error will be given to the learners for their own experimentation concerning map reading and compass reading. They can utilise the information provided on common errors in the earlier stage for their answers here.

Debrief

Learners review their 'creatical abilities' in terms of how far out of the box they are able to think and if their thinking patterns allow for the successful generation of new ideas without being constrained by limitations they set on themselves or assumptions, which may not hold true anyway.

For this case, the learners are encouraged to analyse

- their mindsets about what is right and what is wrong
- their metacognitive processes (or thinking patterns) by asking:
    - In What Ways? (Are the weaknesses or the strengths in our thinking hindering or facilitating performance)?

The Issue of Support

When it comes to group or team support, there are three areas for consideration:

a) Team support (group think)
b) Types of support (constructive, neutral, destructive)
c) Timing of support (pre, during, post- error correction)

Together, these three areas listed above provide a spectrum of sociality related to social and psychological support. What is important is that learners experience some degree of support to motivate them to move forward. There are also possible scenarios whereby confident learners are goaded into deciding based on short timelines and confusing inputs to test their decision-making skills. The learners may be provided information on what the responses of other learners are (e.g. 79% of learners chose option (b) because they felt ….). The false information is to force learners to be clear about their own viewpoints. Hence, by providing constructive as well as destructive feedback with the latter aiming to dissuade or confuse the learner, the purpose is really to get the learners to check their own understanding and rationale. However, the use of destructive feedback must be measured and carefully planned to avoid undue psychological and social damage.

a) Team Support
- Mode of Support (online, face-to-face, coaching support)

With technology, there are now many different options for learners to receive input and support at varying points in time. For example, learners can opt to send out requests for help on group chats on WhatsApp or forum discussion platforms. They can tweet about their current problems and thinking processes. With video clips, they can also record their experiences and what they intend to do with the issues at that point in time. Going onto YouTube to search for possible answers from video clips (especially on procedural errors) is a viable option. Of course, there is also the face-to-face facilitation and class discussion along with coaching assistance from someone who is more competent in the field. By strategically determining the type of support available to the learners, the learning effectiveness can be enhanced or hindered during the DELETE activity.

- Team Errors

'Group think' is a well-known phenomenon based on psychological research on team dynamics and organisational psychology. In brief, group think has to do with group members having similar ideas and assumptions due to the way they have selected or trained. Hence, there are blind spots that the entire group may not be aware of due to their common assumptions and thinking patterns. It may also be due to the team culture if it promotes conformity and discourages diversity of views. Group members may be hesitant to raise issues, just to be seen as group compliant. As a result, group think becomes entrenched as a culture in the group. Based on research on group think, groups that tend to have similar viewpoints among its members may become less competitive and adaptable to changes in the environment. While teams with group think may be seen as efficient in the short term, in the long term, the group actually loses out to other groups due to the lack of diverse viewpoints and creativity. The DELETE approach can also be used to detect group think and assist groups in reversing group think culture as they embark on measures to address errors and propose new solutions. During the engagement process, group members can consciously make an attempt to propose diverse viewpoints, in order to contribute to the diversity of ideas and to the richness of the discussion.

- First Follower effect

There is an interesting phenomenon that is observed in teams known as the 'first follower effect'. In many teams, the leader (whether formally or informally appointed) is only seen as effective if he or she has followers supporting the decisions made. Usually, the first follower (i.e. the first team member to support) makes a difference in swinging the rest of the team to accept the leader's viewpoints and follow the decision or to resist the leader in the team. The perceived reputation of the first follower is the issue here. Often, if the first follower is well-respected, the rest of the team will follow along with the decision, while if the first follower does not have much influence, the rest of the team may subconsciously decide to sit on the fence or not follow the leader's decision. Hence, it is useful to ensure that the leader has obtained some support from a few of the more influential team members so that they can be the first followers. Especially if the first followers are informed of the facts to take the necessary actions, i.e. to follow or to rectify the actions, the entire team can be galvanised to follow accordingly. Again, DELETE activities can be powerful tools to promote group dynamics and leadership skills. It can also be used as a platform to determine the strength of the leader if he has no first follower at the beginning. Will the leader wilt under pressure or be able to convince the team to follow? Is his ability to communicate and convince up to par? These are questions that can be answered using DELETE as a tool for checking leadership abilities. From the team learning point of view, it may be useful to convince the first followers of the merits of the process or concepts to obtain buy-in from the rest of the team eventually. This will facilitate the team moving forward on some of the decisions and learning.

b) Types of Support: Constructive (Positive) feedback versus Destructive (Negative) feedback

As described in an earlier chapter, the degree of support can be either negative or positive, depending on the purpose of the support. In the case of negative support, it may be to force the learner to evaluate the error based on clear rationale and understanding of the concept. As with naysayers and discouragers, learners reinforce their thinking and stand firm with their decision. This is important in the real world where signs may be ominous but being persistent brings success. Hence, negative support can be built into the error to develop resilience and thinking processes, especially for people where time pressure and distractors are evident in their work (e.g. doctors, soldiers and lawyers).

c) Timing of Support

Finally, the timing of support is critical in that support given too early will result in premature abortion of the thinking process since the support dissuades the learner from further thinking through. On the other hand, support that comes too late may be useless especially if the learner has become unmotivated and is prepared to give in. Similar to coaching where timing of support is important, the point when support is triggered, either through observations or by the learner himself, will have to be determined beforehand so as to 'push' the learner forward in order to maximise learning and thinking.

Conclusion

This chapter has been exciting partly because the DELETE model is close to being fully described but more importantly, this chapter fleshes out how using the DELETE approach can facilitate learning and thinking in many different ways, beyond the typical straight-path design and learn approach. For example, asking learners to propose what the possible errors could be is an interesting variety to the typical spot the error task. Hopefully, the DELETE approach opens up a whole new world of instructional design to target learning and reinforcement in specific difficult points of larger concepts.

Chapter 13

The Seven-Step Process in the DELETE Approach

Overview

Since the start of this book, we have examined the error-based learning approach in relation to the roles that errors can play to facilitate learning, especially in the realm of expertise building and metacognition. By layering on the content, I hope you have gained a deeper understanding of the error design and presentation process. This chapter will expand our understanding to the full seven-step DELETE approach where we start with error analysis and end with error refinement.

The seven-step DELETE process is designed to be a logical workflow of tasks and activities, driven primarily by the original outcome of the learning activity. What does this mean? The initial stages in the DELETE process play a key role in determining the subsequent rollout of the rest of the steps as the implementer follows through the designated steps, to arrive at the intended outcomes. Hence, the initial stages involving analysis of collated errors, trialling the eventual task or problem and finally, routing back to initiate the error-solving process are important and should be carefully implemented to ensure learning effectiveness. Based on careful analyses, the difficult concepts are formulated and the errors are then designed.

Process of Designing Errors for Learning

In an earlier chapter, we described the four parameters in DELETE and how they impact the error-based learning process. This chapter will focus on the

Chapter 13

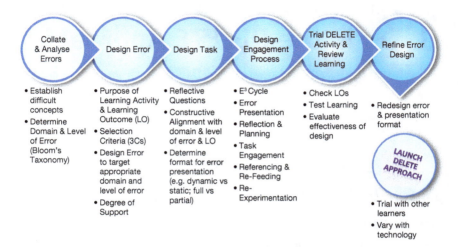

Fig. 25.   The DELETE Design

full *design process* (see Fig. 25) of a DELETE learning activity and how each stage flows into the next to inform the construction of the overall learning activity. More importantly, the means to ensure constructive alignment (making sure the original intent of the activity results in the observed outcome in learning and performance) will be discussed.

The seven steps in the design process feed into each other in a dynamic fashion so when viewing the above process flow, one should be careful to view the process as an iterative, multi cyclical design flow rather than a static unidirectional flow diagram.

We will run through the entire seven steps quickly in this segment before expounding on each step in detail, especially those steps that we have not covered in the earlier chapters.

Step 1: Collate and Analyse Errors

Error analyses and collation are important steps to initiate the design process. From experience, most educators will be able to pinpoint which areas that they teach are problematic for the typical student. The precise

The Seven-Step Process in the DELETE Approach

> Once, I was in a lift with my five-year-old daughter. It was the sort of lift that announced the levels it stopped at. Knowing this, I decided to pull a fast one on her. I told her that the lift we were in was an intelligent lift. The lift would respond to my questions. Just before reaching Level 11, the level that we were stopping at, I asked loudly, 'Which level are we stopping at?' Promptly, the lift responded, 'Eleventh storey'. My daughter's eyes nearly popped out for a second or so. Then she realised she was tricked but still, it was a good lesson for us that sometimes, it is not about having the right answer to the question but rather, asking the right question in anticipation of the answer. In my example above, I asked the right question and so, the lift's answer was inevitably correct.
>
> This brings us to the point of designing learning in view of the errors that learners make typically when they learn. Since these mistakes are common and possibly critical, doesn't it make sense to design the 'right' errors so that the learning is done correctly subsequently? It does make sense, doesn't it?

problem can usually be highlighted with a possible solution to help learners understand the concept. In most of these so-called solutions, the teacher is most likely to relate how the concept should be taught rather than how the concept could be learned most effectively. Focusing on the learning process is the first step to DELETE. The errors are symptoms of the learning process gone awry.

What constitutes a 'Difficult Concept'?

a) Difficult *Procedural* Knowledge — where learners often make mistakes with sequencing of the steps or in applying the rules, e.g. converting direct speech into indirect speech, adding fractions
b) Difficult *Declarative* Knowledge — where learners incorrectly recall the information required, e.g. name of oceans, Newton's first law of motion, Pythagoras' Theorem.

Hence, difficult concepts are simply the stumbling blocks to the learner's understanding of the overall topic and subsequently, the performance required of the learner.

At this point, it may be useful to highlight that the notion of threshold concepts (Meyer & Land, 2006) is somewhat similar to difficult concepts except that besides being difficult, threshold concepts are also definitive points where they identify key areas that need mastery. According to Land *et al.* (2005, p. 198),

> *A focus on these jewels ... allows for richer and more complex insights into aspects of the subjects students are studying; it plays a diagnostic role in alerting tutors to areas of the curriculum where students are likely to encounter troublesome knowledge and experience conceptual difficulty.*

The key difference is that threshold concepts are BOTH difficult and transformative, whereas the difficult concepts mentioned above can be transformative and non-transformative but just complex for the learner. Hence, threshold concepts are likely to be a subset of difficult concepts. Here, we focus on difficult concepts rather than threshold concepts because helping learners overcome potential hurdles in learning will contribute to learning effectiveness. If these difficult concepts are also threshold concepts, the error-based approach will be even more critical for a constructivist solution to making learning happen. What is more important is that the learners have learning opportunities to construct their own understanding of the difficult concepts. It may be that the learners need to traverse the conceptual landscape a few times in different ways before they finally understand the difficult concept. There is no easy or straightforward way for learners to learn some of these difficult concepts.

Examples of the Two Types of Difficult Concepts

Table 9.   Examples of Difficult Concepts

- **At School**

	Procedural (How Questions)	Declarative (Why and What Questions)
1	Find the height of triangles	State the past tense of verbs
2	Perform science experiments	Describe parallel electric circuits
3	Convert direct speech into reported speech	Explain the occurrence of acid rain

- **At Work**

	Procedural (How Questions)	Declarative (Why and What Questions)
1	Serve customers in a retail setting	State the reasons for good customer service
2	Resolve conflicts with key stakeholders	Determine the types of conflicts present in the workplace
3	Manage projects and staff	List the types of challenges project managers face when meeting project timelines

There are implications to understanding the differences between these two types of difficult concepts (see Table 9) as the design of the errors will have to adhere to the nature of the difficult concept that is incorrectly interpreted or applied. To consider an example of a concept with both declarative and a procedural nature, we can look at the application of Pythagoras' Theorem

$$x^2 + y^2 = z^2$$

where x and y are two sides of a right-angled triangle and z is the hypotenuse.

Recalling this equation will be considered declarative knowledge. Someone may remember it incorrectly, resulting in a declarative error. At the same time, the Pythagoras' Theorem will be considered a procedural concept if a learner has to apply the equation to actually find the answer.

Hence, if two sides of a triangle are at right angle to each other and one is 5 cm while the other is 3 cm. What is the length of the third side? For a learner to find the answer, applying the Pythagoras' Theorem correctly will be critical. Hence, the learner needs to first ascertain how 5 and 3 fit into the equation. Following which, adding the square of these two numbers and then, to square root the answer (34 cm) correctly are necessary for the completion of the procedure. Failing which, the learner has committed a procedural error.

Ascertaining whether the concept is procedural or declarative is only the first step. Once we have categorised the error correctly so that our design process is clearer, we can then analyse the errors according to the 3 'C's (Clarity, Commonness and Criticality).

As you can attest, some errors that are common may not be critical. However, due to their high frequency, teachers may want to address these common errors so that learners learn from the error and do not repeat it. On the other hand, there are critical errors that may not be common. These critical errors are worth examining because like the Black Swan theory (where people in the past assumed all swans were white until early immigrants to Australia saw black swans for the first time), it is often the less common errors which may appear during examinations, to test the student's understanding of the more abstract aspects of the theory or principle.

By identifying and categorising the error accordingly, we can then prepare for the next stage, which is to design errors for learning.

Step 1: Collate and Analyse Errors

By having a database of errors associated with a specific learning outcome or concept, we will be able to analyse the nature of the concept (whether procedural or declarative) which will then inform the error design and task design stages.

For example, if it is the procedural aspect of the concept that is difficult, the task design will then focus on getting the learners to complete the procedure with the focus on either analysing or rectifying the key step. Without the initial error analyses, it will be difficult for the designer to determine how best to work out the type of errors to design and the subsequent task for the learner to complete.

The analysis of the error comprises dissecting the error in three ways according to:

- Bloom's Taxonomy (Domain and Level)
- Procedural versus Declarative Error
- Commission or Omission errors

By analysing the actual errors, the design of the new error can be better informed. Errors can be designed at many **levels** (based on Bloom's Taxonomy) depending on the nature of the concept and how the error was made. For example, a learner may apply a rule incorrectly resulting in an error (e.g. the Pythagoras' Theorem was applied to find the side of a triangle without any right angle) or it could be that the error was committed because of a lack of *comprehension* of the question (e.g. to find one of the angles in a triangle not the length) or it could also be an error where the problem was *analysed* incorrectly (e.g. learner assumed that the triangle was a right-angled triangle when it wasn't).

Errors are also designed based on **type**. By this, the various types of errors include those involving *procedural* and *declarative* knowledge. Again, it is important to be cognisant of the manner in which the error is injected into the error-making process and the learning outcomes expected from the activity. If the learner's metacognitive regulation capability is being developed, then the pre-error phase is important. This means that getting learners to be on the lookout for the error injection during the pre-error phases is part of the training. The injection of the error may also be conducted subtly so that the learners will take more effort to detect the error. They may also need to check their assumptions which could blinker their line of sight when it comes to spotting errors.

With the background knowledge of the type of errors usually made, Step 2 will then inform the designer whether it is worthwhile designing a DELETE learning activity centred round the error, using the 3 Cs (criticality, commonness, clarity) as the selection criteria for the decision-making process.

Step 2: Design Error

Based on the types of errors collated, we will have to determine which errors we are to address based on the needs of the learners. As mentioned above, the nature of the error will inform how the errors ought to be designed. Using the 3 Cs as the selection criteria:

- Criticality of error (in completing the task)
- Commonness of error (across different tasks and by different learners)
- Clarity of error (to the learner as in whether the error is debatable)

These three criteria allow the designer to select useful errors to design so that learners will benefit from the DELETE activities. Usually, errors that are critical, common and unclear are worthwhile designing for learning purposes. Examples include reviewing ethical issues such as telling a white lie to a teacher and exaggerating a bully's misdeeds to the authority to get back at the person.

Primarily, the design of the error should be constructively aligned with the learning outcome (i.e. what we want to achieve with the DELETE learning activity) so that we help the learner achieve maximal learning out of the error correction or error analysis exercise.

While, error design is only one part of the DELETE design process, it is possibly the most important. Careful consideration ought to be taken to design the error which then informs the design of the error task. The subsequent step involves the task design which specifies what the learner needs to do with the error, e.g. to rectify the error, to analyse how the error was made or to evaluate if there is a better way to solve the problem and avoid the error altogether. Similar to the design of the error, the design of the task has to be aligned with the achievement of the learning outcome. Anything pitched too low or too high will result in misalignment and possibly the non-achievement of the learning outcome, making the DELETE activity a futile exercise. The task design needs to take into consideration the phase of the error making process that the DELETE exercise is targeting at (e.g. post-error phase).

Step 3: Design Task

Underlying the constructive alignment process is the premise that these efforts are geared towards the achievement of the learning outcome by aligning the error, task and engagement designs. The learning outcome which is linked to the purpose of the learning activity has to be determined early, based on inputs from past and present learners, teachers and other subject matter experts, in order to sufficiently inform the alignment process.

You should also notice that the purpose of the learning activity (see Fig. 26) is not determined till the second stage (under Design Error). This

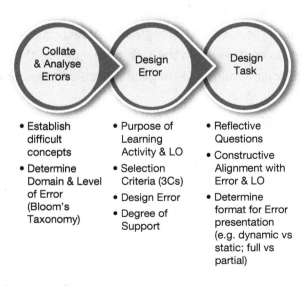

Fig. 26. The Error Design Process

is so that the analysis of errors can inform the crafting of the purpose and the Learning Outcome (LO). The question is then what happens after the error analysis and error design stages. How does the designer determine the task for the learner to complete?

Hence, the three possible relationships between the original task and the designed task are:

1. The designed task is the same as the original task
2. The designed task is more difficult than the original task
3. The designed task is simpler than the original task

The shifting of the task difficulty, whether upwards or downwards compared to the original task, depends very much on:

- Learner ability
- Learning outcome

The first consideration concerning learner ability is to ensure the learner obtains some measure of success (e.g. weak students get to perform simpler tasks even though the error may be the exact replica of the question he or she answered wrongly) so that there is some motivation for the learner to continue with the task. Subsequently, the task can be made more difficult to mirror the original expected behaviour (e.g. solve the problem).

The second consideration on learning outcome is to ensure that the learning is conducted at the level needed to perform behaviour. For some reasons (such as learner ability or to better structure learning), if the learning outcome is simpler such as to understand where one went wrong, the task will likewise align with the simpler outcome. However, if the learning outcome is more complicated than the original requirement, such as to evaluate if there are other ways to solve the

The Seven-Step Process in the DELETE Approach

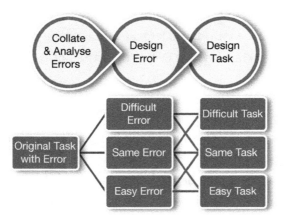

Fig. 27. The Task and Error Design Process

same problem, the task will then have to pitched at the higher and more difficult level.

There is, however, something in between the original task and the designed task — the designed error. This designed error may or may not be exactly the same as the original error made. The designed error can be more complex, same as or easier than the nature of the original error made.

The diagram above (Fig. 27) figuratively represents nine possible permutations when it comes to pitching the difficulty level of the error and the task in relation to the original error and task.

With nine permutations, there are many ways in which errors can be utilised to drive learning. The DELETE learning activity comprises careful design of the error and task so that the learner can appreciate, understand and apply the concept being studied. Not forgetting the importance of learner ability, DELETE ought to be a design process that is learner-sensitive so that learning is enhanced.

To facilitate learning, the placement of the designed error and task ought to be carefully considered so that the learner experience is positive. Depending on the instructional design theory used, the designed error and task can be introduced early, before the explanation of the concept (in the

E^3 Learning Cycle or Kolb's Experiential Learning Theory), or the designed error and task can be introduced late, after the tuning-in and explanation of concept (e.g. in Gagne's nine Events of Instruction).

Step 4: Design Engagement Process

Once the error and the task have been designed, we can consider how best to engage the learner. These three parameters (error, task and engagement process) may be designed concurrently, and refinements may be made in an iterative manner to any of the parameters. As part of the engagement process, the fourth parameter on degree of support has also to be determined.

The preference is to utilise an experiential learning approach as the engagement process. One key value that educators add to their learners is to help learners discover the joy of learning the facts and concepts for themselves. Often, the explanation of the concept prior to practice is deemed as an efficient way of saving time and energy so that learners can focus on the understanding and application of the concept. However, by telling learners what the concept is about, it reduces the need for learners to deeply appreciate and question what the concept is about and if it is really applicable to all contexts. Allowing learners to review and determine the means to solving a problem will allow learners to discover the concept for themselves and thereby, the joy of learning and doing. With the joy comes the motivation to learn something, an inherent human desire to learn and to overcome. Understandably, not all learners will be able to discover the concept for themselves and many will need support and guidance. The key is then to allow learners to attempt and have an experience for themselves so that it will drive their desire to learn about it and to try again. The two compelling reasons to adopt an experiential approach for DELETE learning activities are the increase in learner motivation and a deeper appreciation of the concept and contexts involved. Based on these two reasons and possibly others, the experiential approach is recommended.

However, there are exceptions, these possibly with:

- Learners who have weak cognitive ability and may confuse the process of discovery with the actual concept itself.
- Concepts that are overly abstract and difficult to reproduce as a tangible positive experience.
- Situations where time constraints are real, e.g. with examinations around the corner

With these exceptions, the more direct instruction (via Gagne's nine Events of Instruction) may be preferred. It will be a more traditional teach-and-practice approach.

Nature of Support

We have discussed the type of support at length in an earlier chapter. Here, we will discuss further about other aspects of support. With peer encouragement and group participation, learning becomes fun and enjoyable. It is undeniable that while the acquisition of skills or knowledge is an individual pursuit, the process of learning can be carried out with other learners or experts. Support, either psychological or cognitive, can make or break a learning process for the learner. Designers may choose to include cues for the 'supporter' to provide in event that the learner asks for some help. Alternatively, these cues may be structured into the problem or error so that the learner can automatically trigger the release of the cues upon request.

The timing of the support given is also crucial. Giving support too early robs the learner of the opportunity to work out the problem for himself or herself while giving it too late may result in overwhelming frustration and a loss of time for the learner. Without sounding dogmatic, the support may be given prior or along with the explanation of the concept.

With the degree of support varying from highly positive to highly negative, it is interesting to note that when learners work in teams, there are additional dynamics at play.

The nature of feedback, as those of us who have asked friends, classmates, colleagues or even experts will know, range from useful, confusing, misleading to outright erroneous. Hence, knowing what inputs to accept and what to reject is a key part of the decision structure with regards to feedback sequence. Hence, bearing in mind that learners do have the autonomy to accept or reject opinions, some organisations prefer to provide feedback anonymously or through a third party such as the reporting officer when it comes to work performance.

For DELETE activities, there is the additional element of destructive feedback as opposed to constructive feedback. While uncommon, destructive feedback may be factored in occasionally to build resilience and focus. The learner should know that destructive feedback will be given beforehand so that the learner will not be affected too much psychologically and at the same time, be aware that the feedback given is part of the design, for the eventual purpose of learning.

In summary, along with the error design and task design, the engagement process is a form of instructional design and should be considered carefully, based on learner profile and instructional characteristics. Whether learning becomes a chore or is challenging and fun is a matter of igniting the flame or dousing the fire for the learner. With the latter, the learner is motivated to press on to learn on his or her accord. With the former, it is likely that the learner has to be pushed to find out more, a very tiresome exercise indeed.

Step 5: Trial DELETE Activity and Review Learning

With the initial draft of the DELETE activity (based on a permutation of the four parameters), the activity is then pilot tested with learners to ensure the error, task and engagement process are clearly understood and that the error is appropriately pitched at the right level of difficulty.

Trialling the DELETE activity is important, and the consideration should be from both the perspectives of the

- information (or concept) characteristics, which basically has to do with the error and task designed
- learner ability, which will determine how difficult the error and task ought to be and the degree of support needed.

Usually, it is the learner profile that makes the design of the DELETE activity difficult since there are many different learner profiles (which include ability, personality, experience and motivation). Hence, factoring in flexibility and options into the DELETE activity is useful for the educator to pick one of the options when encountering a different learner profile.

While trialling the DELETE activity, the designer should ensure that the activity helps the learner achieve the learning outcome. If not, either the activity needs to be modified or the learning outcome requires adjustment.

Step 6: Refine Error Design

With the results from the trial, it is expected that the error can be further refined to better engage the learners. Again, the refinement can be conducted to the four parameters: error design, task design, engagement process design and degree of support.

Refining the error design may be iterative and continuous so empowering the teacher to make the necessary changes on the ground may also be another option to make the DELETE approach more responsive to learner needs.

Step 7: Launch Error Approach

Finally, the set of errors is launched for learners to identify and rectify. By putting the errors in a set, the educator can adopt a targeted approach in addressing certain concepts in a progressively difficult manner. This set of errors should be adaptive, meaning that if the learner is able to rectify the errors, then they get more difficult but if the learner is floundering, the errors ought to be easier.

Summary

The seven-step DELETE approach is process-driven and iterative such that there is constant refinement of errors and learning engagement, with the focus on addressing difficult concepts and in the process, helping the learner develop critical competencies, metacognitive, critical and creative thinking skills. By adopting a targeted approach, learners can spend the time meaningfully on the difficult segments and understanding why learners make those errors and more importantly, how to avoid them. Learning from the mistakes of others is possibly the wisest thing to do rather than having to make our own mistakes all the time.

Now that we have briefly covered each step of the seven-step DELETE approach, the next few chapters will describe in detail what each step entails.

Chapter 14

Preparation and Research: Collate and Analyse Errors

The mistakes of the fool are known to the world, but not to himself. The mistakes of the wise man are known to himself, but not to the world.

Charles Caleb Colton

In the previous chapter, we scanned the stages in the DELETE (Designing Errors for Learning and Teaching) rather quickly. In this chapter, we will deep dive into specific steps for greater clarity.

The first step in the DELETE process is to collate the errors made by learners in the past and analyse them for the purpose of design similar errors for effective learning.

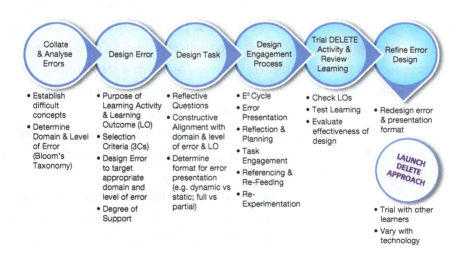

We will examine three ways to categorise errors:

1. Procedural versus Declarative errors
2. Domain Types and Levels of Difficulty
3. Commission versus Omission errors

These three categories are not exclusive. In fact, the errors are likely to overlap. For example, a declarative error is likely to be in the cognitive domain and can be commission or omission errors. By identifying the characteristics of these common or critical errors made by learners or staff, this is now an avenue to inform the design of the errors for learning and subsequently, the task for the learners to deepen learning.

1. Procedural versus Declarative Errors

Among the categories of errors, categorising the error as either conceptual (or declarative) or procedural remains one of the most important. For psychologists and educators (e.g. Billet, 2001; ten Berge & van Hezewijk, 1999), declarative knowledge refers to knowledge about things and issues. Hence, knowing the names of objects and of concepts (e.g. plate tectonics in Geography) would constitute declarative knowledge. Any error made concerning declarative knowledge would be labelled as declarative error. Similarly, procedural knowledge refers to knowledge about a series of steps or procedure. In this respect, there are many errors that stem from a lack of understanding about the procedure, resulting in incorrect sequencing of steps, wrong context to apply the procedure, utilising the procedure based on wrong assumptions and so on. For procedural knowledge, the steps in learning about a topic are often unknown and will add to the confusion if there is no one to guide new learners.

The first step to error categorisation is to identify if the error is a procedural or a declarative error. Following which, the error is then typed according the domain and level in Bloom's Taxonomy. Shown in the following table are further explanations and descriptions of what constitute declarative and procedural errors:

	Declarative Errors	Procedural Errors
1	Mistakes concerning knowledge or naming of concepts	Mistakes concerning carrying out of procedures or steps
2	Mostly cognitive	Can be psychomotor or cognitive
3	Error is made when explaining, labelling or applying	Error is made when implementing the procedure, involving wrong sequencing, missing steps and not adhering to rules when carrying out the procedure

Examples of Declarative Knowledge and Errors

Errors involving Declarative Knowledge are usually factual errors and may entail the testing of rote memory and comprehension ability (see Table 10). There may also be assumptions (such as the concept of 'treaty' and 'selling') which are tested (*Sir Stamford Raffles asked the Temenggong to sell Singapore to him).

Table 10. Differences and Examples of Declarative Knowledge

Conditions under which the Organisational Refund Rule applies	How Singapore was Founded
• Within one week with receipt • Product is returned with the original wrapping (e.g. box) and the supplementary materials (e.g. instruction sheet, ear piece) • Product is in pristine condition without being abused beyond the original purpose it was made for	• By Sir Stamford Raffles • In 1819 • Temenggong was the person managing Temasek (Singapore's name then) • Singapore was a fishing village and was part of the Johor Sultanate • Sir Stamford Raffles signed a treaty with Hussein Shah of Johor to establish a British colony in Singapore.
Errors Include:	**Errors Include:**
• Return the goods within two weeks of purchase • Return goods, preferably with receipt • Damaged goods can still be returned if the damage was caused unintentionally by the user.	• Singapore was founded in 1918 by Sir Stamford Raffles. • The Temenggong was the brother of the sultan of Riau. • Sir Stamford Raffles asked the Temenggong to sell Singapore to him.

As mentioned, errors involving Declarative knowledge are likely to be factual while errors relating to Procedural Knowledge will take on a more sequential nature (see Table 11). What does this mean?

Examples of Procedural Knowledge and Errors

Table 11. Differences and Examples of Procedural Knowledge

Convert from Direct to Reported Speech	Add Fractions with Different Denominators
1) Replace the inverted commas (speech marks) with 'that' at the beginning of the quotation. Remove the comma. 2) Change the tense in the quotation to the appropriate tense. 3) Change the pronouns to the second person according to the speaker. 4) Change the time (e.g. now to then). 5) Move the verb in the quotation for 'wh' questions to after the object. (e.g. What is the time? → what the time was …)	1) List the multiples for both denominators. (e.g. 2, 4, 6, 8…) 2) Find the lowest common multiple for both denominators. 3) Multiply the numerator by the same number as that for the denominator to reach the common denominator. 4) Add the fractions with the same denominator together.
Errors Include:	**Errors Include:**
• Punctuation errors such as not removing the inverted commas • Forgetting to change the tense (e.g. present to past and past to past perfect) • Not changing the pronouns or time • Not moving the verb to after the object	• Listing the wrong multiples • Not getting the lowest common multiple • Multiplying the fraction wrongly (i.e. multiplying only the numerator or denominator rather than both) • Adding the denominator as well

Evaluating the Types of Cognitive Errors for Learning

Table 12 shows the possible instructional methods aligned with the DELETE approach to facilitate effective cognitive learning.

By analysing the types of errors which occur at work or during learning, designers can attempt to design the learning by embedding specific errors to trigger certain types of learning. For example, the designer may focus on extracting procedural knowledge which may be difficult for a particular

Table 12. Evaluating the Types of Cognitive Errors for Learning

	Type of Knowledge	Examples of Errors	Tools	Level of Pitching
1	Declarative knowledge	• Incorrect fact statements • Wrong comprehension of the concept • Wrong application of concepts to the context	• Texts • Cases • Role play, e.g. salesperson citing the wrong specifications	Errors are pitched mostly at the retrieval of facts and comprehension of knowledge within specific contexts
2	Procedural Knowledge	• Inaccurate statements of steps and procedures • Incorrect comprehension of a process • Wrong application of the process within a specific context	• Texts, e.g. Description of the process • Case study with questions • Role play, e.g. salesperson citing the wrong key steps when fixing a piece of equipment	Errors are pitched at the application, analysis, synthesis and evaluation processes whereby knowledge is processed and utilised to achieve an objective.

concept rather than getting the learners to revisit the entire concept including the declarative knowledge. The embedding of the error within the procedure at the critical juncture is one way to make the learning process more efficient and effective since learners can 'skip' the easier segments and identify the errors within the more difficult segments. It also allows learning to be pitched at higher levels, e.g. evaluation or synthesis levels without revisiting the lower levels of comprehension or application. According to Billet (2001), there are three levels of procedural knowledge:

- *Specific procedures*: not requiring conscious thought, e.g. a chef putting together a dish — a basic skill
- *Second-order procedures*: requiring monitoring and evaluation of strategy selection, e.g. what approach to take, deciding prior to the event what is required and the sequence of steps
- *Third-order procedures*: requiring monitoring, organising activities and is strategic in its applications. For example, implementing processes

in new situations, complex problem solving, practicing, planning, monitoring progress and predicting errors and problems.

More specifically, with specially designed errors, there is now a method to focus on difficult concepts (e.g. third-order procedures) for targeted learning. As described in Table 12, these levels of cognitive error correspond to the levels of difficulty in Bloom's Cognitive Domain. Listed below are more examples of the types of cognitive errors generally made by learners (see Table 13):

2. Domain Types and Levels of Difficulty
Cognitive Domain

Table 13. Evaluating the Types of Cognitive Tasks Based on Bloom's Taxonomy

Types of Errors/ Bloom's Taxonomy: Cognitive Domain	Definition	Example
Recall e.g. Remembering wrongly	An error resulting from remembering or transferring information wrongly	Copying numbers or spelling words wrongly from the question or passage The *115ract rested on the treetop
Comprehension e.g. Conceptual misunderstanding	An error resulting from a wrong interpretation of the concept	Not understanding that omnivores overlap with carnivores and herbivores in their diet What do omnivores eat? Answer: vegetables*
Application e.g. Incorrect application of Operational rules	An error resulting from not observing the given rules	Breaking grammatical or computational rules such as using the incorrect tense or adding wrongly $5^2 + 3 = 23$*
Analysis e.g. Under-analysing observations	An error resulting from wrong reasoning	Unable to identify the correct chemicals based on the observations of the reactants in the test tube A colourless, odourless liquid when mixed with a milky edible solution produces a bluish-black solution. The conclusion was that the colourless liquid is bleach*. The correct answer is iodine solution with starch. The reasoning is incorrect as the bleach (or chlorine) has a strong smell.

(*Continued*)

Types of Errors/ Bloom's Taxonomy: Cognitive Domain	Definition	Example
Synthesis e.g. haphazard creation without adhering to rules	An error that is the result of a trial whereby conditions or the context may not be clear	Attempting to create new musical scores using different non-traditional instruments, e.g. glasses and pipes, which do not adhere to basic musical principles
Evaluation e.g. reviewing a problem based on incorrect assumptions	An error resulting from wrong assumptions	Trying to use all the pieces of information in a problem sum on the assumption that every piece of information is important. This may not always be true. The four sides of a garden add up to 50 m. Stretching a 10 m garden hose along one side of the garden, Samuel only managed to reach 2/3 of the side of the garden. What is the length of the side? Answer: 50 / 4 = 12.5 m* The assumption is that the garden is a square. However, there is no indication of that. What is mentioned is that the 10 m hose reached 2/3 of the side, hence, 2 units — 10 m 1 unit — 5 m 3 units — 15 m Answer: The side of the garden is 15 m long.

The cognitive domain is an important one as our psychomotor behaviour and affect often stem from the way we think. The type of cognitive processes (e.g. comprehension, analysis level) we utilised to consider the issue may determine the action we adopt. Whether we choose to analyse the issues thoroughly or to only comprehend the information and then take it as accurate and true impacts the quality of the decisions we make and the potential for errors. Besides being an underpinning process for affect and psychomotor processes, the cognitive processes also works closely with the metacognitive and the belief systems that the individual embraces. To reprogramme one's beliefs and metacognition, a fair amount of cognitive reframing must take place beforehand. Hence, the individual needs to have prior experiences in reflection and evaluative abilities in order to push ahead with the reframing process.

Psychomotor Domain

Listed below (see Table 14) are the types of psychomotor errors generally made by learners:

Table 14. Evaluating the Types of Cognitive Tasks Based on Bloom's Taxonomy

Types of Errors Dave's (1970) Psychomotor Domain	Definition	Example
Imitation e.g. Copying an action incorrectly	An error resulting from copying an action wrongly	Imitating the steps to remove a car tyre wrongly
Manipulation e.g. Incorrect foundational skill that underpins certain tasks	An error resulting from a lack of grounding in basic skills	Incorrect way of holding a bottle of wine when opening it, with instructions
Precision e.g. Not being able to follow through with a routine sequence of actions to be exactly right	An error resulting from a lack of skill practice	Incorrect customer engagement process when upselling other products
Articulation e.g. Not being able to coordinate a series of actions with consistency	An error resulting from a lack of opportunities to coordinate several smaller tasks	Unable to produce a video that involves music, acting and colour
Naturalisation e.g. Not be able to perform a series of smashes, with the ball/shuttlecock hitting the net after a short rally	An error that stems from a lack of guided practice over a long time	Unable to perform optimally under stress such as during sports competitions

Preparation and Research: Collate and Analyse Errors

It is highly obvious that most psychomotor actions do not occur in the absence of cognitive processes, but one often leads to the other. In that regard, the psychomotor domain is the most observable and as such, contributes the most number of measurable indicators when it comes to understanding human behaviour and cognition. Errors in psychomotor domain are also often attributed to conditioning over time (i.e. habits) and retraining by replacing the erroneous actions with the correct ones is the most common approach. However, it is also important to engage the individual in helping him to understand the contextual conditions under which the errors occur. This will empower the individual to make the right decisions when a similar context occurs in the future.

The story of the cat that ran in the wrong direction

A solitary cat sat on the banks of a long concrete drain at the closing of the day. It was fixated on some birds fluttering about near the bush. I was on my way home and the cat was in my path. Quietly, I walked behind it, so as not to startle the cat.

Without warning, the cat heard the sound of my approaching footsteps which intermediately caused it freeze in its movement. Then again, almost instinctively, it turned its head towards me, caught a glimpse of this offending intruder and headed off in my direction, almost knocking into my feet as it charged off into the night.

*What's interesting was that instead of running **away** from me, the danger, it dashed right into me because it looked at me as it ran away. I thought, 'What a silly cat! If I meant harm, it could have been hurt. It should have just run in the direction of the birds, which it has been observing for a while and away from me, the potential danger'.*

However, it dawned on me that many of us are also guilty of the same error. How often have we walk behind someone and the moment they hear our footsteps as we approach them from behind, they veer towards the same side that we are walking on instead of keeping to the other side and letting us pass. It is a common error. We often see this among cyclists and drivers. They move towards the direction they are looking. Likewise, the untrained footballers often look at the goalkeeper just before they kick the ball and as a result, it ends up going straight at the goalkeeper! Our vision has the effect of directing our actions. In view of this natural tendency, it is necessary to condition ourselves so that we override our natural psychomotor reflexes to perform better. World class strikers, on the other hand, condition themselves to look at the unguarded spot of the goal that they wish to kick the ball towards. By designing the conditions for learners to potentially make the errors (e.g. a distraction before the learner kicks the ball), there is a high possibility that the predicted error will be made and thus, forcing the learner to reflect and learn accordingly.

By understanding that vision can impact action (the Manipulation level in the Psychomotor domain), we are in a position to strengthen our performance accordingly. Hence, by identifying the corresponding error of looking at the wrong place (i.e. goalkeeper or centre of the goal), the striker can be trained to avoid the error and score the goal.

Affective Domain

Listed below are the types of affective errors generally made by learners:

Table 15. Evaluating the Types of Affective Tasks Based on Bloom's Taxonomy

Types of Errors/ Krathwohl, Bloom, Masia's (1964) Taxonomy: Affective Domain	Definition	Example
Receiving e.g. Choosing an incorrect belief or value for a particular job role	An error resulting from not understanding the required values or beliefs	The sales staff prioritised sales target over customer experience when asked about the values required in sales staff.

Preparation and Research: Collate and Analyse Errors

(*Continued*)

Types of Errors/ Krathwohl, Bloom, Masia's (1964) Taxonomy: Affective Domain	Definition	Example
Responding e.g. not accepting responsibility when issues arise	An error resulting from a lack of ownership in a particular product or process	A nurse not willing to admit her mistake in administering the wrong medicine when confronted by the doctor, but instead pointed to the illegible handwriting on the prescription form.
Valuing e.g. Not recognising, valuing and displaying the correct value	An error arising from a lack of proper inculcation of values in the person	The teacher did not value the school rules when she chose to turn up in class half an hour late in a short skirt and sleeveless blouse.
Organising e.g. Not willing to accept the values or beliefs of a culture	An error resulting from not bringing the value into harmony with those already accepted values	Despite knowing the organisational SOPs, the long-time supervisor intentionally took matters into his own hands when he volunteered to fix the customer's car even though the customer does not intend to pay.
Internalising e.g. Not having the necessary values as person for the job or in a particular organisation	An error arising from not embracing the correct self-beliefs or values	A manager, without reflecting on his own beliefs or assumptions, dismissed a clerk for being disrespectful when in the first place, the clerk had good reasons for stating the truth clearly.

The table above (see Table 15) illustrates the complexity of errors, especially pertaining to the possible ways of categorising and analysing them. Errors relating to Metacognition and Sociality are not categorised according to levels of difficulty as Bloom's Taxonomy does not include these domains. However, these domains may comprise different levels which require further investigation outside the scope of this model.

3. Errors of Commission and Omission

What are errors of commission and errors of omission? This is an important distinction. Both types of errors are critical and important. The error of commission refers to a learner making an error due to an action, while the error of omission refers to a learner making an error due to not making an action, due to ignorance, forgetfulness or other reasons. What is important is that in the former, the learner makes the error of commission in an attempt to solve the problem but unfortunately, breaking the rules in the process. The latter, on the other hand, probably has the learner missing out steps or concepts.

There is a high likelihood that we will not be able to determine the nature of the error simply by analysing the deliverable or product submitted by the learner as the error could have been committed by breaking a rule or forgetting that the rule existed. The primary way to determine if the error is one of commission or omission is to ask the learner to articulate his or her cognitive reasoning during the problem-solving process. Through the learner's verbalisation of his or her thoughts, the teacher can make a better decision as to whether the learner forgot to apply certain rules, or they were applied incorrectly. Either way, the intervention will be different, between a forgetful learner and one who is not familiar with the rules and applies them incorrectly. In the former case, helping learners remember the procedures or facts will be critical. Developing job aids and memory aids (such as mnemonics) is expected to give the needed support to these learners. If it is the latter case, teaching the learners how to apply the rules and having the respect to adhere to the rules will apply. Again, it is needless to emphasise the need to be thorough and meticulous when applying the rules. Often, it is not the blatant ignoring of the rules but more of a psychological way for these learners to test the system, to push the boundaries and if they can somehow avoid the pain of the consequences, they will.

Chapter 15
Defining the Types of Errors Using the 3 Cs

Introduction

Designing the error to drive the error-based learning process requires the initial step of identifying key errors that people usually make and outcomes that you want to achieve through the learning process. Hence, the foundation of DELETE lies in the rigour of the analysis. We established the various types of errors (e.g. Declarative vs. Procedural; Commission vs. Omission) that people make in the earlier chapter. This chapter takes us into the process of selecting and designing the errors *for* learning, based on the criteria of Criticality, Clarity and Commonness (3 Cs).

With this as our introduction to the chapter, let us dive further into determining the types of errors we can use for DELETE.

Selecting the Error

With findings from the analyses of the errors, we will put the selected errors through a selection process to sieve out less critical or useful errors and to further refine the more useful ones. We can facilitate the selection process with a few criteria. Notably, these criteria must allow us to pick errors which will assist the learners to master the difficult concepts and facilitate the learning process. Generally, the following three criteria can guide us in our error selection process:

- criticality
- clarity
- commonness

These 3 Cs denote the key characteristics of the error and when taken in totality, provide a useful profile of the types of errors we need to focus on when designing learning. Quite sensibly, concepts that are critical to understanding lack a clear boundary to when it is erroneous and are commonly made would present themselves as natural candidates for error-based learning. Finding out how errors are committed pertaining to these concepts is key to designing useful learning activities based on DELETE. Once the difficult concepts have been clearly identified, the error is designed to bring about effective learning.

a) Criticality of Error

To select the types of errors to design, one criterion is the criticality of the error, which simply refers to how fatal the error was in hindering the learner from reaching the eventual learning destination.

For example, when solving engineering problems, every error is possibly critical, as accuracy is essential to resolution of the problem. Even a simple transfer (or copying) error can be disastrous especially if the information is critical. On the other hand, there are errors that may not be critical, especially when the process is not as structured and can still be looped back for recovery. In the case of customer service, not following the sequence of certain service steps (e.g. omitting the key features of a product to customers at the start) may still be remedied subsequently with little adverse effect. Likewise, a facilitator may not have provided a group of learners with the objectives at the start of a discussion. However, if he realises his mistake and clarifies the objectives in the midst of the discussion and elaborates further when the learners ask, he can still redeem himself without too much damage to both the learners and himself. Even then, the image the learners have concerning the facilitator may not be a positive one, especially if the perception is perpetuated over the course of the training. Still, it is good to know that the error is not critical and would not be life-threatening in any way.

b) Clarity of Error

To determine if an error is clearly one depends on how much of:

i. the *rule* is violated and/or
ii. the contextual *boundary* is breached

In both cases, the error becomes evident only if there is there is negative feedback and/or outcome arising from the decision or action.

Currently, the assumption is often that if a learner is able to come up with the correct answer, he or she is sufficiently competent in the concept. However, this assumption may not be entirely true as not all associated issues linked to the concept may be tested through the question. Hence, using DELETE to design errors to test the associated issues will allow for precise testing and checking.

> **Example**
>
> John may think that he knows the topic on photosynthesis well. He claims he knows what is right especially pertaining to the conditions which allow photosynthesis to take place, i.e. sunlight, water, oxygen and chlorophyll and plant. He may also know what is wrong, e.g. To say that animals photosynthesise is an error. There is also the possibility of him now knowing what is right. For example, John may not know that there are cellular animals which have chlorophyll and can carry out photosynthesis. He may also not know what is wrong. For example, to say that ALL plants photosynthesise is wrong. There are plants which do not photosynthesise but rely on other means to obtain food (e.g. mushroom and parasitic plants).

The following diagram shows the possible states a learner may be in, concerning his or her understanding of a particular concept. Not knowing what an error is may possibly be even riskier than knowing exactly when one has made an error. It points to the fact that the learner is not clear on the first principles or the rules being examined.

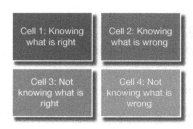

Hence, designing errors to check learners' knowledge in Cells 3 and 4 so that they can move into Cells 1 and 2 respectively is important. To be clear, learning activities involving both rules and boundaries can potentially help the learners to relearn problematic areas in a targeted manner.

In identifying errors that are indicative of unclear boundaries (cells 3 and 4), we have a useful tool to surface these unclear boundaries for critical analysis and learning. By carefully designing errors to highlight the unclear boundaries, learners do not have to stumble upon the boundaries or perform trial and error to uncover these boundaries by accident.

c) Commonness of Error

The issue of commonness or typicality refers to how **expected** is the error since frequency of errors will heighten learners to certain errors being committed for tasks. Hence, any sudden deviation from the norm will create tension and a sense of loss as to not knowing what to do. At this point, learners usually engage in critical reflection and mindfulness to actively figure out the issues and solve the problem. If an error is common (i.e. most learners commit this error), then addressing this error upfront will alleviate the pain experienced by these learners downstream as well as reduce the time to master the topic. For example, many learners often use verbs which are not measurable when crafting learning outcomes (e.g. 'To be aware of concept A' compared with 'To describe concept A ...'). Instead of telling learners about these common errors, which learners are unlikely to register, letting learners experience these errors will be a better

Defining the Types of Errors Using the 3 Cs

learning option to make the learning come alive (e.g. craft a question to measure the *awareness* of learners about concept A).

Overview

Both typical and atypical errors can be categorised according to the following taxonomy, with the red and black spaces being most important:

For typical errors, there is a greater need to focus on aligning practice and establishing understanding for the learners. The chart (see Fig. 28) shows the breakdown of errors according to the three criteria. Most people would agree that the first category of Common, Critical and Clear error would be prioritised, followed by Common, Critical and Unclear (or ambiguous). Due to the commonality and criticality of the errors, these two categories would likely be given preference for rapid resolution.

You can also refer to the error selection matrix (see Table 16) to see how the errors should be typed and described. The examples should also

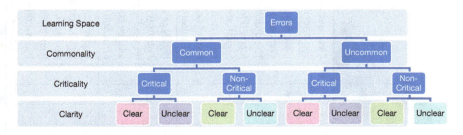

Fig. 28. Hierarchy of Errors Across the 3 Cs Criteria

Chapter 15

Table 16. Error Selection Matrix

	Criticality	Clarity	Commonness	Remarks	Example	Importance
1	✓	✓	✓	Clear mistake that is critical and common. Top priority for addressing.	Contingency management to handle serious customer complaints	✓
2	✓	✓		Clear mistake that is critical but uncommon. Will need to make the mistake obvious to prevent future occurrences. The problem with this type of error is that the people who have learned from incidents arising from this error may have left the organisation before it occurs again. Hence, the knowledge may not be passed on and staff have to constantly learn from this type of error. Codification of this error and solution is essential to ensure organisational learning takes place.	Occurrence of Severe Acute Respiratory Syndrome (SARS) which killed hundreds of people in Asia in 2003. As a result, hospitals in some Asian countries arrived at a code of procedures to manage similar outbreaks. This code of procedures helped countries to react faster to the COVID-19 pandemic, thereby saving many lives.	✓
3	✓			Highly critical error but it is not common nor clear Authority (e.g. senior management or teachers) has to make it clear if this constitutes an error and if so, the accompanying rationale must also be communicated. Due to its low frequency, codification of this error and solution is essential to facilitate organisational learning.	A nurse agreed to witness the formulation of a will for a dying patient due to the urgency of the situation, which led to legal issues subsequently for the nurse and the hospital.	✓
4	✓		✓	Highly common and critical error that is unclear Again, codification of this error and the solution will be essential. However, since the error is common, chances are the learners would have picked up the learning from either themselves or others making this mistake. Hence, communicating the solution or underlying rationale is essential to reduce error rate.	A teacher loses her temper and as a result becomes overly harsh with her students to the extent of committing verbal abuse.	✓

Defining the Types of Errors Using the 3 Cs

5	✓		Clear mistake that is not critical nor common The staff will be aware of the mistake and since it is not a critical mistake, the staff can learn from it and move on. For the organisation, it is probably advisable not to blow this up, just to maintain staff morale since the uncommon error may not occur again.	Wearing clothes of an inappropriate colour when attending a wedding ceremony of an acquaintance from a different culture.
6	✓	✓	Common, clear but non-critical mistake Since it is common, learners may want to stem this error to increase productivity, even though it is non-critical.	Making grammatical errors when speaking to friends.
7		✓	Common, unclear and non-critical mistake Since the mistake is common, there is a need to address it. Due to the lack of clarity as an error, it is possible that the same error was propagated before being corrected.	Making common grammatical errors which are embedded in a culture, e.g. Singlish.
8			Uncommon, unclear and non-critical error In this case, it may be a non-priority since the possibility of it occurring again is low.	Making jokes which are harmless and not funny.

✓ Denotes high

provide some clarity to how errors can be typed. There are likely to be many other examples, especially those which are found in your context.

Conclusion

In conclusion, we can type the error based on:

- Procedural or Declarative
- Domain and Level of difficulty in Bloom's Taxonomy
- Commission versus Omission Errors

With the DELETE approach, the way learners understand the issues can be targeted at critical segments so that potential misinterpretation of key facts and assumptions can be uncovered quickly and rectified. To do this in a systematic and clear manner, learners need to be aware of when these errors are embedded in the passages (*e.g. Between three and five errors are embedded in this paragraph. Find them.*). The clarity in instructions and where errors are found are important to ensure that the learners do not mix up correct answers with intentional mistakes, leading to possible confusion. Especially with weak learners, this embedding of errors must be carried out carefully and possibly only expose them to the DELETE approach when they have assimilated and mastered the facts and skills. Subsequently, it is to move them up to higher levels in the Bloom's Taxonomy such as Analysis and Synthesis with sufficient scaffolding.

(Afternote: Does indicating having three to five errors embedded in the text make you more attentive to the paragraph above? Errors include: 'the manner … targeted at critical segments' (convoluted sentence), 'aware of' (no need for 'of'), 'weak learners' (correct term should be 'less experienced learners' or 'cognitively weak learners') and '… it is to move them up' (should be '… providing them with opportunities to resolve errors at higher levels in …').

These categories of errors should be selected according to the purpose of the learning process. If you as the designer need to determine the level of difficulty and the domain that the *training* should target, then identifying the domain type and level of difficulty of the *error* will help inform the design process.

We also explored how we can select and design errors based on the criteria of Criticality, Clarity and Commonness. The Error Selection Matrix provides a reference guide for designers to determine the construction of the errors and how these errors ought to be presented within the context and workflow. Following which, ensuring alignment of the error design with the learning outcomes is critical and this is discussed in the next chapter.

Part 5

Developing Competences in Five Critical Areas

Part 5

Introduction

Going further, if we are to be specific about the purpose of the DELETE approach, what should we focus on? At the beginning of this book, we discussed about putting competent learners through an experience to facilitate them to acquire expertise. These competent learners may know and can apply the rules within specific contexts. They are also ready to move on to determine further boundaries to the rules for application to new contexts and innovate further.

To identify these errors (based on the 3 Cs criteria), we will require the experts in the field to identify the critical errors in the trade. The experts know where, how and why things will go wrong. They are likely to know how to locate the unclear, critical and the uncommon errors. It often takes an expert to groom another expert in the trade. This was also the basis for apprenticeship and the tradesman guilds which passed the skills of the trade from one generation to the next.

Thus, mastery of skills is one possible context, and with that metacognition (and mindfulness) are areas that we want to develop in our learners to build expertise. In other areas, we can consider using error-based learning to drive competency development by getting learners to identify and rectify errors — errors involving rules and sometimes boundaries. Generally, the focus is to get the learners to review their understanding of

> Keith and Frese (2008) conducted a meta-analysis of 24 identified studies (N = 2,183) with results suggesting that error-based training may be better suited than error-avoidant training methods for promotion of transfer to novel tasks. By allowing active exploration and providing explicit encouragement for learners to make errors during training, there is clear evidence to show that learners are able to make post-training transfers, especially to new activities. This is especially relevant for present-day contexts where volatility and unpredictability forces many workers to deal with new situations on a regular basis.

the rules and how best to apply them in typical situations. Going back to the four domains in the updated Bloom's Taxonomy — Cognition, Emotion, Psychomotor and Sociality, we have these four competences to focus on. Integrating these four competences and metacognition to form a holistic capability development approach is a powerful goal that the DELETE approach can provide.

Focusing on Developing the Competences

To ensure that the design of the error and the learning experience are aligned, the crafting of the learning outcome becomes critical as it forms the common reference point for both processes. As mentioned in the introduction above, error-based learning can target the following outcomes across the various domains, including the holistic development of the individual:

a) Metacognition
b) Cognition
c) Emotion
d) Psychomotor
e) Sociality/Interpersonal
f) Holistic Development — beyond competency to capability

Defining Competences

The concept of work competence is not new, especially in competency-based training and assessment contexts. Performance-based outcomes provide a means of measuring the return on investment and to determine possible compensation for staff or the time spent on learning for students. Hence, across most organisations, competence is carefully measured and rewarded accordingly. While the concept of competence is generally accepted, the operationalisation of competence measurement is problematic.

The primary issue has to do with the breaking up of competence into separate tasks for manageable measurement. This creates problems because the sum of all the tasks does not equate full job competence. There will be gaps that cannot be measured or only makes sense when seen

> The following **five key areas** are identified for intervention through the DELETE approach to improve learning and performance:
> a) **Metacognition**
>   i. To Develop Ability to Evaluate Contexts and Assumptions
>   ii. To Hone Regulatory and Predictive Ability
> b) **Cognition**
>   i. To Strengthen Conceptual Understanding and Skillsets in Targeted Areas
>   ii. To Develop 'Creative-Critical' Thinking Ability
>   iii. To Sharpen Cognitive Adaptability and Flexibility
>   iv. To Build Global (Macro) Perspective-Taking Ability
> c) **Emotion**
>   i. To Develop Values and Beliefs
>   ii. To Strengthen Psychological Resilience for Unexpected Outcomes
> d) **Psychomotor**
>   i. To Develop Behavioural Responses to Situations and Errors
>   ii. To Increase Reflexivity to Errors
> e) **Sociality/Interpersonal**
>   i. To Develop Teamwork Skills Among Team Members
>   ii. To Cultivate Collaborative Skills for Individuals
> f) **Holistic Development — beyond competency to capability**
>   i. To Integrate Skillsets Across Domains to Achieve Mastery for the Individual
>   ii. To Diagnose Skill Gaps and Non-Strengths
>   iii. To Prepare the Individual for Future Skill Needs

holistically in the work context. For example, the willingness of trainers to go the extra mile in addressing learner's needs beyond the classroom training hours is not easily captured when the 'competence' is broken down in the form of key trainer skills. The need to stay back to work with individual learners may not surface all the time. Hence, the aspect of attitude or professionalism is difficult to measure and develop.

Correspondingly, the ability of the worker to see beyond his immediate area of work, to what is required by the client or what the organisation is trying to achieve involves a macro perspective which technically is not part of the job scope. However, this macro perspective is critical in helping workers to see service gaps and stand in, if necessary, to bridge these gaps, especially when other staff may not take on these additional roles outside their job scope. Besides the macro perspective, competence comprises many other intangible skill sets, many of them are non-technical.

For example, a person's metacognitive ability to take a step back to monitor what he or she is thinking about, the person's professional values and beliefs, resilience level and one's ability to read the contextual cues are non-technical but critical core skills that define the expert.

The development of the following areas centre round both tangible and intangible skill sets which contribute to a person's competence at work and in school. The common denominator across all five competences is the framing of these outcomes (metacognition, cognition, emotion, psychomotor, sociality) within the work or school environment. It points to a fellow worker who is able to coach a colleague through a task, with useful sharing of past critical incidents and errors. Likewise, a student who willingly provides inputs to another student on how to solve a Math or Science problem is displaying a level of competence (with regard to the skill) in working with a peer to resolve an issue.

Part 5

Let's work through how the DELETE approach can meet the requirements of these five competences along with the integration of these competences to result in the holistic development of the individual learner.

> A foolish person makes errors and does not learn from them.
>
> A typical person makes errors once and learns how not to make them again.
>
> A wise person learns from the mistakes of others.

Chapter 16
Developing Metacognition

Metacognitive capabilities are difficult to describe simply because they are unfamiliar to many people and many go through their daily lives without reflecting on how they are thinking or feeling. However, that does not mean that metacognition is unimportant. As mentioned in the earlier chapters, metacognition will be a critical capability that differentiates humans from intelligent machines (e.g. AI such as ChatGPT is unlikely to question how or what it is thinking or feeling, at least not the in manner that humans do). Learning from mistakes is also possible when we reflect on the errors that we make. Metacognition is one key process to allow us to process the manner we are thinking and question our assumptions which led to the error!

Metacognition refers to higher order thinking which involves active control over the cognitive processes engaged in learning. Activities such as planning how to approach a given learning task, monitoring comprehension and evaluating the status of a task are examples of **metacognition**.

According to Flavell (1979, 1987), metacognition consists of both *metacognitive knowledge* and *metacognitive regulation*. The first, metacognitive knowledge, refers to knowledge about cognitive processes which can be used to control cognitive processes such as knowing how to regulate the environment to facilitate more effective learning.

Chapter 16

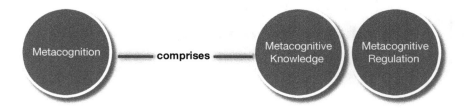

Metacognitive regulation, on the other hand, involves the use of metacognitive strategies. These metacognitive strategies are sequential processes that control cognitive activities in order to achieve a cognitive goal (e.g. understanding how a piece of machinery works). These processes help to regulate and oversee learning, and consist of *planning* and *monitoring* cognitive activities, as well as *checking* the *outcomes* of those activities. For example, when attempting to solve a problem at work, a worker may read a product document on how a piece of machinery works. The cognitive goal is to understand the document and self-questioning may be employed as a metacognitive monitoring strategy to ensure that the cognitive goal of comprehension is met (Livingston, u.d.).

a) **Metacognition**
   i. To Hone Regulatory and Predictive Ability
   ii. To Develop Ability to Evaluate Contexts and Assumptions

Skills involving metacognition, cognitive adaptability and context evaluation require situational awareness and mindset adjustment in order for staff to zoom out of just seeing issues and situations as they are, to focus on the underpinning values, assumptions of these issues and to monitor their own cognitive processes in order to maximise output. Individuals need to place their attention on these processes with sufficient time set aside, to obtain the expected results. With the current rapid pace of life that most professionals face, it is not inconceivable that metacognition is rarely carried out or worse, completely ignored in pursuit of short-term outcomes.

i. *To Hone Regulatory and Predictive Ability*

One of the key differentiators between experts and novices is the ability of the expert to 'foretell' potential errors that may arise and hence, take additional precautions. This capability could be drawn from past experience or from a heightened awareness that 'something is not quite right'. As such, training novice learners in the area of upping their awareness of their own state of mind (i.e. metacognitive regulation) is one useful outcome of the DELETE approach.

Generally, a metacognitive mindset — to analyse the status of their search for the solution in relation to the start and potential end point of the problem is essential in most tasks. However, not everyone possesses this heightened metacognitive awareness to understand what they are thinking and hence, manage their own cognitive and emotional processes optimally. What does this mean? Just as in the case of a trekker looking for a destination, there could be an end point in sight, such as a mountain top in the far distance. However, getting there is another story. The trekker may have to cross rivers, jungles and trudge through swamps, all this while, keeping an eye on the final destination — the mountain top. There will be periods during the trek that the trekker may heading in a direction away from the destination or moments when the mountain top is not visible. During these moments, the trekker must evaluate if he has the physical energy and psychological determination to keep going, whether he is still on the right track and progressing in the right manner. He may determine that his physical and psychological well-being is deficient and having a short rest may help him recuperate and then push on again. This ability to sense one's state of thinking is critical to ensure optimum processing and performance.

Finally, when he determines that his state of being and his approach are appropriate, he can then make the decision to either press on or back track and head up another path. There will be decision junctures that are critical for the trekker to critically analyse his position and progress. He must predict if his decision will result in him getting closer to the intended outcome. Backtracking is one option, but it means a loss of time and resources. Pressing on by heading in a direction that is unclear, with no sign of progress involves risk-taking and courage. However, it may also mean that the waste of resources will be far greater if the path indeed proves to be wrong.

Hence, using errors to train learners to increase their awareness of their thinking processes so that critical decisions are based on careful analyses of the situation through optimal cognitive processing rather than when one is stressed or not engaged fully.

The ability to constantly surface (like a submarine) above one's situation or tasks, to take stock of what's happening, how one is thinking and if one is really on the right track is one aspect of a person's metacognitive ability and is usually not trained intentionally. To know when to stop in one's track to check and when to move on requires practice and guidance. The earlier one picks up this ability, the greater the chances of success or at least non-wastage of resources in the form of abandoning an unsolvable or unwinnable project. In relation to answering questions during lessons or problem-solving at work, the metacognitive ability to evaluate one's status is akin to working smart, not just working hard.

Underpinning the development of metacognitive and predictive ability is a person's level of mindfulness (at a point in time) and reflection (after the point in time when the incident has taken place). Both processes involve a heightened awareness of what happened externally in the environment and internally within one's mind and body. This level of mindfulness and reflection comes about through an intentional and conscious effort to regularly review one's current and recent situations in order to detect patterns and rationale. Stopping to take stock regularly is probably the easiest and most succinct way of describing these two processes.

Developing Mindfulness

How is metacognitive ability linked to mindfulness? Perhaps it is easier to explain mindfulness with an analogy. Among the animals commonly seen, one animal that demonstrates this trait is the ant. Obviously, the ant works extremely hard. It is well known that the ant stores up food for winter during the days of plenty in summer. It is also this hardworking attitude that predisposes it to surviving the extreme changes in environment, weather and threats from predators.

However, while working hard is a pre-requisite for success, it alone does not account for success. There are many other reasons which increase the chances for success.

What Happens When People Become Mindful?

In a study by Richland, Kornell, and Kao (2009), results showed that when participants were unsuccessful in retrieving concepts (i.e. they do not know the answer to the questions), their performance on the same items after learning was better than participants who were not asked those questions. Primarily, the participants in the study read a passage about vision. In the test condition, they were asked about specific concepts before reading the passage, whereas in the extended study condition, they were given a longer time to read the passage but no questions were asked beforehand.

> I recall how my father used television programmes to teach my brother and I about dangers in life. These incidents include befriending people with right values, not picking up bad habits such as smoking and taking drugs. The lessons brought about by the television programmes, especially when the characters end up in prison or in a bad condition, acted as 'errors' for us to avoid. In effect, they were primers for us so that when they actually occur in real life, either when we meet such people or are offered cigarettes, we are already mindful of the dangers found in them.

To distinguish the effects of testing from attention direction, the authors emphasised the tested concepts in both conditions using italics or bolded keywords. Posttest performance was better in the test condition than in the extended study condition — a pretesting effect — even though only items that were not successfully retrieved on the pretest were analysed. The testing effect appears to be attributable, in part, to the role unsuccessful tests play in enhancing future learning. In short, pre-study testing enhances **long-term memory**, possibly due to the increased mindfulness that the questions result in. Learners are primed to look out for the answers to the questions when reading the passage. In like fashion, we expect learners to become mindful when they are exposed to errors BEFORE these scenarios actually occur in real life.

If we go back to the ant, doesn't the ant often put itself in a vulnerable position, exposed to the elements and predators such as man? Yes, it does. It must take some risks in order to find new sources of food. One example of this occurring is when we find ants wandering about alone, probing and sensing the environment with only one objective — to find food to feed its colony. This forward, backward movement across the terrain, trying to determine if there is food in the vicinity posits a tedious and dangerous mission for the ant. Without any forewarning, prior intelligence and little knowledge about the surroundings, the ant has little choice but to proceed with courage and caution, running for cover at the slightest trace of danger. It is in this risky mission to find food that one observes the *mindful* state of the ant. It is aware of how it is proceeding, what vibrations there are in the air or on the ground. It knows where to crawl and how to crawl, to get out of danger quickly. It is also aware of key danger signs (similar to the pretesting experiment) to look out for, based on its past experiences or on the experiences of other ants in the colony. In other words, it is mindful of what is happening around it and what *can* be happening. After all, its survival depends on it. This state of mindfulness contributes to its ability to work smart. Being mindful is about knowing the now and predicting the future, in order to prepare for it. So far, I have mentioned how being mindful aids the ant in escaping from danger. However, that is not about working smart. It is just how mindfulness is important to preserve its life. The working smart part comes in when it forages for food. How is it mindful then? For a start, the ant is constantly monitoring the molecules in the air and particles on the ground with its feelers to determine if there is food nearby. It is aware of when the concentration of food molecules may be thinning and hence, to backtrack or change direction or when the food molecules seem to be increasing in intensity, to move forward. Hence, the tracking back and forth is an intentional motion, with a highly sensitive monitoring system to inform the direction and pace of this motion.

After working with more than 40,000 students, teachers and parents, I have come to realise that for some people tracking back is not be an option. They believe in charging forward and not looking back. They keep on trying and trying. There is nothing wrong with trying and persevering. In fact, it is important to not give up. However, the manner in which they keep persevering seems strange. For one, they seem to make it worse, not better. They also do not look up to see what is happening around them, unlike the ant. They press on, like a bull, breaking up and out, in a fashion that creates more damage, whether psychological or physical, than benefit. Hence, mindfulness when forging new ground, establishing new processes or understanding key issues is critical, to ensure one is on the right track, or at least, not doing or getting into any harm.

How Is This Mindfulness Factor Important in Helping Us Work More Effectively?

Just like the ant, we make mistakes in our learning. Sometimes, we explore the problem or issues and try different ways to solve the issues, without much success. We move forward and backwards, to check our assumptions and understanding, like the ant. In our quest to gain new learning ground, we have to take risks, mostly small and rarely fatal. However, we keep on preserving to get to our destination, in order to understand new topics or skill sets.

To learn well, we have to be mindful, just like the ant. We need to know what is happening and what *can* be happening with the problem so that we can pre-empt and work in the necessary solutions. What we do *not* want is to charge about like a bull in a china store, destroying our self-esteem and venting our frustration on others as well. Keeping an open mind, monitoring our progress or lack of progress and deciding if we need to backtrack a few steps can save us a lot more time as learners. In other words, being mindfulness eventually leads to a heightened sense of metacognition if we take stock of what is happening *inside* us, not just in the external environment.

> *"We cannot afford to have leaders who lead by crisis, whose approach is reactiveness and whose agenda is simply to do what the people want them to do.*
>
> *Leaders must be anticipative and able to communicate a worthy future."*
>
> **Mr. Lim Siong Guan**
> GIC Group President and Singapore's former Civil Service Head

Reflective Practice

Just as mindfulness (and to a larger extent, metacognitive ability) is important when managing novel situations or when the typical rules may not apply for various reasons, reflective practice as a habit (or routine) will allow a learner to constantly improve one's performance through individual critical review. At work and in school, this habit of reflective practice is important to drive learning and review on a regular basis. According to Wilson *et al.* (2005), there are three types of reflection (or learning):

1. Learning in action
2. Learning from action
3. Learning for action

Developing Metacognition

When Sir Alex Fleming was conducting research on bacteria, he stumbled upon an amazing discovery almost by chance. What happened then was a powerful demonstration of how mindfulness can make or break experiments and more importantly, differentiate between fame or oblivion.

It was in the autumn of 1928, after returning from a summer vacation with his family, Fleming was going through his stacks of culture in his untidy laboratory when he noticed that one culture was not covered properly and as a result contaminated with a fungus. Picking it up, he wanted to throw the culture away since he made the error of not covering it tightly enough. Thankfully, before he threw the culture, he took a glance and was mindful that the colonies of staphylococci that had immediately surrounded the fungus had been destroyed, whereas other colonies farther away were normal. Realising that the contaminated culture displayed evidence of a possible bacteria-killing substance, Fleming grew the fungus in a pure culture. Eventually, he identified the fungus as being from the *Penicillium* genus, and, after some months of calling it *'mould juice'*, named the substance it released Penicillin on 7 March 1929. As a result of his error in not covering the culture well, he had the mindfulness to note that something was unusual, leading to his immense discovery and to his winning the Nobel Prize in 1945.

Based on Table 17, one can gather that beyond the typical learning paradigm or process of learning during work or practice, there is the learning from work (or action) which simply is reflecting on one's action, to question one's assumptions and beliefs. More importantly, Wilson et al. (2005) propose a third category of learning for action which implies a conscious effort at applying the learning to new contexts.

In the context of reflective practice, error detection and rectification as a learning design can facilitate the learning in action, from action and for action mechanisms by simply focusing on the key or difficult concepts where the errors are made. The ensuing task/s could be structured to focus on the application of the concepts to new paradigms and situations so as to allow for prior planning and a heightened sense of mindfulness for similar events in the future. The pitching of the errors at the right level (of difficulty) will also help to match learner profile and ability so that motivation is maintained through the achievement of success by the learner.

More importantly, both mindfulness and reflective practice will contribute to the development of one's metacognition. Why is the focus on one's thinking important? The primary reason is the assumption that

Table 17. Reflective Practice — Affordances and Challenges

	Learning In Action	Learning from Action	Learning for Action
Primary Affordances	Occurs during the behaviour or response Observed during daily routines Immediate feedback from the environment and actors	Occurs as part of an intentional response Focus on deriving patterns and insights Possibility of checking assumption and belief Facilitates double-loop reflection and transformation	Focus on applicability of learning Intentional effort to develop new competencies Mitigate risks at work
Challenges	Can be formal, informal and non-formal especially at work Issues of scope of content, time constraints and lack of learning support	Need for deep reflection to drive learning Social or peer support critical for deep learning Facilitation is key	Designing for *transfer* is critical Work or school context determines applicability Relevance and validity of the content are issues
DELETE Approach	Group discussion, facilitated activities to drive the reflection and subsequent learning	The learning moments before, during and/or after the error presentations would present these moments to learn from action (typically the error/s).	The call to action for the learners to re-experiment their learning in other contexts or problems (e.g. case studies, role plays, simulations, group discussions) would be the key to learning for action.

once we are aware and in charge of our own emotional and cognitive strengths and weaknesses, we can do well to address them and make our cognitive processes better. It is akin to monitoring our speed when driving a car. We can choose to ignore the speed dial or the AI voice that tells us to slow down, but these tools act as useful speed checks. Hence, it is up to the person whether to take the advice. In addition, developing a person's frequency and depth of reflection also means that the person needs to check the tools more often and with more deliberation. In our case, the tools will be our thinking output and content.

While it is not the intention of this chapter to provide an in-depth treatise of metacognition, mindfulness and reflective practice, the inclusion of these various cognitive processes and skills here is to emphasise the functionality of the DELETE approach to develop these rarely mentioned, yet essential metacognitive skills.

> *If I had an hour to solve a problem,*
> *I'd spend 55 minutes thinking about the problem*
> *and 5 minutes thinking about solutions.*
>
> Albert Einstein

ii. *To Develop Ability to Evaluate Contexts and Assumptions*

The second metacognitive outcome is about the ability of staff to evaluate the appropriateness of contexts for certain SOPs to be applicable and along with that, evaluating the underlying assumptions sufficiently. It is the norm that training and classroom lessons focus on developing the skillsets of learners to perform at work or in an assessment and rightly so, since this is what the learners eventually need to do most of the time. If the context is consistent and unchanging (e.g. highly controlled situations), then there are few issues with this approach. In the event when contexts do not remain stable but vary frequently (e.g. stock market behaviour or jobs involving frequent contingencies), then being aware of the appropriateness of the SOPs becomes critical so that errors do not arise.

Carefully designed errors can send a strong message to learners that the correct implementation of the SOPs under contexts that the SOPs were not crafted for can be disastrous and highly inappropriate. Hence, one key teaching point is 'not to follow SOPs blindly' but to think through when contexts have changed and require a review of how SOPs are carried out to the T. To be fair to learners, especially novices, it can be difficult for those who are not familiar with the tasks to understand fully the SOPs, much less the contexts behind the SOPs.

For example, there is an authentic case of a curtain designer who provided several measurements for the contractor to install the curtain fixtures in the living room and two toilets in the client's house. After attempting to install the fixtures, the contractor left to return another day as he started late in the day. However, what he did not realise was that of the two toilets that the new maid led him to, one of the toilets was incorrect. It was the toilet in the Master bedroom that needed the curtains. The curtain designer and the contractor did not know that there were three toilets not two in the apartment. Needless to say, the house owner was furious with the curtain designer for failing to give proper instructions to the contractor. As the curtain designer was new to the job, he failed to have considered that the apartment, despite its small size, could have three toilets.

In this case, the SOPs were followed conscientiously with careful recordings of the measurements which were passed to the contractor. However, the context that the house owner would be at home to guide the contractor to install the fixtures did not apply then. When the new maid came into the picture, the context was quite different (from the norm) and as a result, the original SOPs were insufficient, with the measurements and descriptions being incomplete to facilitate the correct installation of the fixtures. Either the SOPs can now be further enhanced to include drawings of the precise location of the fixtures or the context should be stated clearly that the house owner must be at home to guide the contractor before the fixtures can be installed.

Using these errors to vary the contexts allows learners to pick out the boundaries that the SOPs will or will not apply and so, be aware of the moments when contexts have changed when some consideration of the appropriateness of SOPs will be needed.

Chapter 17
Developing Cognition

Following on from metacognition, developing cognition is another feature of DELETE approach that can enable expertise and competency building. For most students, this is what they do predominantly in school over the first two decades of their lives. Over abstract concepts (such as differentiation and theorems, physical and chemical rules), our students struggle to grapple with these concepts, climaxing in their performance at tests and examinations, effectively translating their gargantuan efforts into benefits as they snare lucrative job offers based on their excellent academic scores. Increasingly, there is a shift to non-academic skills, but the underlying cognitive capabilities remain important as our students choose to develop their capabilities in a myriad of contexts outside of schools and classrooms, for purposive application of 'real-time, real-place, real-work' learning.

In this segment, we will focus on four cognitive learning outcomes, to keep the discussion relevant to the DELETE approach:

i. *To Strengthen Conceptual Understanding and Skillsets in Targeted Areas*
ii. *To Develop 'Creative-Critical' Thinking Ability*
iii. *To Sharpen Cognitive Adaptability and Flexibility*
iv. *To Build Global (Macro) Perspective-Taking Ability*

These outcomes shift from the more observable skills and knowledge gaps (such as technical skills) to skills which are difficult to quantify but critical for the purpose of improving work performance. Most training focus on getting the tasks done, but the DELETE approach facilitates work competence involving areas beyond specific tasks, such as possessing problem-solving capability, empathy and identification of and pre-empting problems before they occur.

For a start, we will focus on the typical training objective of strengthening conceptual understanding and skillsets in problematic areas.

i. *To Strengthen Conceptual Understanding and Skillsets in Targeted Problematic Areas*

The DELETE approach focuses the learning on the specific step of a procedure (e.g. solving Mathematics questions, decision-making) or segment of the concept (e.g. the irregular past tenses in English, limitations of AI usage at work). We will revisit this delineation between procedural and declarative concept in a later chapter under error analysis and difficult concepts. It is useful to know that this differentiation is important as declarative (or facts) knowledge is usually aligned with the 'what' and 'why' questions, while procedural (or steps) knowledge requires the learner to apply the 'how to'. For learners who may exhibit certain strengths or weaknesses in either faculty, the design of the errors will have to consider the characteristics of the errors associated with declarative and procedural knowledge respectively.

For example, learners often have to work through the initial steps of the procedure or to recall the easier segments before reaching the critical or more difficult area. As such, they may be waylaid by the earlier steps in the procedure or confused by the other areas without reaching the more critical or difficult area which the teacher is focusing on for that lesson. Hence, by designing learning using errors, learners can zoom in to focus on the specific step or segment of the procedural knowledge without being confused by the earlier steps or segments. I have listed two examples to illustrate my point:

1. Solve 3 + 2 + 2 (32 + 52 × 2) / 2
   3 + 2 + 2 (32 + 52 × 2) / 2
   = 5 + 2 (32 + 52)
   = 5 + 2 (84)
   = 7 (84)
   = 91

Find the errors in the earlier solution. More importantly, what conceptual understanding does the solver still lack? Which of the following errors is this solver likely to make again if he does not correct his misunderstanding?

a) 4 + 3 × 2 = 14   b) 5 (3 + 1) = 16   c) 6 / 2 + 3 = 1 1/5

The key concepts include:

- functions next to the brackets will apply to all the numbers within brackets (e.g. /2 should also apply to the number '32')
- the functions next to the brackets should be carried out first before summation or subtraction (e.g. 5 + 2(84) is not the same as 7 (84))
- the number next to the brackets imply multiplication not addition

Given that the solver has issues primarily with the concept of brackets, he or she is likely to commit the (b) error as it involves brackets.

More importantly, the learner who needs to spot the errors and articulate the concepts has the added task of being clear what concepts are being violated and hopefully, not to make these errors. Try a question involving conjunction and semantics.

2. Form one sentence from the two sentences below using a conjunction.

Tom likes to eat mangoes that have a tangy taste.
Mangoes with a tangy taste are usually slightly green in colour.

Answer 1: Tom likes to eat mangoes which are usually slightly green in colour.
Answer 2: Tom likes to eat slightly green mangoes that have a tangy taste.

Find the errors in the above answers. How are these errors different? What conceptual errors are embedded in them? What are the assumptions made behind these errors?

The errors are not obvious. Answer 1 is erroneous because being slightly green is not the criterion, but the tangy taste is the critical factor for Tom and leaving out critical information such as 'tangy taste' is not acceptable when it comes to combining sentences. Answer 2, on the other hand, claims that Tom likes green mangoes with a tangy taste, but the original two sentences were not stated that way. Tom just prefers mangoes with a tangy taste but may have no preference when it comes to colours.

The solver assumed that the logic in the individual sentences can be combined and extrapolated to make further assumptions and conclusions. However, this changes the precision of the sentence, and it is this attention to precision that the solver needs to develop further.

The errors force the learner to take on a more analytical stance and not jump into making decisions too quickly. It also allows further questioning of the learner's own understanding of the concepts.

Based on these two illustrations on how errors can drive cognitive understanding, learning designers and educators have a tool to design activities which target specific concepts at the appropriate level of performance for both practice and to check understanding. Using errors allows educators to present uncommon principles or rules which seldom surface unless the learner encounters them in rare contexts. More importantly, learners can be asked why these errors occur. By intentionally surfacing the workings of these principles or rules through the errors, learners can now make a conscious effort to avoid making the same mistakes and hopefully, apply the rules or principles in the correct manner. You will also realise that when learners can answer a question correctly, it does not mean the learners have fully grasped the concept or skill set. They just happen to answer that particular question correctly.

For example, a four-year-old girl was quizzed on her ability to tell time. She could show correctly using a paper clock with movable hour and minute hands, the time for 3 o' clock, 7 o' clock and 1 o' clock as shown in Figure 29. That seems like she has grasped the concept of reading time (at least on the hour).

However, it is only when she was tested using specially designed error (targeting the difficult concept of the meaning of the hour and minute

Developing Cognition

hands) that her true understanding of telling time was tested. She was asked if the clock face on the left (see Fig. 30) shows 3 'o clock. She replied in the affirmative.

It goes to show that being able to move the clock hands correctly for three different times does not mean she can tell time. She does not know the difference between the hour and minute hands. In this regard, knowing what is correct is insufficient. Knowing what is wrong is equally important and completes the picture. This is an area that not all educators do well in — getting the full picture of what the learners really know — what is right and what is wrong.

With DELETE, it provides the possibility that educators can now test if learners know how to answer a question some of the time but not all the time. It also tests the assumption that knowing how to answer a question equates to knowing the concept in its entirety. Often, a wrong answer tells us a lot more about a learner's ability than a right one. For example, when asked what number this is (3), a child responds with 'six'. This implies the

Fig. 29. Time-Telling Competencies for Four-Year-Old Girl

Fig. 30. Time-Telling Competencies Using DELETE Approach

child does not know how to read '3' as well as '6'. Hence, a wrong answer can be more informative than a correct answer and should invite reflection rather than immediate correction. Asking the same child how '3' looks like and why he read it as 'six' can be useful questions to trigger reflection at least at the basic level.

At the Workplace

From the workplace training point of view, DELETE presents an alternative approach to helping experienced staff gain further competence without needing retraining in the entire curriculum all over again. Staff who are already trained for the job but lack the experience to reach mastery status often will benefit from the DELETE approach as there may not be many structured training programmes which will address their skill gaps. Most of the time, these staff just need more practice and experience. They don't face too many issues at work, and they can problem-solve whatever that comes their way. However, they are also not experienced enough to become a mentor and so, are often left out of the senior management or mentoring programmes. It is common to find workers undertaking 'refresher' courses for the simple reason that they have to clock training hours. What is frustrating to these experienced staff is that the training duplicates what they do at work, something they are inherently familiar with after years of working in the environment on those issues. Hence, the DELETE methodology provides a more targeted approach to providing errors in a different context for these experienced staff to work through, not just to train them in those similar concepts they already know but to get these staff to reflect and work through unfamiliar contexts with uncommon errors. In this way, they become mindful of the existence and possibility of these errors. This exposure to uncommon errors is a means of accelerating their acquisition of experience within the work context. This is important as the experience will prepare them to handle future cases with similar issues or contexts.

A case in point is the pool of schoolteachers (and it can also refer to medical professionals and real estate agents, accountants and other professionals) who have to attend continual professional development (CPD) programmes year after year, to clock CPD points. Many of them are experienced professionals with a number of years of relevant work experience. For them to undergo training on areas that they already know (e.g. pedagogical principles or basic teaching methodologies for teachers) is not a productive use of their time. Hence, by designing errors for these professionals to rework their assumptions and become a more mindful professional may be useful to drive new behaviours and outcomes. Don't we agree that doing the same task and expecting a different result is unrealistic? We need to do something different to get a different and hopefully, better result.

From the design point of view, this outcome is likely to be the most common for the DELETE approach given that most learning is geared towards getting the specific task done correctly with full knowledge of what is wrong and right. We will further discuss how we can design appropriate errors to target specific gaps in understanding and skill sets, for both declarative knowledge and procedural skill sets. More examples will also be given for the training of staff at the workplace.

ii. *To Develop Creative-Critical Thinking Ability*
The first DELETE design centred round developing competencies using typical case studies to exemplify mistakes and learners to correct these mistakes as part of technical skill training or knowledge acquisition. Going forward, the remaining DELETE designs under the Cognition section will target relatively different capabilities, beyond the typical skills performance and understanding. In fact, the value proposition of DELETE is to empower the designers with a wider range of tools when crafting learning activities for the development of learner capabilities. Not many design tools allow learners to reflect deeply, develop metacognitive ability or build awareness of contexts that SOPs operate in. The DELETE approach may provide this

Chapter 17

additional avenue for designers to utilise errors as trigger points for building capabilities beyond just task skills and knowledge to job performance and life skills.

The second outcome that the DELETE approach hopes to achieve is likely to be familiar to you — the development of creative and critical thinking skills, which unlike the first outcome, does not belong to the typical set of task skills although they are necessary skills for daily functioning to create new solutions to solve problems. What is slightly different here is the argument that creative and critical thinking skills should not be separated artificially but allowed to assimilate and integrate seamlessly for optimal functioning in real life. After all, most people intermix creative and critical ('creatical') thinking at pace without even realising it. The question is the extent that people consciously force themselves to think a little further before switching modes.

Developing 'Creatical' Thinking

Increasingly, there is an understanding that creative and critical thinking while different do not operate in the absence of each other. In fact, during daily life routines, one can often find the intertwining of creative and critical thinking processes as one encounters and solves issues in life. The intentional extension of  creative or critical thinking to allow ideas to grow or to be pruned should be a conscious effort and again, this requires careful training of the learner to carry out the required thinking process at the right time. Hence, the literature usually talks about the use of creative OR critical thinking to achieve one's learning goals. I would like to propose that an intertwined creative and critical thinking process or what I term as 'creatical' thinking, much like a peel of a fruit with both the insides and outsides stuck together but performing different functions (outside for protection and inside as flesh of the fruit) is a more authentic reflection of our cognitive processes. Unlike current models of critical and creative thinking where ideation precedes idea analysis, the intertwined approach takes the perspective that the brain can manage to carry out both processes, switching between the two at rapid speed, to generate new ideas and to critically analyse the idea in quick succession.

Typically, the generation of a new idea or a new process of solving a problem would be considered as a creative process. One would also consider something creative as extraordinary and 'not thought of' by most people. Sometimes linking two very different concepts found in different fields can yield very startling results. For example, what comes into your mind when we put 'thermos flask' together with 'earphones'? Some of us may generate very interesting permutations, 99% are probably frivolous and useless at this point in time. However, there may the 1% who can think of something useful as a result of this combination. Perhaps, some of us can think of how the vacuum in the thermos flask can also act as the same deterrence for sound. Hence, ear plugs with vacuum in them may be more effective than the ones we have now. Can that work? I am sure if we give our imagination some room to explore, some of these thoughts may be useful.

Determining the usefulness or viability of an idea is usually a critical thinking process. Critical thinking involves careful analysis of the context as well as the issue so as to determine the next step of action. Good judgments depend on the extent of consideration of the contexts. However, over-analysing the contexts or issues may lead to a waste of precious time and resources or in the extreme case, paralysis where the learner does not know what to do.

If we combine both creative and critical thinking processes in an intertwined manner, then one becomes cognizant to the fact that critical and creative processes do not exist independently but that a person can switch quickly between the two processes. This is important in that knowing when to switch from critical thinking to creative thinking and vice versa will save the learner precious time and reduce engagement in unfruitful processes. The question is not so much how fast to switch but when to switch — the right moment to ideate and the right moment to analyse. This ability to determine the appropriateness of 'when' needs training. Metacognitively, the individual has to tell the brain to switch gears when the time is 'right'.

For example, if the learner has spent substantial amount of time on critically analysing the error without making any headway in understanding the issue or underlying theories, then switching over to a creative thinking process may be more fruitful. By doing so, the learner may engage in generating solutions which do not depend on the analysis of the problem (e.g. trial and error approach). At times, by engaging in creative thinking, the learner may stumble upon a possible opening or certain theory may come to mind, resulting in the learner switching back to the critical thinking mode to determine if the theory is truly applicable or not. Hence, 'creatical thinking' requires careful training, to allow learners to switch between thinking processes in a conscious and purposive manner.

In short, this outcome is to create and to critique almost simultaneously; the ability to switch gears quickly with clarity and control, allowing for optimum thinking. At the same time, it requires great metacognitive control which many are not capable of. It is about the control of our minds — the way we think — forcing ourselves not to judge too early but to allow the brainstorming and creative nature of our minds to explore and wander is useful when the situation allows it, when speed is not of essence and there is liberty to push frontiers and try new approaches. Conversely, if there is urgency to push ahead and to make decisions, one must switch quickly enough to a critical mode once the list of acceptable solutions becomes available. Deciding what to do requires good judgment and a narrowing down of options and pursuing the actions which follow. Hence, while performing both functions of creating and critiquing well is important, the ability to switch quickly back and forth at the RIGHT moment in time

> **Example of 'Creatical' Thinking**
>
> Someone may have missed his train and the next one will take another 20 minutes to arrive. As he is trying furiously to think creatively how to get to his destination on time, he is generating new possibilities and thinking out of the box, which may include hitching a ride from a colleague who may stay nearby or taking several buses for that matter. Sooner or later, he has to quickly narrow down the options and critically make a decision. This switching between creative and critical thinking is essential for daily normal cognitive functioning. The speed of switching from one to the other and knowing when to switch can determine success or failure in achieving one's goals. For example, if the person described above takes too long to generate all the possible means of transport before critically narrowing down the options, he will have missed even the second best option, resulting in him being extremely late. On the other hand, if he shoots down all possibilities too quickly, he may be denying himself other innovative solutions that he would have thought of if he dwelt a little longer on the creative thinking spectrum. Developing the ability to decide when a particular lead is not productive and quickly moving on to the next one is what this DELETE objective is about.

is of even greater criticality. That ability to switch at will is an important and difficult one.

One approach to developing creative-critical ('creatical') thinking is to task learners to add missing information to the problem for creative solutioning process. What does this mean?

For example, an incomplete problem with a partially described context may be presented to the learners. The task for learners is to make good the error which based on the problem and context above is an obvious one. How then can learners add information to the context or problem which will convert the obvious error into one that is justifiable and possibly non-erroneous? This calls for creative solutioning and one that requires rapid critical judgement, especially if there is a time limit added to the task.

A group of surgeons when operating on an old lady realised that they made an error in diagnosing the tumour. Instead of it being benign as the initial biopsies showed, the tumour appeared malignant and in fact, highly aggressive. The error seemed to have been made by a new lab technician who interpreted the biopsy results wrongly.

Task: Suggest possible scenarios or contexts which will make the above error a non-issue. You have 5 minutes to propose as many scenarios as possible.

See box on the right for possible scenarios.

By thinking of contexts in which the initial error presented could be nullified, it allows learners (in the above case, possibly nurses or medical students) to take a step back to consider if the assumption that an error has really occurred is truly correct. If it is correct, is the error of any consequence? Hence, there is a place to develop a person's ability to switch between creative and critical thinking at a rapid pace for effective daily problem-solving. The key question is whether this particular activity is useful

(Context 1: The old lady was hit by a car and was already dead to begin with. The surgeons were operating on her as part of their medical training.

Context 2: The tumour was found on the part of her leg which has to be amputated, due to gangrene. As long as the cancer hasn't spread to the rest of the leg, she can still survive the tumour scare.

Context 3: The surgeons realised that the malignant tumour was found in another part of the organ which was not detected by the scans. The results from the biopsy on another tumour were actually correct. That tumour was benign and the lab technician did not actually make a mistake.)

Context 4: Actually, the lab technician did not make a mistake. It was the doctors who diagnosed the cancerous cells wrongly.

when it comes to developing creative and critical thinking. Noticeably, the learners are asked not to generate or analyse solutions but to review the contexts that the error was made to make it a non-issue. Hence, the switch in focus is key for learners to take into consideration both the solution and the seemingly innocuous context that it is based in. As you may be able to see in the above case of the cancer patient, the context may render the problem a non-issue.

The closure of the exercise is important to draw together the critical elements of questioning our own assumptions, contexts and not making a decision or judgment too early.

iii. *To Sharpen Cognitive Adaptability and Flexibility*
Similar to the earlier outcome of metacognitive development, this outcome is also a reflection of the pressures exerted the fast-paced environment we work in. In a world where the situation is constantly changing, one's ability to cope with the dynamism of the issues can be severely tested. However, a constant struggle for course designers when it comes to developing real work competence where adaptability is required is to factor in the dynamism of the interactions with the environment and people. While role plays and simulations may capture some of the dynamism, often it is dependent on the learner's actions and decisions and may or may not lead to the difficult concepts that may not surface if the required action is not taken by the learner.

What DELETE errors do as a design mechanism is to use the errors to force the learners into the situation whereby the difficult concepts or skills surface to provide opportunities for the learners to experience and react accordingly. Hence, the learners must cope with a constantly changing wicked problem and error. There is a case presented on the next page illustrating how a dynamic case can present the case facts in such a manner that challenges the cognitive adaptability and flexibility of learners to respond. The targeted learners are new immigration officers undergoing induction to the job.

Chapter 17

Example of a Case — Immigration Officers at Checkpoint

Task: You will be presented with the partial cases in quick sequence. Before the next sequence is presented, you are to answer the questions within 7 minutes either alone or in pairs. Provide as many possible answers as possible. Think of the SOPs, contexts, assumptions and actions which should be taken when providing your answers. Remember that speed and breadth of thinking are essential here. Question what and why certain behaviours are not presented in the case.

Phase 1: Partial presentation of key facts and context

Two immigration officers, Kenneth and Sophia, were at the checkpoint for outgoing cars examining the boot of a BMW. It was the evening peak hour with a long line of cars waiting to clear immigration. Based on SOP, they checked the boot, undercarriage and the driver's seat along with the backseat for any illegal substances or persons. There was a pregnant lady in the front, next to the driver who was her husband. Not finding anything suspicious, they handed the passports back to the lady and waved the driver on. He drove the BMW away promptly.

Strangely, as the BMW sped away, there was a loud 'pop' sound as if a balloon exploded from within the car. The car screeched to a halt about 50 m away. Kenneth ran over to investigate.

Questions
- What do you think happened? Discuss if Kenneth's actions were appropriate?
- Under what context would Kenneth's actions be inappropriate?
- What would you do if you were Kenneth or Sophia?
- Do you consider Kenneth to have committed a critical error? Why?

Phase 2: Further presentation of errors

As Kenneth ran over to investigate, the driver of the white BMW waved him over and asked for help. He said that his wife's vacuum flask exploded when she wanted to take a bite. Kenneth walked to the other side of the car to check the condition of the lady. She looked startled, with hot food spattered over her face and body. Kenneth radioed back to inform his superiors of this incident. Meanwhile, Sophia continued to check the next car (a black SUV) alone as the line of cars was increasing and as she waited for support to arrive.

Questions
- Now that you know the context, discuss if Kenneth's actions were appropriate?
- Were there other errors committed in the above case?
- Under what context would Kenneth's or Sophia's actions be inappropriate?
- What would you have done if you were Kenneth or Sophia?
- What will you do next if you were Kenneth?

Phase 3: Presentation of the context
After checking the car, Sophia handed the five passports back to the two men, two women and a girl in the car. The silver SUV moved off and Sophia was in the midst of checking the next car (a minivan) when her colleague, Boon Hui, arrived at her checkpoint about 7 minutes later. 'Any problems'? asked Boon Hui. Sophia glanced up, 'No problem. I am about done with this car. You can take the next one. Kenneth should be back soon'. Boon Hui shrugged his shoulders, 'OK'! He turned to the next car to begin checking. Sophia waved off the minivan.

Questions
- Were there errors committed here?
- Do you see any linkages or development of possible errors from Phases 1 to 3?
- What would you do if you were Boon Hui or Sophia?

Chapter 17

Phase 4: Final presentation of the context

Three weeks after this seemingly innocuous incident where the lady in the white car was checked for some light scalding, five persons were arrested in the neighbouring country for trafficking of illegal workers. The mastermind, along with four illegal workers, was caught when the minivan they were in overturned due to the deep potholes in a rural road, masked by the puddles of water after a heavy shower. Their passports were not stamped despite having passed through the immigration checkpoint.

Questions
- What do you think actually happened?
- Did any of your earlier assumptions or predictions match the above ending?
- Looking back, what were the contexts and the assumptions made that allowed the illegal act by Sophia?
- Now that you know the outcome, what would you have done if you were Kenneth or Boon Hui then?
- Are current SOPs sufficient to prevent such incidents?

Debrief

Naturally, in a case, there are many assumptions including the integrity of the characters (e.g. Sophia). However, it is useful to always question assumptions and contexts and to rethink issues especially when the SOPs, seemingly correct, may become wrong when the actual contexts are not in line with the assumed contexts when the SOPs were set up. In this case, the context was that we assume impartiality of all immigration officers. When the context is different, the SOPs may then need to be reviewed on the ground. Did Boon Hui or Kenneth question the correctness of the SOPs they followed?

Obviously, this is a hypothetical case to showcase possible application of the DELETE approach and is not intended to cast doubt on the integrity

Developing Cognition

of immigration officers. It does allow the error (in this case, the assumption that Kenneth made about his colleague) to surface.

More importantly, this approach is useful to develop staff who need to respond to emergencies or contingencies which are unpredictable. When the critical and/or common errors has been captured from the subject matter experts and stakeholders, the error is allowed to evolve based on intentional design and the dynamism of the error is then demonstrated through the partial presentation of the error and solution taken by the case characters. As shown in the example above, more details are revealed as the learners analyse the situation, actions taken and the errors in real time. Compared to unscripted role plays and game simulations, the DELETE approach is more focused by getting to the difficult concepts and skillsets quickly. With role plays and simulations, there is the possibility that the learner may not choose the actions which trigger the difficult concept. Hence, while it is noted that the design is a lot more intentional and hence, provides less autonomy to the learner, it is more effective in driving home key messages and critical learning points. Sharpening the learner's cognitive adaptability and flexibility is a possible outcome when using the DELETE approach in a dynamic manner.

iv. *To Build Global (Macro) Perspective-Taking Ability*
Having a global perspective, or systems thinking (Gharajedaghi, 2011; Meadows, 2008), also referred to as having 'helicopter vision' or the 'ability to see the big picture', is a crucial skill for workers as they advance in their roles and need to make decisions beyond their typical responsibilities. For instance, they may be asked if they can approve an exemption request from a client. With a broad understanding of the processes and potential consequences gleaned from experience, the worker can confidently make these decisions. On the other hand, less experienced workers who lack the knowledge and understanding of what happens before or after their specific task *may* struggle with this decision-making process and may not have the desired outcome. Often, it is the understanding of how

the organisation behaved in the past which informs the decision-making process. Many of these past decisions by management are tacit knowledge and are undocumented, thereby making experienced workers valuable in the context they operate in.

The design of the DELETE approach for this learning outcome will require the inclusion of the workflow, the various rectification options with the corresponding consequences. The logic is to expose the learners (especially those new to the context) to as many 'cause-and-effect' relationships as possible so that they will draw the necessary conclusions about how the rectification actions and consequences are linked. The patterns or principles underpinning the relationships should become obvious over time so that the macro picture can be generated for future decision-making.

Example of a Case — Senior Management Staff of a Training Organisation

Task: You will be presented with a case (a global training organisation) with numerous rectification options and the accompanying consequences. Your task is to evaluate the given options and consequences and determine new rectification options. You will also need to make conclusions based on what you observe from the relationships between the options and the consequences. Your eventual rectification options will determine if the training organisation is ready to take on the new world of technology-enabled learning. Review the workflows, contexts, assumptions and the actions to be taken to as none of these are objective nor permanent. Remember that speed and the ability to take perspectives of the issues involved are essential here.

Phase 1: Presentation of Case with Context and Workflows
You are in the senior management team of a large, global training organisations (GoLearn) based in Tokyo. It has a long history of more than

50 years with more than 500 staff worldwide. Annual revenue is USD 50 million although profits have been diminishing in the past 5 years at less than USD 2 million yearly. The primary reasons include a more competitive landscape and the influx of technology-enabled learning programmes which have undermined the classroom training approach which is highly facilitative and experiential taken by your organisation.

The workplan for the next three years has been proposed although the consultants brought in to conduct the studies and make the recommendations are not in agreement over some of the major pieces of the proposal. They have made a total of five recommendations based on different reports (e.g. the New Horizon report, e-learning blogs).

The typical workflow to generate the workplan is to review the proposal and determine what works and what doesn't, then implement those which work accordingly and dispose of those items which are not feasible. Typically, senior management makes the decisions on the workplan.

Questions
- What do the challenges to the organisation really mean?
- Is technology-enabled learning really so formidable?
- Is the workflow of generating the workplan problematic and what alternative workflows are there?

Phase 2: Presentation of Errors
The consultants proposed five recommendations, some of which are disruptive and will require change management processes, including the termination of some of the long-term staff. Others require a change in mindset coupled with new skillsets such as computer programming skills. Most importantly, the proposal is seeking USD 5 million in budget to fund investments in new technology and pedagogy. The five proposals are summarised below:

1. From 'brick-and-mortar' business to online learning engagements through creation of online learning assets — this entails replacing the

senior facilitators and assessors with younger (and cheaper) e-designers and e-facilitators
2. 'Glocalising' the learning content — training materials and resources which have mass appeal globally are enhanced and contextualised by in-country designers to meet local learners' needs. On the other hand, resources which are highly specific to individual country's requirements or needs are discarded to increase productivity and return on investment.
3. Outsourcing of training and administration to e-facilitators and administrators based in cheaper localities — these e-facilitators and administrators will be given additional opportunities to upskill in order to cope with the new demands.
4. Enterprises will be the focus of new initiatives not the learners — this sets out that employers and enterprises are the real customers. The rationale to this recommendation is that employers pay for 80% of the training that GoLearn provides. Hence, making these employers happy implies happy customers.
5. Market certifiable programmes courses more aggressively, and focus less on short continuous professional development courses, so as to generate more revenue with less marketing.

Questions
- Which of the recommendations do you agree with? Why?
- What possible consequences could result from these five recommendations? How can we mitigate the possible fallout from the implementation of these recommendations?

Phase 3: Presentation of Errors, Rectification Options with Corresponding Consequences

After the five recommendations were accepted, some with much apprehension and resistance from the ground, the outcomes did not pan out the way the consultants expected. After one year of implementation, a lot of the damage was done and staff morale was at an all-time low. Revenue dropped considerably as a result of cancelling the classroom training programmes when online programmes are still a new phenomenon. While employers are happy with the lower cost of online training, employees are not taking to the e-courses since they entail additional time outside of working hours. GoLearn management has called for a review of the recommendations given the current outlook and results. The rectification options are listed in Table 18 for consideration. As part of the senior management, you are expected to list the possible consequences arising from the suggested recommendations. What else can happen? Would the rectifications make the situation worse?

Phase 4: Rectification Options with Corresponding Consequences
In phase 4, the consequences (from the subject matter experts) arising from the rectifications are checked with the learner's own list to determine alignment and to trigger reflection.

Debrief

Finally, review the list of possible consequences with your own to determine what the underlying principles are and lessons to be learned. These lessons could be drawn from many disciplines such as marketing, leadership, management, training methodologies and pedagogies so having the 'bigger picture' in mind will allow you to make connections especially when management decisions need to consider the technical issues and human resource factors for implementation success.

While the above case is lengthy, the long engagement process centring round errors and their consequences provides learners with the opportunities to draw from their current work and experience and push for connections to be made between past actions, present decisions and future results. The difference between DELETE and other management case studies is that by designing errors into the case, specific skillsets can be developed. In this case, the systems thinking or 'big picture' mentality is addressed by looking at how rectification efforts have resulted in further

Table 18. GoLearn's Recommendations and Options

Recommendations	Subsequent Issues	Rectification Options	Suggest Possible Consequences	Your Decision as Part of Management
1. From 'brick-and-mortar' business to online learning engagements	Drop in revenue; industry is not ready with online engagement	Resurrect classroom training, rehire old staff and reduce the pool of e-learning developers to cut staff costs. Rebrand GoLearn into a blended learning organisation.		
2. 'Glocalising' the learning content	Contextualising global content is difficult especially with video clips with foreign actors and accents	Produce generic materials (e.g. scripts, storyboards) which can act as the framework for contextualisation. Given the reduced revenue, the contextualisation efforts will have to be carried out in phases. In the meantime, reuse the old local content and develop interim resources based on the local content.		
3. Outsourcing of training and administration overseas to reduce cost	Customers get frustrated because the overseas admin staff did not appreciate their issues. Some e-facilitators were not competent in their subj. matter and facilitation.	Provide another layer of assistance at the local office to manage cases which the outsourced admin office cannot resolve. Get these staff to also cross sell products when they interact with customers. E-facilitators will remain as outsourced personnel as their costs are more competitive.		

4. Enterprises will be the focus of new initiatives not the learners	The learners who are employees are not receptive to e-learning so they do not sign up for courses despite employers' encouragement.	Refocus on learners by conducting more training needs analysis on the needs of the learners. Provide incentives such as serious gaming options for these learners. Develop non-work–related courses such as parenting and relationship e-courses.
5. Market certifiable programmes courses	The reduced number of courses resulted in fewer options for customers. They did not see value in the programmes offered. The short courses acted as 'tasters' for learners to sign up for the longer programmes.	Introduce complimentary 3h courses as a marketing tool. Modularise certifiable programmes for flexibility so that learners can take the modules in any sequence.

Table 19. GoLearn's Recommendations and Options, with Consequences

Recommendations	Subsequent Issues	Rectification Options	Possible Consequences	Your Comments
1. From 'brick-and-mortar' business to online learning engagements	Drop in revenue; industry is not ready with online engagement	Resurrect classroom training, rehire old staff and reduce the pool of e-learning developers to cut staff costs. Rebrand GoLearn into a blended learning organisation.	Disastrous outcome as conflicts arose between old and new staff, leading to staff resignations. On the other hand, blended learning worked better than e-learning for learners.	
2. 'Glocalising' the learning content	Contextualising global content is difficult especially with video clips with foreign actors and accents	Produce generic materials (e.g. scripts, storyboards) which can act as the framework for contextualisation. Given the reduced revenue, the contextualisation efforts will have to be carried out in phases. In the meantime, reuse the old local content and develop interim resources based on the local content.	The local content was appreciated by the learners while some global content provided alternative perspectives so it was win-win for GoLearn and the learners.	

3. Outsourcing of training and administration overseas to reduce cost	Customers get frustrated because the overseas admin staff did not appreciate their issues. Some e-facilitators were not competent in their subj. matter and facilitation.	Provide another layer of assistance at the local office to manage cases which the outsourced admin office cannot resolve. Get these staff to also cross sell products when they interact with customers. E-facilitators will remain as outsourced personnel as their costs are more competitive.	The layer of local staff helped in resolving complex issues but cross-selling by overseas staff was disastrous as information was misunderstood. The Interview process for e-facilitators needs to be tightened with face-to-face interaction. A regional rather than a global e-facilitation strategy may be more effective.
4. Enterprises will be the focus of new initiatives not the learners	The learners who are employees are not receptive to e-learning so they do not sign up for courses despite employers' encouragement.	Refocus on learners by conducting more training needs analysis on the needs of the learners. Provide incentives such as serious gaming options for these learners. Develop non-work-related courses such as parenting and relationship e-courses.	This should have been the strategy right from the start as learners determine which courses are consumed although HR engagement is critical to get your foot in the door. Going forward, direct sales to learners (e.g. MOOCs) are also possible.
5. Market certifiable programmes courses	The reduced number of courses resulted in fewer options for customers. They did not see value in the programmes offered. The short courses acted as 'tasters' for learners to sign up for the longer programmes.	Introduce complimentary 3 h courses as a marketing tool. Modularise certifiable programmes for flexibility so that learners can take the modules in any sequence.	The complimentary courses will provide some marketing power but you will be targeting the wrong crowd. Learners who look for free courses generally do not sign up for fee-paying ones. Reintroducing the short paid courses may be a better option.

problems for the organisation. These issues and errors help learners uncover deep underlying principles which a typical case may not embed or if they do, then the reflection could be at the 'first cycle' where the case may close once the solutions are provided (in phase 1 — see Table 18). It is when the learners are taken through the second and third cycle (see Table 19) that the learning is deepened, and certain recommendations made by the learners are then evaluated for quality of thinking. Hence, the intentional design to develop specific outcomes (e.g. 'Big Picture' thinking) in DELETE makes for a more effective learning experience.

Conclusion

Moving through metacognitive development into cognitive competencies, the focus so far has been about improving information processing and thinking capabilities. For most professionals managing information, such as lawyers, IT professionals and teachers, the logical sequencing of thoughts is part of what makes one's work efficient and effective. The error-based learning incidents typically target the higher order skillsets (e.g. evaluation and creation) from the cognitive domain as these skillsets take a lot more time and effort to develop. The advent of AI (e.g. ChatGPT) has expedited this urgency for information professions to relook what areas AI is not yet able to perform competently and push into those areas. One possibility is for professionals to acquire systems thinking, gaining insights into how teams, organisations, sectors and industries operate and progress into higher levels of authority with this competency. The other option is to develop subject matter expertise where boundaries to rules remain fuzzy, resulting in such knowledge being valuable. This is where the DELETE approach can fine-tune these capabilities to plug specific skill gaps in individuals where needed.

To be clear, what makes us distinctly human is our emotional make-up, and that differentiates us substantially from AI. The next chapter will focus on the affective domain where we will discuss the development of values and beliefs, psychological resilience.

Chapter 18
Developing Emotion

Introduction
Relative to cognitive development, emotional development tends to take a backseat in formal schooling and training even though it is acknowledged to be important, especially in the growing years of a child. Emotional stability and resilience are especially critical when the adult worker is undergoing job role transitions (e.g. lost a job or promoted to a new role). The assessment of emotional stability and growth can be less straightforward compared to test items for cognitive development and require self or observer ratings to determine some of these traits (e.g. mental strength) and the underlying values and beliefs that facilitate the healthy growth of one's emotional response system. In general, the emotional maturity of a person can determine if he or she can maintain the level of performance and beyond, especially in stressful circumstances. Keeping calm and remaining collected are important traits for all, more so for those in leadership positions, as their decisions will be far-reaching and impact more people. To what extent can we facilitate the emotional development of our learners, and to drive positive development of values and beliefs?

Emotion

i. *To Develop Values and Beliefs*
Beyond the acquisition of technical skills (whether solving actual or paper-based questions in examinations), the development of values and beliefs in the learners should take priority especially in shaping the young or when

Chapter 18

inducting a new worker into the profession. These values and beliefs will guide the person to do what is right besides doing it right. Performing the task correctly is important but prior to performing the task, one must question the motives behind the task and if doing it will be detrimental to anyone.

Getting learners (especially the young and impressionable) to adopt culturally accepted values and beliefs should not be an incidental process. It should not even depend solely on the mentor or teacher to impart these values, but most people will agree that values development process should be crafted intentionally into the curriculum for reflection and assimilation by the learners during the learning process. Where possible, the learners will have the opportunities to debate or even fight the values and beliefs and eventually, make these values and beliefs their own.

How can this development of values and beliefs be implemented? Through careful design of the errors, learners can make their own errors or be allowed to choose options which may test their resolve and beliefs concerning controversial matters related to the task at hand.

> *"Dealing with the VUCA world requires young people who have self-confidence, courage, integrity, wisdom, judgment, energy and imagination."*
>
> **Mr. Lim Siong Guan**
> GIC Group President and Singapore's former Head, Civil Service

To give an example of a DELETE case, a business executive, Sam, is attending a social gathering organised by a client and suddenly find himself face to face with a competitor who is trying to source for information about a particular tender submission. To make matters worse, the dinner bill is sponsored by the competitor. What decisions should the business executive make that will not make the host look bad but at the same time, not compromise his own professional standing? Eventually, the business development manager decided not to make a fuss at the dinner. He was cordial towards the competitor but kept his distance. At one point in time, the competitor smiled at him and slipped him a business card with his contact number. Sam entertained the competitor with a smile but looked away quickly. Many days later, the competitor contacted Sam again for a meal. He also sent a photo of them together at the gathering. Sam and the competitor looked really close and friendly in the picture. At that point, Sam realised that there was a danger of being accused by his organisation of selling out.

By starting with the end scenario (or errors), the learners can retrace the journey and determine the exact point where the path of rightful judgment was crossed. With DELETE, the designer can also incorporate other unforeseen errors into the learning activity so as to inoculate the learners from making similar errors in the future. Being aware of the values and beliefs underpinning the decisions is critical so that learners comprehend their decision-making process and go back to first principles when there are no SOPs or rules to aid them.

Key questions for reflection include:

1. *Was there anything wrong with Sam's decision in the first place?*
2. *Do you think Sam made an error? If so, what kind of error was it? Moral, ethical, professional or operational etc.?*
3. *What was his underlying belief when he responded in such a way?*
4. *How else could he have responded?*
5. *What would you have done? Why?*
6. *What is your own set of beliefs with regards to professional behaviour?*
7. *What would have your organisation done if you duplicated Sam's behaviour?*

Based on the case described above, the ambiguity in terms of the correctness of the rectification work helps to uncover the underlying values and beliefs of the person. Hence, you may be able to see the learners' own viewpoints and values during the discussion and reflection. Whether it is a correct or incorrect behaviour is immaterial since the case is fictitious but the rationale that the learners provide will be critical. In the same manner, the values and beliefs shared during the discussion are also very illuminating in locating the learner's standpoint on the ethics scale. Obviously, the organisation will have to determine the moral and ethical standpoint with regards to an ambiguous situation. The DELETE approach will have achieved two objectives through the case:

1) Organisation's viewpoints on possible conflict of interest will be made clear
2) Staff's underlying values and beliefs will be tested, reconsidered and aligned, if the staff decides to do so. If not, then at least, the organisation is aware of the staff's stand with regards to certain important values.

Other examples include bribery and corruption even if the local culture demands it. For example, in 2013, GlaxoSmithKline's drug sales team attempted to bribe some Chinese officials and doctors to take on and dispense their products, despite some patients not needing the medicine. Eventually, GSK's market price slumped 61% in the third quarter, heavily hit as a result of the bribery scandal that damaged its ability to market products in the country. It also likely strengthened their competitors' position in the market.

Likewise, corporations globally also had their fair share of management staff siphoning off money to pay off their personal debt in recent years. There are others who fall prey to temptations and commit extramarital affairs with customers. What can we draw from these incidents? It is easy to criticise and judge others when they make mistakes. One key principle underpinning these examples is that work values and beliefs are critical to effective professional decision making. In summary, it will be the personal beliefs and values that will drive decision-making such as those mentioned above. When these lessons are taken together, it appears that achieving alignment in ethics and values through focused training is one important activity for organisations going forward.

ii. *To Strengthen Psychological Resilience for Unexpected Outcomes*
Falling prey to temptations and making errors during crucial moments at work or in school can be expensive. I recall making an 'unforgiveable' error during my Additional Mathematics O Levels examination when instead of performing 'differentiation' on the variable, I performed 'integration' instead. It only dawned on me that I made a mistake on my way home after the paper! I ended with an 'A2' grade instead of my usual 'A1' grade. This incident was an awakening call to remain alert even with seemingly simple tasks. It was an expensive lesson and one that will stay with me for life.

What many of us do not realise is that we learn as much from what the educators teach as the mistakes that we and our classmates make during lessons. Learning from mistakes is a natural part of the learning process. In fact, it is an experiential process that learners can capitalise on to deepen their learning. The primary reason is that errors are made when there is an attempt to apply the learning. For example, a student may have tried to add two improper fractions. When he added the denominator as well, the teacher becomes aware that the student does not grasp the concept of fraction which relates to part-whole relationships. The denominator is only describing the 'size' of the whole and does not contribute to the actual quantity of the fraction (e.g. 1/12 is much smaller than 1/7).

Results from a meta-analysis (Keith & Frese, 2008) of 24 studies that explicitly utilised errors as a tool for training showed that the error-based approach may be more effective than error-avoidance (i.e. trying to get the answer correct) when helping learners to apply learning to new situations. What the study suggests is that by facilitating learners to identify and manage these errors head-on, the learners are more able to manage their performance when it comes to new situations when errors may occur at a significantly higher rate than a familiar context.

Hence, one of the characteristics of the **DELETE** (*Designing Errors for Learning and Teaching*) approach is to capitalise on typical and atypical errors to direct the learner's attention to specific error-prone sequences or areas in the curriculum. By doing so, it is expected learner's motivation and interest in the topic will increase, along with learning effectiveness since the outcomes may be unexpected. As what the experiment described above suggests, learners generally become more alert to the unexpected stimulus and put in the attention to learn better. While this sounds more cognitive than psychological, the increased resilience and confidence that comes from being cognitively prepared can make a big difference during moments of crisis.

By intentionally subjecting learners to different types of possible errors within a safe learning environment, it is equivalent to immunising the learners through small doses of 'paper-based shocks' so that in the event that a variant of any of these situations were to arise, the learners can fast track their thinking and move ahead quickly to the crux of the matter because prior thinking has already been carried out during the DELETE training sessions. Hence, when using DELETE to train psychological resilience, the focus is on helping learners to develop their reasoning processes and confidence in managing these novel situations. Getting learners to consider different perspectives to the situation may be useful in helping learners eliminate the unhelpful options later if these situations do occur. Described below is an example of how DELETE can used to strengthen the psychological resilience of people to deal with unexpected outcomes. I must also emphasise that regular practice and reflection on the part of the person is key to maintaining that cognitive sharpness and psychological resilience.

> *"The failure to change in good time and in good times is the triumph of complacency or the shortage of courage ...."*
>
> **Mr Lim Siong Guan**
> (2013, p. 195)

The following is a case which may be useful as an example in

Developing Emotion

building up learners' psychological resilience to unexpected outcomes. The context for this case is that you, as the learner, may be currently the main caregiver for your parents while the other siblings are still supportive by contributing financially and caring for them on the odd weekends. Given that the situation is still manageable, how do we (as hospital or community support officers) prepare caregivers for different scenarios whereby the current caregiver may end up being the sole caregiver with limited resources to continue with the level of care for the patient? This case is to achieve a certain level of preparedness on the part of the caregiver so that appropriate discussions can take place, while times are still good.

Video Case Part 1

As the sole breadwinner in your family, you take good care of your dependents because you feel an obligation to do so. At times, you wonder if you should ask your siblings to take on some of these roles such as taking your elderly parents to the doctor or cleaning their home to reduce the likelihood of lice and vermin. However, over time, your siblings become desensitised and less willing to chip in to take care of your parents due to time constraints and increasing job demands. Everyone, except you, is pushing the responsibility around. You sense that your parents are feeling a sense of rejection. Just a few months, your father has become quite bed ridden.

"... things have gotten somewhat awkward now since Mom and I are no longer so mobile and depend on you and others to help us move around or even to take us to the toilet. It is not easy for you, just as it is not easy for us. I hope you understand that. When you were young, we took care of you without wanting to burden you in our old age. There is really no need to take care of us when we are old. We can get the maid to help us. We are fine. I am just so glad that we have you as our child. We love you."

His cancer is now at Stage 4 and the pain appears unbearable. On the previous page is an excerpt of a letter you received from your father...

Reflections

1. What are the three possible endings which may result from the above scenario?
2. How will you respond to each of these three endings?
3. How do you try to engineer the best possible ending for your parents and siblings?
4. What would happen if the worst ending occurred? How would you feel and react?

Video Case Part 2
Continuation from the case ...

Unfortunately, this was the parting letter before your parents took their own lives by an overdose of sleeping pills. They left together, laying on their bed as they did so, with a slight smile on their faces. They did not want to be a burden to anyone, especially their beloved children. Leaving together was the best way they knew how.

Reflections

1. How will you respond now to this ending?
2. How will you perceive your siblings' role in contributing to this ending? What about your own role?
3. How will you do things differently if you knew that your parents intended to take their lives?
4. Finally, what is the likelihood of the above ending occurring to you in your current situation?
5. How are you going to respond now?

Developing Emotion

The learners can present their responses to the class, for their peers to give inputs and support. Following which, the facilitator will share self-directed learning resources for theory building. The facilitator will pose questions to glean insights from the learners, check understanding and cover knowledge gaps pertaining to caring for the seniors.

In the final stage of the lesson, the learners will proceed to apply their learning to their own context, to identify key issues, make a plan caring for their own relatives and suggest areas of change to better cope with the downstream transitions.

While the earlier case appears to be somewhat extreme, it was intentional to provide an element of 'shock' so that some immunity and thinking through can take place, in order to prepare the learner for possible difficulties ahead. It is not unlike scenario planning although in the intention here goes beyond just preparing cognitively for the eventualities, but to focus on building psychological resilience, especially for instances where the learner may not have many choices to act upon.

Referencing the DELETE Model, can you find the four elements in the above DELETE scenario? What are the type of error, the type of task, the engagement process and type of support?

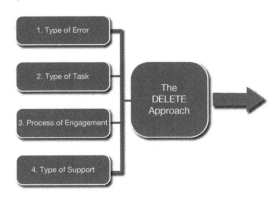

The type of error based on the 3 Cs model is Critical, Uncommon and Clear. The error is in the affective domain, underpinned by cognitive analysis (involving critical reflection).

The task is to engage with the learner's affective (emotive) domain by triggering specific beliefs concerning caring for relatives and predicting errors (to build metacognitive capability). The engagement process is the DELETE Error Engagement and Experimentation (E^3) Learning Cycle with the error mentioned after the first round of information presentation but without the error being presented. The type of support can be peer inputs, guided by reflection questions.

Conclusion

The scenario shown is one out of the many possible means of DELETE approach. By varying any of the four elements in the DELETE approach, you can achieve a wide permutation of designing and implementing the learning activity, to achieve the corresponding learning outcomes. While the affective domain is not as common in adult education, it will increase in importance in the future as AI takes over some of the cognitive tasks. One key differentiator between humans and intelligent machines will be about values and beliefs in the affective domain.

Chapter 19
Developing Psychomotor Skills

Unlike developing cognitive skillsets, the DELETE approach to developing psychomotor skills targets behavioural responses, which have a larger kinaesthetic component. Hence, the learner's ability to carry out the physical task according to the required standard will be the focus here, in this chapter. Naturally, when we discuss the development of physical skillsets, it will not exclude the need to hone the finer aspects of psychomotor accuracy, consistency and dexterity, just like how time and effort are required to develop cognitive competencies. Psychomotor training involves cognitive processing, especially where decision-making is needed to determine how to execute the movements. Hence, the DELETE approach will view the training of psychomotor skills in a holistic manner, with the cognitive skill development underpinning the performance.

Psychomotor

i. *To Develop Behavioural Responses to Situations and Errors*
ii. *To Increase Reflexivity to Errors*

The psychomotor training of accurate behavioural responses and the reflexivity to errors are described in an authentic approach to using DELETE in the healthcare industry where nurses and first aiders have to learn cardiopulmonary resuscitation (CPR). The first segment of the case outlines the behavioural training using typical errors while the second

Chapter 19

segment focuses on the behaviours of these first aiders and nurses in responding to situations and issues arising from errors. The third segment addresses the speed of responses to these situations.

Case on Psychomotor Training

Progression from Level 1 (training correct responses to casualty situations for novices) to Level 2 (responding to critical errors during casualty situations) and finally to Level 3 (responding in a timely fashion to critical errors) is determined by the learner's readiness (see Table 20). He or she may decide to repeat Level 1 numerous times before going on to Level 2. The rationale for having three levels is made stronger by the fact that a number of these first aiders and nurses have to refresh their skills every two to three years based on regulation. Hence, moving them up the expertise ladder makes sense, to help them gain mastery of the skillsets.

By utilizing the error-based learning approach, these first aiders and nurses are trained to respond quickly, have metacognitive awareness and

Table 20. Psychomotor Competencies for the Levels of Novice to Expert

Level 1 - for the Novice	Level 2 - for the Competent	Level 3 - for the Experienced

• To learn the basics of CPR with little error infusion • Ensure competence before going to Level 2 • Determine level of confidence and clarity to reduce possible confusion when errors are introduced	• To acquire mastery through infusion of error-based learning (DELETE) • Focus on the psychomotor process of CPR with reflection questions to drive learning • Conduct detailed debrief through discussions with expert instructors in final session	• To acquire mastery through timeliness of resonses • Increase pressure by reducing time allocated • Build metacognitive awareness of potential issues by introducing other possible consequences and eliciting decisions

be ready for any unpredictable situations which may arise (e.g. relatives objecting to the female casualty being touched by the male first aider).

Progression from Level 1 to Levels 2 and 3

1) Level 1 — *For the Novice*
   - Cognitive checks — recite procedure
   - Model the expert to carry out sequences of actions
   - Practise accuracy of actions within time limits
   - Reflect based on feedback

2) Level 2 — *For the Competent*
   a) Error-based psychomotor checks and responses
   b) Learners are to demonstrate their skillsets; Facilitators will inject errors into the routine and the learners are to respond accordingly (see Table 21 for errors)

3) Level 3 — *For the Experienced*
   a) Complex error-based psychomotor responses within time limits
   b) Learners are to exhibit metacognitive planning, monitoring and evaluation (Pre-error and Error phases — to detect anomalies and respond accordingly)

Content for the CPR Programme

Three parts to the content:

a) Check for danger and prepare victim for CPR
b) Begin CPR (within 120s timeline)
c) Handover to ambulance or paramedics

Learning Object is an interactive e-resource for learners to engage in self-directed learning prior to or after the classroom training, in this case.

Table 21. Example of Psychomotor Competencies Cardiopulmonary Resuscitation

	Segments	Difficult Concepts/Skillsets	Manner of Instruction (Level 1 — for Novice)	Manner of Instruction (Levels 2 and 3 — for Competent and Experienced)	Description of Errors and Metacognitive Checks
A	Check and prepare victim for CPR	1. Open airway 2. Seal mouth 3. Call for ambulance 4. Ensure safety of all	Video Clip (with correct demonstration) Learning Object (theory)	Video Clip (with errors) — stopped at specific points for learner to take over Feedback video by expert on errors (triggered when errors are not addressed) Video Clip (with reflection questions)	Forgot to ask bystanders to search for AED Checking the pulse first and then breathing rather than concurrently Not tilting head back sufficiently Q: What may happen next? (*metacognition*)
B	Begin CPR (120s)	5. Position self 6. Right pace 7. Complete CPR cycle	Video Clip (with correct demonstration) Interview with expert on proper procedure (theory)	Video Clip (with errors) Feedback video with expert on errors (triggered when errors are not addressed)	Arms are bent during chest compression Wrong counting rhythm Casualty was turned away from first aider to recovery position Q: What may happen next? (*metacognition*)
C	Handover Procedure	8. Documentation	Learning object (conditional branching)	Learning object with errors (conditional branching)	Forgot to give documentation to ambulance staff

Debrief

Due to the high degree of psychomotor skills in CPR, it is suggested that the learners watch the video clips with the correct demonstration before they attempt to practise on the mannequin. The facilitator will observe and give feedback to the learners during and after the demonstration. After completing level 1 where learners are somewhat competent, they move into level 2 where they are to watch the demonstrator carefully for errors in the procedures. At a specific point, the demonstrator stops, and the learner is asked to comment on what may happen to the casualty. After the verbal response, the learner takes over to manage the situation and to rectify the errors where possible.

Metacognitive regulation through pre-error checks is developed by exposing the learners to reflective questions prior to each segment in level 2. Subsequently, the learners are timed to rectify the errors and mitigate any negative consequences as well as complete the psychomotor procedure within specific timeframes to achieve efficiency and effectiveness. Lives could be compromised if the procedures are not carried out in a timely fashion.

The learners are expected to complete the training with consultations with the facilitators to close any gaps and for pre-assessment briefing. Some of the reflections include restating the importance of certain procedures and how the errors (e.g. bent arms in chest compression) highlight the negative impact on the casualty's well-being.

Rationale for the DELETE Approach in CPR Training

You may question the rationale for using DELETE approach in CPR training since it is highly likely that the same first aider will start and end the resuscitation procedure with the casualty. Why bother with rectifying errors if the trained first aider should not make those errors in the first place? In fact, the value of the DELETE approach lies not so much in the rectification process although that is still important, but in the reflection

Chapter 19

and review of why certain procedures are carried out as such. It is only through errors (i.e. boundaries of the SOPs are breached) when the learner appreciates the importance of following the SOPs. For example, pressing with bent arms when carrying chest compressions results in less force being transferred to the chest and a less effective compression. The heart is not sufficiently compressed to push blood out to the vital organs including the brain. Understanding the effect of this error deepens the learning for the learner. More importantly, if there are variations in the situation (e.g. casualty with knife in chest, broken ribs or is trapped in a face-down position), the first aider can go back to first principles which in this case, would be to get blood to the vital organs regardless.

Physically getting the learner to address the errors (e.g. performing the chest compressions despite having a knife stuck in the chest) ensures the learners are competent with the behavioural response within a timeframe required to get the job done well.

Referencing the DELETE Model, can you find the four elements in the above DELETE scenarios? What are the types of error, the types of task, the engagement process and types of support?

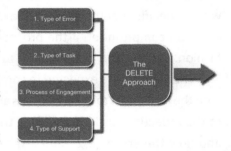

For the error of compressing the chest with bent arms, the type of error based on the 3 Cs model is critical, common and clear. The error is in the psychomotor domain (likely *manipulation* level where learner is still memorising the steps).

The task is to identify and rectify the error of bent arms when performing external compression, within the video context. The engagement process is likely Kolb's experiential learning cycle with the error presented to the learner as a trigger and the theory to ensure learners practise the right method of compression. The demonstration by the learner is the final stage of application of the learning. The type of support can be via peer and facilitator inputs, guided by the video resource.

Conclusion

The scenarios are shown as a series of errors presented intentionally in sequence, to 'overwhelm' the learner, so that the stimuli are authentic, and the pressure exerted on the first aider reflects real life context. The challenge is stopping the demonstration to elicit the responses from the learner to understand the decision-making process. One option is to ask the learner to verbalise the thinking so that the peers and facilitator can follow the logic of the psychomotor decisions made by the learner.

The psychomotor performance often involves manipulating equipment and tools. With error-based learning, the design of the error can be about the tool (e.g. tool is faulty) and the way in which the learner uses the tools.

Chapter 20
Developing Sociality and Interpersonal Skills

Social learning and collaborative skills are important 21st-century competencies, which emplace the learner within the social work environment where managing others and oneself will be needed to get the job done. Keeping oneself firmly within the social fabric of work teams is one way to acquire new competencies where work can drive learning, especially if feedback is forthcoming and constructive. The positive strokes that come from positive team vibes and achievement are useful motivators to get us moving along on the career trajectory that is expected to be unpredictable and potentially rewarding if we are adaptive and forward-looking.

For the purpose of discussion, the DELETE approach can be used to develop your competencies in the Sociality domain at the team and the individual levels:

Sociality

i. *To Develop Teamwork Within Teams*
ii. *To Cultivate Collaborative Skills for Individuals*

Naturally, the teamwork competencies will require the team to develop the skills together, thereby focusing on the cohesion and synergies within the team.

Chapter 20

i. *To Develop Teamwork Within Teams*

Complex work is often completed through teams as tasks get more layered, requiring deep expertise, from contributors, sometimes with teams in other countries and time zones. Hence, using errors to build team spirit and inculcate the synergy among team members, helping each other to look out for potential errors and pitfalls is one possible useful outcome from DELETE.

For example, we can get the team to work as individual members to resolve an error and determine the quality of the combined work compared to having them to work together as a team to resolve the error. While the latter may or may not help resolve the error faster, the process of solving the error is likely to be different due to the team dynamics at play. How to make the difference count can be explored and enhanced so that teamwork can result in a better resolution process for everyone, including an improved problem-solving capability of the entire team. Part of this process will also involve understanding how each member operates and the strengths that he or she brings to the team. The way in which each person resolves the error can be analysed by the entire team so

> The Institute of Medicine (1999) published a study stating that between 40,000 and 50,000 people die in hospitals a year as a result of human error and poor coordination among healthcare providers. In view of the high fatality rates, considerable research on teamwork within the field of medicine (e.g., Carayon, 2012; Gaba, 2000; Manser, 2009) has been conducted to mitigate human error. By focusing on the deployment of team training programmes (Kanki *et al.*, 2010), both the healthcare and aviation communities have conducted targeted research to understand the factors that lead to human error and how training can be used as an effective countermeasure. The results seemed to indicate that training can lead to life-saving consequences.

that in a strength-based approach, future resolution processes can allow members to operate based on their strengths with minimal overlaps among members, resulting in more efficient and effective teamwork.

Case
Learning Outcome
The team members work together to mindfully spot and cover each other's failings, resulting in stronger ownership of the work by the team members.

Context to be Given to the Team Leader
You are the Academic Director for a training organisation, taking charge of the quality of the programmes offered to the adult learners. One of the key performance indicators in your portfolio is to ensure that the programmes are refreshed every three years to meet the changing needs of the industry. As the three-year timeline is drawing near, you have activated your three teams of academic advisors and consultants to review the 30 programmes (10 programmes per team) offered by your organisation based on a list of five criteria:

- relevance to industry
- frequency of runs (as proxy for popularity)
- quality of curriculum
- learner feedback
- potential for growth

Their role is to use the checklist to determine the current standard of the programmes based on their specific subject matter expertise. In addition, reports and data (tweaked to include errors and irregularities) are provided to the teams for their evaluation. These consultants and advisors also engage with the faculty and learners to obtain feedback from the ground. The deliverable is a three-page report on each programme which will then put together with the other programme reports for submission to the senior management of the training organisation.

The three teams are given one month to come up with the report and recommendation for the Academic Director to make the necessary decision. Together as a unit, they conducted a brainstorming session to detect any patterns observed from the data collected. At the two-week mark, the teams are to provide an interim scan sheet to give an indication of their findings and the general direction the teams are taking.

First Injection to the Project/Role Play

Upon submission of their interim scan sheet, the academic director issues an announcement that it was recently uncovered that some of the trainers have been enticing the learners to give positive feedback on the training they attended. Two key questions are asked by the Academic Director:

- Did any team spot irregularities in the data and reports given to them? Why or why not?
- What do the teams need to be mindful of when conducting the evaluation process, as part of the reflective practice?

The teams are to submit their answers to the Academic Director together with the report at the end of the four weeks, as scheduled. Once the submissions are in, the reports are then handed to the other teams for review and comments.

Second Injection to the Project/Role Play

- Did any team realise if anything else was wrong with the evaluation process or the reports?
- More importantly, can they identify and remedy any errors made over the past three years and were not detected till then?

- One of the educators attempted to excuse his behaviour by downplaying the seriousness and trivialising his 'joke' with the learners at the end of the lesson

Debrief

Following the evaluation exercise, the three teams are asked to reflect on their learning through the exercise. Some of the key take-aways for the teams could be:

- Being more mindful when looking through the data and reports
- Be close to the ground to identify educators who embrace wrong values or show a lack of integrity
- Working with other team members to spot possible errors
- Taking a more proactive role when carrying their work and not to take senior management's word as always correct

The facilitator presents a teamwork model for the team to link their experience with the theory. The learners determine their gaps in communication, sharing information and resolving conflicts. Following which, the team members proceed to work on a task together (e.g. to rework the evaluation process) and apply their learning.

Through this DELETE approach, the objective is to strengthen the teamwork by working round core values, and developing mindfulness with the teams undertaking change and innovation at work.

ii. *To Cultivate Collaborative Skills for Individuals*
Likewise, at the individual level, there is a need for each member to develop strong collaborative skills. Knowing when to support others and when to stand up to make your own voice heard are examples of workplace sensitivity. Supporting ideas of fellow colleagues is the easiest way to grow one's relationship with colleagues. At the same time, you also want to ensure that you maintain your objectivity in providing opinions and contribute by

adding value. Through dynamic error resolution, the team can work through issues with increased or decreased levels of stress and conflict designed into the team collaboration so that gaps and crack lines can be revealed and rectified. The level of trust can also be built up through the collaboration process through subsequent video analysis of the team building process.

> *"Once a certain level of trust has been built up, the next stage is to cultivate a strong collaborative culture within the workplace."*
>
> **Salas *et al.*** (2012, p. 79)

Injections of DELETE scenarios through weekly sharing sessions about how teams collaborate or fall apart due to individual member's contribution and/or destructive tirades can utilise a range of DELETE options:

- Describe the end outcome of a team (e.g. a team that collapsed when the pressure increased, with individual members carving out their own space and working alone to resolve their own issues. Get your team members to review the story and work backwards to suggest possible tipping points and what brought about the demise of the team being mentioned. Conversely, share a story about a successful team and ask your team members to suggest how this team came about, what measures they took to grow the team. What critical success factors made the difference? Get the team members to list the underpinning structures which could be present to limit the risk of members crossing the boundaries of team dynamics and interaction. What are these boundaries?
- Paint the dynamics and interactions of three teams with different personas and outcomes — where the goals were achieved in varying degrees, negatively correlated with the synergy of the teams. What it meant was that the team that achieved the highest output had the lowest level of synergy and likely, highly dominant players who drove the team hardest while the team with an average/acceptable

Developing Sociality and Interpersonal Skills

output displayed a very high level of cohesion and motivation. They worked together and took time to listen to each other's ideas and that contributed to a lower output, but the positive culture made the process more enjoyable.

Get your team members to review the teams' dynamics and debate the 'errors' made by the three teams and which team resonated with their own beliefs about team performance and purpose.

There are other possible means of designing scenarios with errors for teams to review. Role playing the scenarios as a team with respect and candour would also be useful to iron out differences and establish norms of behaviour. For example, there was a real story of a team member voicing her displeasure with receiving emails and text messages over weekends several months into the project. It took an email expressing her frustration that got the team to reflect on what the acceptable norms were. This was probably unnecessary to begin with and if norms were discussed and established at the onset, the process of regulating team dynamics might have gone on more smoothly.

> *Life can only be understood by looking backward;*
> *but it must be lived looking forward.*
>
> Søren Kierkegaard

Referencing the DELETE Model, can you find the four elements in the above DELETE scenarios? What are the types of error, the types of task, the engagement process and types of support for the error of enticing learners to give positive feedback on training evaluation scores?

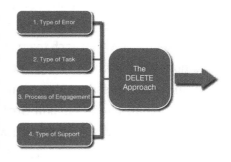

The type of error based on the 3 Cs model is non-critical, common and unclear. The error belongs to the social domain as the team needs to arrive at clear demarcation to what constitutes 'enticing' and is unacceptable. It would require the team to agree what the boundaries and rules are pertaining to learner evaluation.

The task is to conduct a discussion among the team members on the issue, to arrive at a consensus on the issue and issue the standards for all that adheres to in the subsequent training sessions. The engagement process is likely the DELETE E^3 learning cycle with the error presented to the learner early on, as an error trigger. The engagement of the learners and the learner experimentation of the social rule setting work to drive team cohesion and alignment. However, the rule setting session is not always uneventful. Some members could raise issues with the idea and get aggressive with others who oppose them. Hence, putting learners through the various scenarios, aids the formulation of social rules and establishes the process for doing so. A strong facilitator will be a useful support as teams need to be transparent in asking and answering difficult questions.

Conclusion

The social domain is often a neglected domain, when it comes to skills upgrading, often due to the need to address complex social structures and dynamics. However, it is an important area given the speed at which teams form and fall apart due to external and internal pressure. Team dynamics differs across teams so the use of DELETE approach requires contextualisation to the specific team characteristics. What are the needs for each team? How can each team leverage their strengths? What are the limitations and can errors be crafted to help strengthen those areas? These are some of the questions that each team needs to ask.

More than ever, the skill profiles of individuals and teams are scrutinised over and over again, to drive productivity and profits. What the DELETE approach does is to help individuals and teams focus on building up their strengths and address underlying weaknesses by using errors to target those areas. You tend to focus on the area in which the errors are located (e.g. social skills).

However, one should also not forget the integration of these skill gaps to make the holistic person. Our capabilities comprise the skills found across the various domains and overlaid together. As a result, the DELETE approach needs to drive holistic training of individuals across all or most domains. Let's take a look.

Chapter 21
Holistic Development — Beyond Competency

In the previous few chapters, we examined the development of competences in the critical areas of metacognitive, cognitive, affective, psychomotor and social domains through using the DELETE approach. This chapter will examine how we can integrate these critical areas for the holistic development of the individual, beyond competency to capability. How does an integrated DELETE approach look like? Listed below are three areas (out of many other possibilities) for discussion:

Holistic Development — Beyond Competency to Capability

　i. *To Integrate Skillsets Across Domains to Achieve Mastery for the Individual*
　ii. *To Diagnose Skill Gaps and Non-strengths*
　iii. *To Prepare the Individual for Future Skill Needs*

The purpose of the skillset integration is to develop holistic mastery to perform the job role.

i. *To Integrate Skillsets Across Domains to Achieve Mastery for the Individual*
By addressing all forms of competencies including metacognitive, adaptive thinking, creatical skills and attitude development in addition to the typical competency development, the individual will go beyond passing the assessments to performing effectively in the real world. What this means

is real job competence, which leads us to the purpose of this DELETE approach — to develop a person's capability to perform the job which is beyond task competency.

While most people may associate one's ability to implement tasks (e.g. writing a report and managing customers) as key to performing the job, we will be able to relate to skills which are not technical in nature, but are critical to complete the job (e.g. high level of emotional quotient to empathise with complaining customers, resilience and flexibility when instructions change suddenly). These are horizontal, cross-sectoral skills (sometimes known as 21st-century competencies), which keep a person in the job over the long term. These skills enable one to complete the job in a satisfactory manner. For example, having a poor attitude or an inflexible working style may offend clients and result in losses for the company. Doubtless, the worker may be able to perform the majority of tasks most of the time, but critical moments when engaging with customers or resolving complex problems determine if a worker gets promoted or fired. These are moments when performance matters. Depending on what horizontal skills, attitudes or beliefs need to be developed for the job role, the DELETE approach ensures these cross-domain skills are addressed within the appropriate work contexts.

Example of Holistic Development for Aircrew and Pilot

Training pilots and air crew can take a long time partly because there are numerous competencies which the pilots and air crew need to be familiar with. From understanding how the airplane works to reading the meters in the cockpit and serving irate passengers or to sense if there are any issues with the airplane, pilots and air crew face a litany of issues and are expected to resolve all of them. Hence, achieving competency for these workers in the air is not an option. The question is whether mastery is also expected. In view of the possible loss of lives from any error made by air crew and pilots, practitioners would argue that mastery is not a nice-to-have; it is a must-have. Some of the crew members should be experts at specific job tasks to lead the team in the event of any mishap. Being an expert at the trade implies that the person is able to draw from his or her wealth of experience and deal with any unexpected incidents. The training of metacognitive ability to spot danger cues early, the honing of the individual's decision-making skills during the error and post-error phases and the development of emotional and sociality domains to work as a team underpinned by strong moral values are capabilities that pilots and air crew will need in an emergency.

How then, does the DELETE approach work for these workers in the air? Metacognition is a critical capability that air crew need in order to be aware and to spot passengers who may pose a threat to other passengers. The capability to decide quickly, followed by the actions to be taken needs to be developed. To grow the emotional domain, there needs to be a clear set of affective areas to be targeted. For example, a deep concern for passengers' lives and safety, courage to sacrifice self in order to save others, having the discipline to sleep sufficiently and avoid intoxicants before flights are important professional values and beliefs which pilots and air crew need to embrace. In addition to these capabilities, how can designers inculcate other values and beliefs into air crew during the training process?

Case

One hour before the flight home, Captain Tom found out to his shock, that his wife and five-year-old son were involved in an automobile accident back home. They were back-seat passengers in a car driven by a friend when a truck rear-ended them and sent the car flying forward more than 10m. Both mother and child were rushed to the hospital with life-threatening injuries. They were undergoing surgery at the point when the aircraft was undergoing preparation for flight. Captain Tom was severely shaken and informed the flight authorities and his superiors about his predicament. As there was no other Flight Captain available to take over his flight and it was also the earliest flight home, Captain Tom was advised to fly the plane but leave most of the flying to his co-pilot. Besides, it would be extremely expensive for the budget airline to postpone the flight to find another pilot. Captain Tom accepted the recommendation reluctantly, but he was not in

Chapter 21

the most optimal state to fly the plane. Thankfully, it was not a full plane, and the co-pilot took on most of the responsibilities in conducting the pre-flight checks. At the same time, Captain Tom was anxious and constantly distracted by messages on his phone. He did notice that his co-pilot was not familiar with all the procedures and had asked the control tower a couple of odd-sounding and irrelevant questions. Captain Tom attributed it to the co-pilot being transferred recently from another type of plane to the A320. Finally, the plane took off in good weather. There was little that Captain Tom could do except to sit tight throughout the 6-hour flight.

Midway through the flight, the chief flight attendant notified the cockpit that a passenger was getting rowdy and wanted to see the Captain. His co-pilot left the cockpit to attend to the passenger. Captain Tom then took over to monitor the flying, which was on autopilot anyway.

Q: What can possibly happen? What workflows were being contravened? What should Captain Tom or the co-pilot have done instead? Discuss with your team members.

He could hear the argument escalating between the passenger and the co-pilot behind the locked cockpit doors and wondered what was happening. Through the intercom, the chief flight stewardess informed him that the passenger wanted to see the Captain and kept shouting despite being told to quieten down. Finally, Captain Tom told the co-pilot to take over while he attended to the irate passenger.

Q: What can possibly happen? What workflows were being contravened? What should Captain Tom or the co-pilot have done instead? Role play with your team members for 10 min, what Captain Tom should have done.

When he walked out of the cockpit, Captain Tom realised that it wasn't just one passenger but four in total who wanted redress. There were three middle-aged men and a 10-year-old girl. They wanted to fly to a neighbouring country to ask for political asylum. It would take a 3 h detour but it was on the way, they claimed. Returning to their country of origin would result in them being detained and imprisoned. They looked desperate and knelt on the floor in plea for assistance. The conversation took more than 50 minutes and by the time Captain Tom managed to convince them that they needed to talk to the authorities after they have landed, he was exhausted. Besides needing to manage these issues, his mind was still preoccupied by the state of his injured wife and son.

Returning to the cockpit, he was greeted by the sight of his co-pilot looking intently at the gauges. 'Is anything wrong'? he asked. The co-pilot shook his head but did not look up. As Captain Tom took his seat and took a quick glance at their location. He was horrified to find that they were behind schedule and they were losing fuel fast. A quick check showed that the plane was flying too low, creating a lot more drag than necessary. The amount of fuel left was barely sufficient to reach the destination but even then, it had to be in good weather. The alternative was to land and re-fuel at a nearer airport before flying again which meant possibly 3 more hours before he could reach home.

Q: Were there other options? What should Captain Tom do? If you were Captain Tom, would you take the risk to fly back home or refuel? Work on the flight simulation to perform flight recovery. How would you fly the plane now?

Taking hold of the controls, Captain Tom took the option to fly home direct since the weather reports indicated fair weather. He instructed the co-pilot to look out for inclement weather ahead. Feeling anxious, he flew higher and at a faster speed to make up for the lost time. However, that also meant that fuel consumption was not optimal and the risk of not making it to the airport became higher.

Chapter 21

Q: What should the co-pilot do? Should he interfere and ask the Captain to land at the earlier airport, since it was his fault to begin with? However, that would result in the airline losing tens of thousands of dollars in revenue and compensation. Can he afford that?

Subsequently, the plane landed with emergency vehicles on standby. The amount of fuel left was only 5 minutes' worth. Captain Tom was chastised and disciplined for failing to put his passengers' safety before his own concerns. He was also demoted along with his co-pilot for risking more than 80 lives.

In this case study, the learner's metacognitive capability is tested through questions posed at specific points in the activity. Learner reflections provide the deepening of learning and the application to work contexts. There could be many other possible endings to the scenario presented, including the co-pilot crashing the plane or hijacking the plane, using the false accident as a ploy to distract the Captain. Hence, in the pre-error phase, taking the learners through the considerations in order to develop their metacognitive capability could be the focus, according to the case above. Regardless of whether the predictions were right or wrong, the process of being aware and to plan ahead is more important. The focus is in developing metacognition where air crew learn to be *alert* to any changes in standard procedures and potential consequences. Hence, taking pre-emptive measures to mitigate any risks is dependent one's *understanding* of the first principles to the procedures.

In the error phase, the manner in which the Captain responded to the dilemma is the focus, coupled with the consequence of risking his passengers' lives. Was the Captain putting his concern for his family above that for his family? What if the passengers perished? Would that be more costly than any time savings? While there was little description of the 'rectification' process due to the safe landing of the plane, the consequences of demotion are also worth reviewing for the level of 'worth-it-ness'. These would be questions for reflection and more 'experimentation' so that better outcomes could be achieved during the learning process.

In the post-error phase, learners engage in experimentation (reviewing other possible actions) leveraging the first principles (e.g. passengers' safety and equipment reliability) to govern the Captain's actions. In this phase, the learners focus on shaping their reasoning process, in view of the limited information provided to the Captain at that point in time. Values such as respect for passengers' lives should be inculcated during this phase.

ii. *To Diagnose Skill Gaps and Non-strengths*
Using the same case described above, you can also design the learning to diagnose skill gaps and non-strengths. Based on the responses to the questions, the learner's skill gaps (e.g. metacognitive ability to pick up contextual cues and evaluate danger) can be ascertained. Likewise, the learner's ability to propose reasonable rectification options or to apply social skills can also be diagnosed and documented. The critical aspect to achieving this outcome is having a comprehensive framework of required skills which can be used as a list of competencies for diagnosis. To some extent, this approach will be similar to a situational test although the errors will generally make the situations more volatile, requiring more on-the-spot thinking and reflex responses.

Unlike the first outcome (to integrate skillsets across domains), this second outcome is to diagnose skill gaps across domains. The trigger to elicit learners' skills (and possible gaps) needs to be holistic, covering a range of skills stretching into cognition, affective, sociality (and psychomotor, if necessary) domains. In the earlier example, the review of the emotive factor (e.g. worrying about wife and child) and how it impacts the Captain's responses is part of the affective considerations, besides the technical considerations (e.g. sufficient fuel to last the trip) and sociality factor (i.e. whether to trust the co-pilot's competency in spite of initial apprehensions).

iii. *To Prepare the Individual for Future Skill Needs*
Finally, to prepare individuals to cope with the challenges ahead is always a tall order. In the first place, knowing what the future challenges are can be difficult, given the ever-changing world that we live in today. These

capabilities such as having a mindset for innovation and creativity, specific technical skills to develop cybersecurity and automation and other service-oriented industry such as nursing may be in high demand going forward. As such, developing these capabilities using the DELETE approach, so that individuals reach a level of mastery is politically and economically logical from the perspective of setting national policies. Helping the individual learner to develop a diversified set of capabilities (such as flexibility and metacognition) to cope with new challenges in a VUCA landscape is nevertheless, an important economic strategy.

In the case of the pilot training, the trainee pilots will have to review their professional values and belief system pertaining to the value of human lives compared to the value they place on their own families. It is a dilemma. If the latter is more important, perhaps another job may be more suitable since pilots have to be away from their families for a high proportion of time. By constantly asking the trainees to review their value system, it prepares them professionally for the long term as they make important decisions in their career or during their work based on sound values.

Similarly, metacognitive development by getting learners to review their underlying assumptions (e.g. to always trust their co-pilot) may be useful. It is about developing a healthy sense of checking assumptions to pre-empt downstream issues. By promoting the holistic development of the individual, moving him or her from competency to capability, DELETE distinguishes itself from typical training approaches, which usually focus on developing skillsets and knowledge compared to holistic development of expertise across domains.

Summary

The integration of competences through the DELETE approach will require learning design skills which may not be commonly found in most designers. Thinking out of the box, with an emphasis on incorporating contexts, tasks and errors that may be outside of their routine job scope, will require exceptional design skill. For the learner, it is this capability, to do the job well that differentiates the responsible from the nonchalant, the capable from the somewhat able and the willing from the non-committal. With the DELETE approach, learners can be developed further in their thinking, problem-solving contexts, macro perspective-taking and attitude formation to become a more holistic and thinking worker or student.

This section of the book has provided key reasons and cases to illustrate how the following areas can be used for learning from errors:

a) Metacognition
b) Cognition
c) Psychomotor
d) Emotion
e) Social
f) Holistic Development

Having examined the various use cases through the DELETE approach to achieve different types of learning outcomes, we will next switch focus to look at how we can design the errors for learning to improve performance. Errors are platforms whereby we can check and reflect on the process and what we can do to change the situation. They present useful opportunities for us to make good what has gone wrong or can go wrong. Hence, being mindful becomes critical to help us respond quickly when the solutions become less clear cut and are more convoluted. In this regard, designing the right errors to enhance the learning and mindfulness process, to spring on threats and capitalise on mistakes to improve performance. In the long run, it is on an important role, from prime learners and facility managers.

It is also critical to consider that the DELETE approach goes beyond just error design but that it comprises *the entire learning process*, including the manner in which the *error presentation*, is infused into the case study. The key factor is to consider carefully to ensure learning is deep and sustainable. The next few chapters will illustrate how the learning process can be designed by capitalising on the error as a stimulus for active learning.

Part 6

Selecting and Designing the Errors to Trigger Reflection and Learning

Part 6

We have covered over several chapters key concepts on the designing of the learning process using the DELETE approach to achieve learning outcomes across various domains including metacognition.

In this segment of the book, we will examine the construction of the errors and the tasks designed to facilitate the achievement of the learning outcomes. To achieve constructive alignment, these learning outcomes should be made visible, where the intentional error design will then point the learners to acquire the expected skillsets.

Specifically, we will examine how errors and the accompanying parameters can be designed and presented, as complete, partial (static or dynamic) or absent. These parameters as shown in Table 22 are:

Table 22. Error Design and Four Other Design Parameters in DELETE Approach

	What Does This Mean?
Context	The scenario in which the error is framed within and this context can refer to the organisation, job role, topic (e.g. Math problem), issue and outcomes expected etc. Providing the context aids the learner in setting up a mental structure to go about resolving the error and to achieve the outcomes
Workflow	The part of the process in which the error occurs. This workflow may be known as the SOP or rule. Questioning the workflow is part of the error-based learning approach.
Error	What is wrong although errors can be partially hidden from the learners to stimulate curiosity and endeavour to find the issue and error
Rectification	The efforts to correct the error can be useful information as the boundaries to the workflow/SOP/rule are made clearer if the rectification efforts work or do not work
Consequence	The eventual outcome from the error and/or the rectification efforts is feedback to the learner on the issues encountered and how far from the expected outcome as caused by the error

Selecting and Designing the Errors to Trigger Reflection and Learning

Table 23. The Visibility and Dynamism Dimensions in the Error Design Considerations

Complete	Partial Static	Partial Dynamic	Absent
The relevant information (e.g. context) is completely presented to the learner. This option requires learners to determine what information is more critical, informing the decisions to be taken and the learning of the skill.	The relevant information is partially revealed at the start. There is no further information provided as this is a 'static' option (like a snapshot of the issue), which makes this design more straightforward when it comes to unpacking the issues, workflow and error.	The relevant information is partially revealed and will be further revealed as the case unfolds. The 'dynamic' presentation implies the information is dished out over time, likely over several phases, making this option more challenging and interesting.	When the information is absent, the learner needs to make assumptions. On one hand, it presents some challenges to guess but leaving out some of the less critical information keeps the design streamlined and likely, simpler for learners to unpack the issues.

The *Visibility* (*Completely shown*, *Partial* and *Absent*) and the *Dynamism* levels (*Static* and *Dynamic*) are the variations that designers can consider when presenting the errors and the parameters listed in Table 23. What do these imply for the learning experience? Let's dive deeper.

Chapter 22
Linking Error Design with Learning Outcomes: Metacognition

There are numerous permutations of error designs based on the Visibility and Dynamism dimensions. We will examine some use cases of how these permutations can lead to different Error Designs as described below based on the learning outcomes that were described in the earlier chapters for the various domains:

a) **Metacognition**
   i. *To Hone Metacognitive and Predictive Ability*
      — the learner must constantly determine *whether* a solution is forthcoming, and whether he or she is on the right track when analysing and predicting the error. Some possible permutations to develop the learner's metacognitive and predictive ability include (see the ticks):

Table 24. Permutations of Design Parameters to Hone Metacognitive and Predictive Ability

	Complete	Partial Static	Partial Dynamic	Absent
Context	✓	✓		
Workflow		✓	✓	
Error			✓	
Rectification			✓	
Consequence			✓	

What the table indicates is that context can be presented completely or partially (static). The partial workflow can be presented in a static or dynamic manner. The error, rectification and consequence should be presented in a partial dynamic manner, unfolding over time.

With the gradual revealing of the workflow, error, rectification and consequence to the learner, the learner will need to predict what is going to happen next based on the limited information given at that point in time. The learner also needs to check his or her own assumptions and beliefs to ensure all grounds are covered, just like how an investigator needs to question the information sources and to gather other data where possible.

To be clear, there are other possible permutations of information presentation to achieve the same outcomes, but what is shown in the table are likely to be the more straightforward options, which laypersons can adopt and implement easily.

The reason this approach is suitable for the development of metacognitive/predictive skill is that the learner attempts to identify and resolve the upcoming or evolving errors before the errors is full blown, or if the workflow has gone off track and is making the context and error worse. To control the situation, the learner must possess a strong foundation in the concepts and theories underpinning the work process. In addition, one's experience with the nature of the problem is critical.

> Typically, ants do not walk about blindly in a reactive fashion. They predict if a particular route will yield possible returns (i.e. food) by constantly picking up cues from the environment (e.g. tremors or taste of food molecules in the air). Often, they feel their way as they move forward.

This approach is to sensitise the learners' ability to monitor and evaluate the development of a solution by constantly comparing with what they are familiar with or what they have experienced. Hence, the learner needs to spot the error *before* or *when* it is just about to occur. To present the scenario according to this approach, it may be most effective to do

Linking Error Design with Learning Outcomes: Metacognition

this as a video case so that learners can stop the video clip at any point in time to indicate when they feel the error is about to occur and rewind accordingly or propose a new course of action. As such, the permutations of error design depicted in Table 24 can be used to develop mindfulness, hone metacognition and predictive skillsets.

ii. *To Develop Ability to Evaluate Contexts and Assumptions*
   — identifying contextual cues and assumptions to review current workflows and the boundaries to these workflows

It is not uncommon to hear of errors which stem from workers following the correct procedures as lay down by the organisation. These errors arise as a result of 'blindly' following workflows or SOPs and not taking exceptions into consideration. These exceptions are too numerous to be fully documented and they usually vary with contexts. These varying situations do require workers to be flexible, mindful and empowered to make the decisions to deviate from the workflows in non-standard contexts.

To illustrate, the following is a true story of how a training administrator nearly made an error by merely following SOPs. This officer was in charge of learner enrolments for workshops and the guiding principle was that once the number of enrolments has reached the stipulated figure, no new enrolments can be allowed. Some of the workshops were extremely popular and hence, were well subscribed to. There was a workshop on e-learning that fell into this category and registration was closed a few weeks before the date of the workshop. Two days before the workshop, the personal assistant of the CEO of a public listed company called up to enquire about enrolling her CEO into the workshop. The reply from the administrator, following SOPs, was not unexpected. There was an apology followed by rejection of the request for enrolment. Credit to her, the personal assistant was persistent and made a phone call to the administrator to make an exception for her CEO. Subsequently, with approval from his superior, the administrator allowed the personal assistant to register her CEO for the workshop. Given that about 20% of the registrants would be absent for various reasons, it was quite possible to allow the CEO into the workshop if space constraint was an issue. More importantly, having the CEO attend the workshop provided useful links for future collaboration between the training provider and the listed company. From the training organisation's perspective, it would have been an error on the part of the administrator in not making the exception to the rule in view of the potential businesses the connection could have brought in.

However, from the administrator's point of view, it can be a difficult decision to make since the SOPs are in place and the rest of the participants may experience discomfort if the room was too packed or the trainer to participant ratio was not ideal. It would take an experienced enrolment staff to know where the boundaries to the SOPs are and how to make those decisions and the kind of information needed to make exceptions if necessary.

Table 25 indicates how the parameters can be designed to facilitate the learners' ability to evaluate contexts and boundaries to the SOPs.

As with the example of the training administrator described earlier, the scenario can be presented with the context being partially presented (full class with no space and request came in only two days before workshop). As the learner makes certain decisions, new information comes in, with pressure from the personal assistant for the officer to grant an exception. There may also be a waiting list so should the administrator allow the CEO to leapfrog over the rest of the waiting list to join the class?

Table 25. Permutations of Design Parameters to Hone Ability to Evaluate Context and Assumptions

	Complete	Partial Static	Partial Dynamic	Absent
Context		✓	✓	✓
Workflow	✓			
Error	✓			
Rectification		✓	✓	
Consequence		✓	✓	

Linking Error Design with Learning Outcomes: Metacognition

What happens if there are complaints from other learners about the class being too cramped and unconducive for learning? The rectifications may also be included such as giving the CEO the first available date for the next run of the same workshop or providing the trainer to go to the CEO for an individual coaching session. The partial consequence could be that the CEO perceived the rejection as a slight and so, declines all other rectification or service recovery measures. What should the administrator do then?

As illustrated, the partial static context is presented with missing or wrong information. For partial dynamic contexts, the presentation of the context could be to have someone, or a group of persons articulate the problem through a video or verbally via a role player so that different perspectives are presented simultaneously. The learners are expected to spot what the issues are as the officer recalls the issues. The multi-fold issues related to the problem can then be related using different 'lenses' (akin to Brookfield's Four Lenses model to reflective practice). On the other hand, the complete workflow may be made known to the learner (e.g. no new registrants when class is full).

The advantage of this dynamic partial context is that there are a lot of possible answers that the learners can propose to address the issues in the context, with some of these answers being out of the box and unconventional. What is important is that the learners determine the contextual issues which led to the possible error. To obtain this level of competence, the learners must be able to associate the types of problems which lead to consequences. The rectifications and the accompanying consequences will also throw some light on the context that the scenario is operating within. Hence, a review of the contexts and workflow could ensue following the DELETE approach, if the scenario is authentic.

Conclusion

You may be getting the grasp of how the various parameters can be presented to good effect. Whether the information is presented completely,

Chapter 22

partially or not at all (absent) and in a dynamic or static manner, the learning experience will vary. In line with these permutations, the facilitator competency in bringing out the learning is critical. Asking reflexive questions for the purpose of eliciting responses to drive constructivist learning is part of the facilitator skillset. Similarly, if learners can play an active role in driving the learning and supporting each other's thinking, the outcomes can be achieved more effectively.

Chapter 23
Linking Error Design with Learning Outcomes: Cognition

Moving into the Cognition domain, the parameters and the information presentation remain the same although the outcomes for the Cognition domain are markedly different. Let's look at the four outcomes that we discussed earlier on in this book.

i. **To Strengthen Conceptual Understanding and Skillsets in Targeted Problematic Areas**
   — presenting scenarios from different perspectives to facilitate the acquisition of new insights

At the basic level, learners should be able to understand and identify an error within the context of the scenario presented. To keep the process simple, the context, workflow and error could be presented either completely or in partial (static) state (see Table 26) so that the learner can see the issue at the first reading or exposure. What is critical is the

Table 26. Permutations of Design Parameters to Strengthen Conceptual Understanding and Skillsets

	Complete	Partial Static	Partial Dynamic	Absent
Context	✓	✓		
Workflow	✓	✓		
Error	✓	✓		
Rectification				✓
Consequence				✓

way these three parameters are presented. To start, the learner will be put through the error-making process (pre-error, error presentation and post-error) with the context being part of the pre-error phase. However, the focus here is to strengthen conceptual understanding of the skillsets and issues involved. To do that, the reflection and subsequent theory-building components will provide support to the learners to explain why and how the errors occur. It is a good idea to keep the design simple and straightforward so that the learners do not get overwhelmed by the amount of information presented. Scaffold the activity for incremental learning to ensure the gradual acquisition of the concepts and skillsets. As such, the rectifications and consequences may be kept out of the picture too, if they do not value add to the learning process, at least until the debriefing stage where the learners may want to understand how the situation panned out and the consequences that followed.

The approach described is suitable for learners who are still grappling with the skillsets. The tasks designed in association with the error ought to focus on the lower levels of Bloom's Taxonomy such as comprehension (e.g. identification of error) and application (e.g. rectification of the error). On the other hand, if the learners are competent in the skillsets, then the strengthening of the skillsets and understanding can take on a more convoluted and complex approach.

Presenting the context, errors and workflow in a Partial (Dynamic) state could be effective in facilitating learner reflexivity while keeping these learners motivated to want to find out and investigate more. A description of the consequences and the rectification efforts would also help close the loop for these learners interested to know the outcome of the error.

ii. **To Develop 'Creative-Critical' Thinking Ability**
— adding missing information for creative solutioning process

Compared to the other approaches, this approach is interesting because the learners get to modify the context, which includes the problem

Table 27. Permutations of Design Parameters to Develop 'Creative-Critical' Thinking Ability

	Complete	Partial Static	Partial Dynamic	Absent
Context		✓ (allowed to add details)	✓ (allowed to add details)	✓ (allowed to recraft context)
Workflow		✓		
Error		✓		✓
Rectification		✓ (allowed to add details)		
Consequence				✓

or issue they want to solve or troubleshoot. Hence, learners may creatively add other information, either to make their lives easier (i.e. easier to solve the problem) or to make the rectification more creative (i.e. to allow other atypical ways to resolve the issue). There is also the critical analytical element that requires learners to evaluate what the issues are.

For example, a problem on soil erosion in the vicinity of a village may require the learner to add other possible details (e.g. near a chemical plant and a river) to the issue so that the error (e.g. to plant more trees) can be more obvious (with chemical pollution, the trees will not survive either so planting more trees will not help). The learner can then proceed to rectify the error by suggesting the removal of the plant and to clean up the river in order to ensure vegetation can thrive and grow, thereby reducing soil erosion.

In the case where the error, rectification or context are absent with a partial workflow (see Table 27), the learner can propose other rectifications with the additional details to the context to further justify the rectifications. This example is just one of many possible ways in which the learner can now 'manipulate' the context and propose new rectification measures to reflect the effectiveness of the measures, in a reverse engineering manner!

To recapitulate, the focus here is to develop the *creatical* capability of the learners and there needs to be a fair amount of space for learners to push the boundaries without overthinking the logic or the justification.

Bearing in mind this flexibility in design and implementation will ensure that learners are given the laxity in their exertions, within a safe environment.

iii. **To Sharpen Cognitive Adaptability and Flexibility**
   — Coping with a constantly changing wicked 'problem' (context), workflow and error

This section addresses the process of developing one's cognitive adaptability and flexibility within an authentic context. To keep the DELETE activities realistic and the learning practical, while at the same time, pushing the learners to reconsider the rules that apply, a more dynamic approach is proposed. What this means is the ever-changing context, workflow and error as these parameters are presented partially over time (see Table 28). In a world where the context is constantly changing, one's ability to cope with the dynamic nature of the issues can be severely tested and generating the rectification measures that correspond to the requirements is an important competency to be developed. In short, to achieve this learning outcome, the learner has to work with all three parameters (context, workflow and error) undergoing change at any point in time. The rectification and consequence may also be absent at the beginning of the case with some possible insights being provided as the case unravels. However, there is also a possibility that the rectification and consequence may not be included in the case so that learners can propose the rectification and think through what the consequences are for each rectification proposed.

Table 28. Permutations of Design Parameters to Sharpen Cognitive Adaptability and Flexibility

	Complete	Partial Static	Partial Dynamic	Absent
Context			✓	
Workflow			✓	
Error			✓	
Rectification				✓
Consequence				✓

Linking Error Design with Learning Outcomes: Cognition

For example, the context may be presented to an engineer in the form of statistics and input variables for him to work with. Subsequently, as he or she engages in the workflow, to carry out a task (e.g. determine the amount of chemicals to be added or duration of process), the numbers or variables may change, which requires the engineer to modify the workflow so that the situation will not result in disastrous consequences. At this point, there may not be an error yet. However, the designer may now inject the error by attributing a consequence to the engineer's earlier actions. As such, the learner (watching the video) or the engineer involved in the role play must be able to quickly point out where the error is and suggest rectifications. Continuing with the rectification, there may be new errors which emerge as a result, adding to the myriad of issues which hypothetically may happen in an authentic work situation. Hence, the learner must then be able to quickly address and rectify the error. Verbal explanations should be provided by the learner in selecting various options so that the reasoning process is articulated and documented. There should also be considerations of the least negative consequence when selecting the rectification option.

Besides being flexible, the learner has to quickly grasp the issues and the dynamic conditions, in order to propose new solutions within a certain period of time. One's ability to see the issues within a larger framework (i.e. Big Picture ability or Helicopter Perspective) is also tested here.

To emphasise, the difference between this fourth approach and the second approach (on developing 'creatical' ability) is the dynamism that this fourth approach presents. The context, workflow and error are being presented in a dynamic fashion at the same time, with these parameters changing every minute, thereby making rapid decision-making capability critical. The second outcome (on *creatical* capability), on the other hand, has some of the parameters (e.g. context) presented as partial static or even complete so the learners will have a good idea of what the issues are at the start. For this fourth outcome to be achieved fully, the learners will not be given any brief beforehand and have to watch the video case unfold (or be part of the evolving role play) and react accordingly at the right moment in time.

While similar to some extent to situational tests in terms of the dynamism and ever-changing scenarios, this DELETE approach differs in that critical errors are intentionally designed into the scenarios so that the learners will encounter an error or several errors (attributed as a result of the learners' prior response) to facilitate learning and mastery of skillsets.

iv. To Build Global (Macro) Perspective-Taking Ability
— Managing a work environment that is volatile, uncertain, complex and ambiguous

Managers and leaders are expected to have a global perspective-taking ability to assimilate information from different fields and disciplines and in so doing, connect the dots to formulate an overall strategy to navigate the ever-changing landscape for survival and growth. Hence, developing the global perspective-taking ability is more critical than before. The difficulty is in finding the means to develop this ability. Using an error-based approach is only one of the many means of addressing this developmental need but it could be the most effective one. The reason being that errors often define the boundaries for the learners to make their own conclusions about how certain rules behave within different contexts, especially when the stresses are placed on the individuals to pick certain options. These choices result in consequences, which can be useful lessons for the individuals to strengthen their perspective-taking ability.

As described in an earlier chapter, this design approach emphasises the associations among the workflow, error, rectification and consequences. It is only when one sees how the various rectification responses affect the consequences that the learning becomes real and that the relationships among the various parameters are established. How then do designers work out the parameters for the DELETE approach to work well? See Table 29 for suggested design arrangement:

Table 29. Permutations of Design Parameters to Build Global (Macro) Perspective-Taking Ability

	Complete	Partial Static	Partial Dynamic	Absent
Context	✓		✓	
Workflow	✓	✓	✓	
Error			✓	
Rectification			✓	✓
Consequence			✓	

Referring to the case on the training administrator allowing the CEO of the client organisation to participate in the training, the approach was to present the context and workflow in their entirety with the rectification options being presented partially and in a dynamic manner. As the rectification options and the corresponding consequences unfold, the learner is tasked to reflect and propose new rectifications based on the new consequences. Through the dynamic approach, the learners are brought through the reflection and task engagement process step-by-step in order to develop their cognitive processing, especially by considering all possibilities and factors to the issues. A facilitative style with a small coach-to-learner ratio is preferable to ensure a thorough discussion of the issues takes place. The epistemological stance is that of collaboration and experimentation. The learners generate the perspectives with an eye on the consequences. Sweeping through the various outcomes in quick succession is intentional and contributes to the learners developing macro perspective-taking competencies as they take on different lenses when reviewing the options in line with the outcomes generated. Peer inputs given during the small group experimentation process can sensitise the learners to understand how factors impact each other, leading to consequences which can be unimaginable at the onset.

In summary, the process of building perspective-taking by strengthening the learner's comprehension of how the rectification responses to errors are associated with the consequences within the context and the workflow presented can be convoluted. An expert facilitator can help unpack the process for the learners in a clear and systematic manner. Presenting different types of rectification options so that different perspectives are considered will also prepare learners for future decision-making processes.

Chapter 24
Linking Error Design with Learning Outcomes: Emotion

Moving on from the cognitive domain to the emotion domain, the emotive learning outcome presents a different set of challenges. As what we have done in earlier chapters, we will examine these two outcomes among other outcomes:

i. **To Develop Values and Beliefs**
   — Enculturating the values and beliefs of the organisation or industry for application in different contexts

Using the DELETE approach for the emotional domain requires the designers to look at the learning activity with a different lens since the outcome requires emotive and mindset shifts. To begin with, developing a professional's values and beliefs is a long-drawn process with numerous life-changing moments which define the person's identity and character. Hence, to manage expectations, the DELETE activity will only be part of the many milestones that the person will cross. Looking at Table 30, the

Table 30. Permutations of Design Parameters to Develop Values and Beliefs

	Complete	Partial Static	Partial Dynamic	Absent
Context	✓	✓		
Workflow	✓	✓		
Error	✓	✓		
Rectification		✓	✓	
Consequence		✓	✓	

context, workflow and error can be either fully or partially presented to the learner. The options are relatively varied compared to the other domains. The purpose of the DELETE activity is to allow the learner to evaluate the moral and ethical standing of the issue and make his or her own value judgement on what can be or should be done to rectify the error. Hence, what is most important is the degree of awareness and value formation that the learners currently have and how to move them to become more aware, in preparation for value and belief formation.

For example, if the organisation made a mistake with the online pricing of some of its items and customers bought the items at a marked-up price. Knowing the error subsequently, should the learner then decide to reimburse the customers even though many may not have realised the mistake? This calls for an evaluation of one's values and beliefs concerning fair consumer principles and practice. Again, rather than having the scenarios presented as right or wrong, it is critical to link possible consequences to the actions (or rectifications) taken. If true incidents can be used to underpin the design of these DELETE activities, there will be greater credibility when the learners question the authenticity of the consequences.

If the partial dynamic design is taken, the rectification action can be presented as a series of responses to the issues cropping up at various points in the learning process. Accordingly, the consequence will also evolve based on the learner responses. What will be interesting is to add the time element to the scenario so that there is significant pressure on the learner to act in a timely fashion or else risk further implications. Placing a peer to dissuade or influence the learner in a positive or negative manner can also part of the learning process for the learner. Subsequent reflection on the process will reveal deep-rooted values, which may hidden even from the learner himself or herself. It is also important for the learner to uncover the values of the organisation and industry during this activity and to decide if these values are worth embracing. There are values and beliefs which may not be aligned with one's own belief system and so the de-conflicting process has to take place or else the misalignment will result in the learner being unwilling to conform to organisational or industry procedures and processes.

A final word on this design is that the learner must be willing to be open and not be too guarded when undergoing this learning process. To achieve this, create a psychologically safe environment for the learners to share their deep-felt attitudes and thoughts. Having peers with whom trust is established is important. Otherwise, the results will be non-authentic, and the value of the learning is limited to what the learner chooses to be open about.

ii. **To Strengthen Psychological Resilience for Unexpected Outcomes**
   — Developing psychological resilience to cope effectively with unexpected situations

The development of resilience is a difficult process, not unlike the enculturation of a staff into an organisation or industry. The difficulty lies in the deep-seated nature of the resilience within a person's psyche. Hence, to reach deep within, the contexts and error should be highly emotive with high stress, to prepare the learner for such situations in the future. Obviously, there should be limits to how far this activity can go so as not to cause post-trauma stress disorders or other mental and psychological impairments. Shown in Table 31 are possible combinations

Table 31. Permutations of Design Parameters to Strengthen Psychological Resilience for Unexpected Outcomes

	Complete	Partial Static	Partial Dynamic	Absent
Context			✓	
Workflow			✓	
Error			✓	
Rectification			✓	✓
Consequence	✓			

of the learning design. To infuse stress into the scenario, a partial dynamic approach is taken so that there are responses required all the time, within very short timelines. The rectification actions may be absent to force the learner to take the necessary steps to reduce the impact of the error. The consequences, on the other hand, ought to be made clear so that the learner is aware of the negative impact of his or her error and actions. The learner should also be able to withdraw from the activity without any adverse impact to his or her career development.

For example, a fireman may be put in a situation to break down a door in a burning warehouse to save his colleagues who are trapped in the room containing explosive material. He touches the door which is extremely hot and has to decide if he is to break it down or to take a different route in. The danger to breaking the door down is that it may cause any fire within the room to suddenly engulf the inhabitants as the rush of oxygen fills the room. Given that there is limited information and the pressure to act, the fireman is urged by his team mates on his walkie-talkie to respond quickly. He has no choice but if he makes the wrong decision, he could kill not just his colleagues but also himself. Inserting peer pressure and realism into the scenario would be useful to push the learner to act fast and with clarity and courage.

The psychological resilience is developed as the facilitator takes the learner through the various scenarios including those with errors, i.e. the explosion did occur and kill everyone in the warehouse. Getting the learners to wear the uniform, carry the equipment and experience the scenario is also important to get the learners into the right frame of mind for action and decision-making. Most importantly, the errors designed into this approach have to be realistic and authentic so that the learning can be transferred to actual situations if they occur.

The escalation of the difficulty levels (either with more complex scenarios or a reduction of response time) should be gradual and in step with the learners' competency and comfort. Besides developing psychological resilience for individuals, this approach can also be used to develop resilience for teams. For the latter, team-based decision-making would depend on creating roles within the team which can upset the original power base residing in individual members (e.g. the supervisor now takes orders from his subordinate who is role-playing a senior position).

Chapter 25

Linking Error Design with Learning Outcomes: Psychomotor

We have examined the permutations of the parameters to achieve learning outcomes from metacognitive, cognitive and affective domains. In this chapter, we will examine how we can create multiple error-based learning scenarios to drive deep learning to achieve learning outcomes in the psychomotor domain. There are two psychomotor outcomes that we will focus on here:

i. **To Develop Behavioural Responses to Situations and Errors**
   — Building prompt and accurate psychomotor actions to resolve issues

Obviously, most complex behaviours will be initiated or accompanied by cognitive decision-making. In the case of training Cardiopulmonary Resuscitation (CPR) skills to first aiders and nurses described in an earlier chapter, the learners were taught to identify errors in the procedures and to rectify them accordingly, when the learners are tasked to take over the situation.

Besides quick thinking, the first aider needs to respond promptly with action. During training, the learners work through the problems within the contexts in a systematic manner, likely under time constraints. For example, the first aid trainees have to address the deterioration in the casualty's condition because a bystander tried to help by pulling out the knife which was originally stuck in the chest cavity of the casualty. As a result, when trying to resuscitate the casualty, the first aider now needs to also stem

Table 32. Permutations of Design Parameters to Develop Behavioural Responses to Situations and Errors

	Complete	Partial Static	Partial Dynamic	Absent
Context	✓	✓	✓	✓
Workflow	✓	✓		
Error		✓		✓
Rectification		✓		✓
Consequence				✓

the blood flow from the chest cavity that is interfering with the chest compression process. It gets more complicated as the first aider proceeds with the procedure. Movement-wise, the first aider needs to carry out the chest compression without aggravating the casualty's condition. It will take a fair amount of eye-hand skill underpinned by understanding of first aid procedures, all occurring within a very short period of time.

Table 32 shows possible options when designing the DELETE learning experience to achieve the required behavioural responses. For example, the context and workflow can be partial and dynamic, with partial information about the issues being presented (e.g. how the casualty injured himself or a car stalling on the highway). The workflow may be partially clear since there may be different parameters involved (e.g. the resuscitation workflow for a child is different from that for an elderly person and the first aider may not be fully aware of the workflow). The partial presentation is intentional, as a reflection of authentic first aid situations where the first aider has to uncover the context, causes and consequences within the short time provided. A lot of information will be hidden as a result.

The focus for this learning outcome is to develop timely behavioural responses to situations to resolve the issues. To take the learner a step further, the reflexivity to errors needs to meet the tight time constraints placed on the learner.

Linking Error Design with Learning Outcomes: Psychomotor

ii. To Increase Psychomotor Reflexivity to Errors
— Developing psychomotor responsiveness in a timely fashion

Similar to the behavioural training described earlier, the psychomotor reflexivity training refers to a more dynamic approach where new parameters are injected to result in more real-time responses from the learners. As depicted in the CPR training, the reflexivity training can be considered one more level higher than just the behavioural training for the learners. Here, we are training automated responses to situations where there is little to no time to think.

The table of parameters (see Table 33) shown below differs from that for behavioural training in that there is a lot more dynamism and evolution of the scenario involved. The degree of dynamism required in this approach is high where timelines are kept strictly to present the stressors as found in authentic work situations.

Table 33. Permutations of Design Parameters to Increase Psychomotor Reflexivity to Errors

	Complete	Partial Static	Partial Dynamic	Absent
Context	✓	✓	✓	✓
Workflow	✓		✓	
Error			✓	✓
Rectification			✓	✓
Consequence				✓

To achieve a highly responsive psychomotor outcome, the casualty presents additional complications, e.g. cardiac arrest in rapid fashion. Bystanders may also interfere with the process and cause additional interference. The error and rectification are dynamically presented to elicit real-time psychomotor responses from the learners. The extent and speed at which the first aider is able to address the evolving situation while maintaining calmness will be measured for performance.

For these types of training, role plays or simulations are likely to be the only options available to train time-sensitive responses. Besides healthcare, defensive measures in self-defence or military manoeuvres can also be addressed in this DELETE design.

In summary, the learning outcomes associated with psychomotor development tend to be about achieving:

- accuracy of the psychomotor response
- appropriateness of the response based on the context and the known causes
- the most desired outcomes given the circumstances

The DELETE approach provides the complexity and authenticity of the scenarios required to train learners to respond quickly and in a reflexive manner. Targeting specific outcomes can be achieved with the errors designed into the learning as markers for learner attention.

Chapter 26
Linking Error Design with Learning Outcomes: Sociality

Incorporating the sociality dimension into the learning process adds authenticity and enables learners to better work with others. Here, we are looking at how teams and peer-to-peer relationships can be developed. On top of cognitive or psychomotor competencies, which often discussed and developed individually, development of social skills requires others to be involved.

i. To Develop Collaboration Skills Within Teams
— Providing Opportunities for the Team to Build Mutual Understanding and Rapport

Depending on the maturity of the teams, the context and workflow could be simple (using either complete or partial static approach) for the new teams so that the members can focus on getting to know each other rather than resolving the error. For more mature teams, a partial dynamic approach could be taken to allow the team to forge their own understanding of the context and issues involved. Build flexibility into the learning process so that the leader emerges from the team with supporters to provide inputs or get additional resources to move the team forward. Ultimately, the test for the team is when the actions undertaken are erroneous and whether the members start blaming each other or seek to defuse the issue and start afresh as part of the rectification process. The consequences can be weighted accordingly to add or decrease the pressure on the team.

Table 34. Permutations of Design Parameters to Develop Collaboration Skills within Teams

	Complete	Partial Static	Partial Dynamic	Absent
Context		✓	✓	
Workflow		✓	✓	
Error		✓	✓	
Rectification		✓		✓
Consequence		✓		✓

For example, the context (see Table 34) given to a team may be to complete a project and present the findings to the management team. The workflow would be to split up the project, conduct research on the various segments and come together to discuss and decide on the eventual project before going off again to work on the various segments. Subsequently, the team members decide who is to present the various segments to senior management. The 'partially static' error may be that the team received misinformation about the date of the presentation and hence, has much lesser time to work through the project to get it ready for the presentation or the original scope given was much smaller than the expected. The team would have to adapt and change direction accordingly.

What would be the rectification process and the consequences which follow? The team members will have to discuss and decide given their own tight schedule and commitments. Naturally, there will be trade-offs and rescheduling especially since the team members work in different locations in Asia. Part of the scenario would be that each member is given a set of information via character cards including the areas they can compromise and those they cannot (e.g. no meetings on Tuesdays and Fridays or no flying off over the weekends). Based on the character cards, the members now have to negotiate and determine the best- and worst-case options and the corresponding consequences, to arrive at the final decision. Some of these characters could be superiors and subordinates, just to add the power play element into the interaction.

Linking Error Design with Learning Outcomes: Sociality

Through this DELETE approach of focusing on building sociality among the team members, it is imperative that the members are given the space and time to work out the knotty problems themselves. If they can be 'locked' in a room or a physical space, the discussions can be video recorded and examined later to determine findings.

Besides actually conducting team simulations, presenting the case parameters (e.g. reduced timelines) via a case study method is also possible. With this approach, the team members can discuss what they would do if they were faced with the same issues or constraints. The eventual rectification and consequence of the case can also be presented (as partial-static) at the start of the learning process to allow the team members to consider other options so that the outcome can be improved.

ii. To Cultivate Collaborative Skills for Individuals
  — Fostering individuals to adopt a collaborative mindset and skillset

While the earlier outcome is about creating a cohesive team, this outcome is about getting individuals to adopt a collaborative mindset. Working together is an increasingly important activity at workplaces but not everyone is well-equipped with the right attitude and behaviour when it comes to working and learning together. It is essential that to forge strong bonds among working teams, individuals need to possess self-motivation and team motivation. Hence, this outcome is targeted at transforming the individual to embrace collaboration for the good of the team or organisation.

To put the recommended design into context, the individual may be presented with a designated job role within an organisation or school and given a task which requires collaboration with other team members to complete. The workflow (see Table 35) is partially stated (could be either static or dynamic) so that the individual has to reflect on the issues, especially the manner in which he or she needs to work with others. The learner has to check his or her attitudes towards the team as the scenario evolves. More importantly, the injections of provocations and inconsiderate remarks by team members could trigger certain behavioural and cognitive responses on the part of the learner. These responses ought to be recorded for self-reflection and coaching subsequently. In any case, the dynamic nature of the scenario is important to add pressure and stress on the learner who has to respond in a timely and appropriate fashion. The agent bringing about the error/s could be by team members or attributed to the learner as part of the case. The rectifications with the accompanying consequence are to be determined by the learner during the scenario.

Assuming the learner faces a hostile team that he has to work with to improve Human Resource (HR) processes in a manufacturing firm with 100 staff based in the country, the critical questions would be the kind of mindset he goes into the collaboration with and what he does when provoked or ridiculed. Does he rise to the challenge or withdraw and let others lead? The partial static case would describe the characteristics of each of the team members with the exception of one or two of the more eccentric members. HR simply does not have their details.

The error is then committed by the team leader who passes a snide remark on colleagues from a certain department that they only talk and don't really work. The learner feels very uncomfortable. As the meeting closes, the team leader asks the learner to stay behind and attempts to sway the learner over to his side. He makes further disparaging remarks about individuals in the department and after about half an hour of ranting,

Table 35. Permutations of Design Parameters to Cultivate Collaborative Skills for Individuals

	Complete	Partial Static	Partial Dynamic	Absent
Context		✓	✓	
Workflow		✓	✓	
Error		✓	✓	
Rectification				✓
Consequence				✓

he asks the learner for his views on the department he mentioned. Does the learner share the same view? Why? What does the learner do now?

At some point, the learner may think this is not just an issue of trying to develop collaboration skills but of ethics and conscience. This will be a valid consideration. What happens before this consideration takes place is critical too. Does the learner attempt to understand the team leader's perspective? Why does he say those disparaging remarks and in what context? What are the avenues that the learner can tap on for help? The team leader obviously made an error. Does the learner even try to make the best out of the situation to get the project going? Depending on the choice of rectification, there will be consequences, not just for the learner but also for the team, who may lose this opportunity to showcase their capability to senior management.

To add complexity, the team leader turns negative towards the learner and chooses to ostracise the learner in the same manner. What does the learner do? How can the team come together to collaborate in a cohesive and cordial manner?

Similar to the earlier outcome, we can also consider the case study approach to achieve this outcome of transforming the learner's mindset to collaborating with others. With the case parameters (e.g. members' characteristics), the learner proceeds to deconstruct what he or she would do if faced with the same issues or constraints. The eventual rectification and consequence of the case can also be presented (as partial-static) at the start of the learning process to allow the learner to consider other options so that the outcome can be improved. What is important here is the need to challenge the learner's mindset through questioning the learner's decisions and getting the learner to reflect critically based on one's assumptions and beliefs regarding collaboration and teamwork.

Chapter 27 | Linking Error Design with Learning Outcomes: Holistic Development

Sennet (2008) describes the development of master craftsman as an arduous process whereby the master craftsman develops psychomotor and cognitive skills through many hours of practice and through the practice develops skills of imagination to reflect and learn from the experiences. Notably, craftsmanship is one example of mastery and something that we can make more effective in the light of Artificial Intelligence (AI) and automation development. There are some crafts which people will still value and pay for despite machines taking over (e.g. artisanal tea making, premium glassware and carpentry). Developing mastery takes time and a concerted effort by the craftsman to keep honing his or her skills (psychomotor, cognitive, affective, sociality and metacognitive etc.) to perfection. Hence, it is not sufficient to develop skills in only one or two domains. The competency development needs to be integrated across the various domains in order for the mastery to reach maturity. When the focus is on the holistic development of the individual craftsman, the focus is to go beyond competency to capability. How do learners develop themselves holistically, to focus on capability and not just competency growth? We will review the following three outcomes:

i. **To Integrate Skillsets Across Domains to Achieve Mastery for the Individual**
   — Strengthening the connections among different types of skills to ensure a holistic and skilful approach to resolving issues

Table 36 provides many options for designers to select from. One of the considerations is to determine where the focus of the holistic development is going to be — at the pre-error, error or post-error phase. If there is more emphasis on pre-error capability, the learner is expected to acquire the capability to observe, be aware, to predict, plan, strategise and navigate using his or her social, cognitive, psychomotor, affective skillsets in order to minimise the risk and possible negative consequences before any adverse events (i.e. error) are to occur. Even if the error occurs, the learner has also pre-empted the error and is ready to carry out the rectification process. This set of mastery skills is usually not obvious nor observable to the novice as much of the planning occurs in the mind and data gathering through questioning and the five senses. Sometimes, one notes a heightened sense of alertness on the part of the expert or master who may have picked up possible signs of error. Hence, at the pre-error stage, the capability to be developed remains very much error prevention or minimisation with cognitive planning (to pre-empt and to develop alternative courses of action for different scenarios) underpinning the process.

At the error stage, one must have skills of adaptability and flexibility to manage the situation. Leadership skills underpinned by moral strength, courage and decisiveness (part of affective domain) can be severely tested in this stage. Learners are expected to demonstrate their capability to read and take charge of the situation, minimise immediate danger before taking rectification actions. This stage can be short, depending on the urgency

Table 36. Permutations of Design Parameters to Integrate Skillsets Across Domains to Achieve Mastery for the Individual

	Complete	Partial Static	Partial Dynamic	Absent
Context	✓		✓	
Workflow	✓		✓	✓
Error	✓	✓	✓	
Rectification		✓	✓	✓
Consequence		✓	✓	✓

Linking Error Design with Learning Outcomes: Holistic Development

of the situation (from life endangering to reviving a project that is going downhill).

Finally, the post-error stage requires a level of humility to accept better solutions as the learner seeks ways to rectify the situation, to mitigate the negative impact and increase the positive impact of the consequences. Often, through the rectification process, the learner taps on his or her psychomotor and cognitive expertise along with leadership and communication skills to move forward. The impact from this stage will be determined by the actions undertaken in the pre-error and error stages.

The key difference between this holistic development and the earlier designs (e.g. developing teamwork) is that there is no specific competency being targeted but rather, the learner is expected to perform ALL necessary planning and actions to make it work, notwithstanding the severity of the error.

The designer can thus choose to provide a complete pre-error picture to the learner so that there is a clear canvas for the learner to work on and following which the rectification process could be the focus. On the other hand, the partial dynamic or partial static modes are useful to test responsiveness at the error and post-error phases. Learners are expected to provide rectification actions based on the assumptions of possible consequences if these are absent.

Using the CPR case mentioned earlier, in the holistic development of the learner, besides the psychomotor skills, cognitive skills requiring understanding of the tools and situation are expected, mobilising others (e.g. other first aiders or bystanders) to support the work (social skills) and being aware of one's cognitive or affective bias when providing the first aid (metacognition) will be critical in pulling together a credible performance in saving lives. The errors designed into the scenarios at different phases of the learning experience will be important. Naturally, when the learners are competent, it is useful to vary the errors, to develop the individual more holistically. For example, the casualty may suddenly reveal that he has a deadly communicable disease after the CPR has been carried out for more than 2 minutes. Is there an endangerment to the first aider and the bystanders supporting the first aid procedure? Adding on, the driver of the car (who hit the casualty) may get agitated and attempt to interfere with the life-saving procedure, to try to get the casualty to absolve the driver of any blame.

There are many permutations to the error design. It would be useful to consider that if the rectifications and consequences were provided to the learners, midway through the procedure (i.e. based on your current actions, fast forward by 10 min, the casualty suffered a cardiac arrest and the driver of the car fled the scene. Rewind to present … what are you going to do differently now?). If necessary, the learner can exercise a 'thinking card' for a quick huddle with his/her team members to discuss for a short period of time before engaging in the exercise again.

Due to the need to integrate competencies across domains, the likelihood of the learning engagement to be a role play or simulation is very high. Using a virtual reality scenario is also possible although the cost is usually more prohibitive, but the ability to repeat the scenarios consistently, across different locations, is a benefit, especially for teams operating in different countries.

ii. **To Diagnose Skill Gaps and Non-Strengths**
   — Uncovering gaps in specific skillsets through non-routine error-based learning designs

Often, individuals do not find themselves incompetent at managing or completing routine tasks. It is only when errors or a crisis emerges that the individuals may discover that their skills to cope with the task are lacking, for example managing a team when morale is low, and fraud is suspected of one of the members. Hence, using the DELETE approach, one has to deftly manage the issues as a whole, going through the financial irregularities with sensitivity so that one does not deflate morale further but at the same time, presenting transparency and fairness to all concerned. Managing team members' needs while at the same time, self-regulating one's own emotions will require the team leader to draw from his or her reserves. Uncovering one's skill gaps before any such event occurs, followed by targeted development will be useful for the individual.

You will realise that all the parameters are presented partially, either in a dynamic or static manner (see Table 37). The rationale is to diagnose one's metacognitive ability, followed by rectifications and understanding of the possible consequences. As this design is targeted at diagnosing the individual's capabilities, a competency framework or checklist is to be drawn up beforehand (e.g. management skills, technical skills, metacognitive abilities, problem-solving skills) as indicators.

The critical difference between a gap profiling exercise and a learning experience is that an observer (preferably with a checklist of indicators) assists with monitoring responses and the thinking process (with the learner articulating thoughts aloud). Letting the scenario run and injecting new information at specific moments to test if the learner is able to respond appropriately are part of the gap profiling exercise. If there are doubts about the learner's cognitive, psychomotor, social or metacognitive capabilities, further injection of errors or issues should be carried out (sparingly) to expose the learner's skills gap and for confirmation subsequently. Obviously, the purpose of the exercise is to determine the learner's non-strengths and strengths for downstream learning for the learner.

The reason for the context, workflow and error to be given partially (none are complete and none are absent) is to set some boundaries and

Table 37. Permutations of Design Parameters to Diagnose Skill Gaps and Non-strengths

	Complete	Partial Static	Partial Dynamic	Absent
Context		✓	✓	
Workflow		✓	✓	
Error		✓	✓	
Rectification		✓	✓	
Consequence		✓	✓	

parameters for the learner to observe and align with current SOPs/rules. Likewise for rectification and consequences where these two parameters can provide useful feedback to the learner on the outcomes if he or she responds in specific ways. The consequences can either be positive or negative.

The design of the error and other parameters is to ensure that the activity will result in learner responses which are observable and measurable.

iii. To Prepare the Individual for Future Skill Needs
— Building skills for future needs

This is somewhat of a tall order but an important one as the global environment demands a new set of skills for every generation, based on the rapid technology development. Hence, the task of preparing individuals to take on new jobs cannot rest solely upon the shoulders of school teachers only. Employers, adult educators and individuals have to take responsibility to push lifelong learning for society, to maintain the competitiveness and productivity of the workforce.

In this DELETE approach, the potential skillsets relevant for the future are first identified and embedded into the training. These relevant future skills may stem from any of the domains, including being part of one's metacognitive capability. Once identified and designed into the learning, the individuals can proceed to undertake the training, which should still take on a holistic approach to training the individual with some emphasis on the future skillsets.

Table 38 resembles the integrated approach to holistic training because the focus on integration of skillsets should remain. What will reduce the complexity of the design is to provide a full picture of the workflow, especially for future work. The contexts can vary along with the error, rectification and consequence since these could constitute part of the training for metacognitive and problem-solving skills. For

Table 38. Permutations of Design Parameters to Prepare the Individual for Future Skill Needs

	Complete	Partial Static	Partial Dynamic	Absent
Context	✓		✓	
Workflow	✓			
Error	✓	✓	✓	
Rectification		✓	✓	✓
Consequence		✓	✓	✓

example, if prompt engineering (fine tuning prompts to AI) and training of AI are now deemed as a 21st-century skill as some futurists have argued, then these skills could be embedded within the context of group projects where collaborative learning skills and digital literacy are taught. The errors infused into the codes (said to be generated by the AI) will require rectification and reflection. With the partial dynamic approach, the group has to arrive at a consensus to uncover assumptions in the prompts, supported by a facilitator to provide or inject more errors or consequences into the situation. The focus is on building conflict resolution skills while working through the issues, a common work context in many organisations. This approach combines cognitive skills (problem-solving), sociality (collaborative learning) and affective management (patience and perseverance) in the integrated approach to prepare our workers for such future skill needs.

Conclusion

The intentional design of the five parameters: errors, with context, workflow, rectification and consequence involves two dimensions:

- *Visibility* (*Completely shown*, *Partial* and *Absent*)
- *Dynamism* (*Static* and *Dynamic*)

These dimensions provide the variations that designers can consider when presenting the errors and the parameters listed earlier.

These dimensions allow for numerous permutations of the DELETE approach, achieving the various outcomes set out across the five domains (metacognition, cognition, affective, psychomotor and social). Not forgetting that we are also looking at a holistic approach, where all or most of the domains are integrated for better work performance.

The design tables shown over the past few chapters are suggestions on how the parameters can be presented across the two dimensions of *Visibility* and *Dynamism.* These permutations are not fixed and depending on the outcomes, can be designed accordingly to achieve the desired competencies.

When located within the Error Engagement and Experimentation (E^3) Cycle, the five parameters can work together to create an impactful learning experience. The errors trigger learner responses, while the remaining four parameters provide the constraints and boundaries within which the learner needs to navigate. It is in the intentional design (despite the seemingly ad hoc presentation of the parameters) that the learners are brought through the experience. The facilitator will need to be cognisant of how the learner is journeying through the (E^3) Cycle to ensure that the learning is broad and deep.

Chapter 28 Refining Errors

We examined the DELETE Error Engagement and Experimentation (E^3) Cycle in detail, early in the book, along with some use cases. In this chapter, the focus is to encourage you to carry out continuous improvement reviews through validation and checks on how the errors and tasks are aligned to create useful learning opportunities for learners. No instructional design is perfect. With an evolving work and job landscape, the review process will have to be timely and granular. Hence, continuous monitoring of the situation and learner profile is crucial to ensure fidelity of the tasks set and to keep making learning happen for the learners.

Recapitulation

The DELETE learning design constitutes four elements:

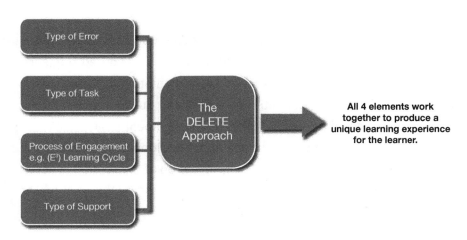

Given that each learning activity is designed for different outcomes, the designer has on hand a vast range of design permutations by tweaking each of the four elements that will specifically target the required competencies to achieve the outcomes.

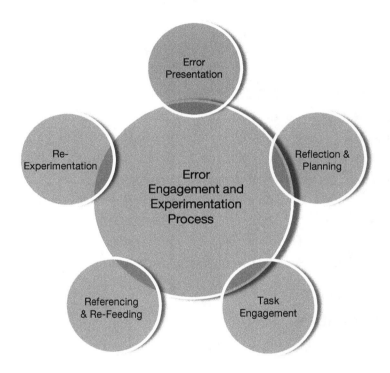

Subsequently, the way the DELETE learning process is carried out is determined by the sequence of activities. Here, the proposed sequence is based on the Error Engagement and Experimentation (E^3) Cycle where the learner is given opportunities to reflect and question assumptions and build metacognitive abilities. The Task Engagement stage is critical in which the designed task should bring about additional learning beyond error identification and rectification. Examination of the context in which the error was made along with the assumptions held by the error maker makes this stage essential to maximise learning.

Refining Errors

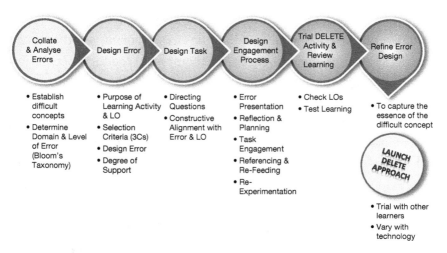

Fig. 31. The 7-Step Process to Designing the DELETE Approach

Setting Up the DELETE Learning Approach

The previous segment discusses the make-up of the DELETE learning process. To arrive at the 4 elements of error, task, error engagement and support types, the designer undertakes a full design process starting from analysis to error crafting and trialling with the eventual refinement of the learning process. Akin to the ADDIE process, this instructional system design model is tailored to the DELETE approach where specific elements such as error and task design are highlighted.

As Fig. 31 shows, the entire DELETE approach requires careful analysis and error crafting to set up an effective learning approach. It is a purpose or outcome-driven design with highly difficult concepts or skills being the target of the activity to reinforce the competencies and to reduce preventable errors.

Error Refinement Considerations

Since DELETE is outcome-focused with clear intents for the learner, the refinement of the error naturally should adhere to the principle of closing

331

gaps between the desired outcomes and the actual learning result. Hence, the designer's task is very clear in that the changes made whether to the error design, task design, task engagement process or the support type, will strategically align the learning activity to achieve the learning outcomes.

a) *Learner-Centric Design*
Even though the outcomes can be clearly stated, the imperative is to go back to the learner to understand if the original learning outcomes set for the activity meet the learner's needs. Here, the learner profile in terms of his or her job role, capability, cognitive and collaborative styles, and more importantly, the learner's beliefs and values will affect the nature of the learner's needs. Being learner-centric implies a need to constantly check back with the learner on the effectiveness of the learning process. With the DELETE approach being so targeted and specific, the learner will have a very good idea of how the learning activity is meeting his needs.

- *Purpose-Driven Error Design and Refinement*

Being purpose-driven is not necessarily bad. It can be useful too as the purpose directs the designer, educator and recipient to focus their energy and resources on the particular concept or skill that the learner has to acquire.

If we recall the possible outcomes that we have described in detail are likely to be a segment of all the outcomes that designers are interested in. We will have to be cognisant of the changing needs of learners over time. The outcomes we looked at so far are:

1. **Metacognition**
    i. To Hone Regulatory and Predictive Ability
    ii. To Develop Ability to Evaluate Contexts and Assumptions
2. **Cognition**
    i. To Strengthen Conceptual Understanding and Skillsets in Targeted Areas

ii. To Develop 'Creative-Critical' Thinking Ability
   iii. To Sharpen Cognitive Adaptability and Flexibility
   iv. To Build Global (Macro) Perspective-Taking Ability
3. **Emotion**
   i. To Develop Values and Beliefs
   ii. To Strengthen Psychological Resilience for Unexpected Outcomes
4. **Psychomotor**
   i. To Develop Behavioural Responses to Situations and Errors
   ii. To Increase Reflexivity to Errors
5. **Sociality/Interpersonal**
   i. To Develop Teamwork Skills Among Team Members
   ii. To Cultivate Collaborative Skills for Individuals
6. **Holistic Development — beyond competency to capability**
   i. To Integrate Skillsets Across Domains to Achieve Mastery for the Individual
   ii. To Diagnose Skill Gaps and Non-strengths
   iii. To Prepare the Individual for Future Skill Needs

These outcomes reflect only the *tip* of the iceberg of capability development. With the choice of the outcomes determined, the designer can then go about designing the error, task and level of support. Prior to that, the designer may 'guesstimate' and imagine how the error design ought to reflect authentic working considerations and difficulties. For example, designing a learning error to highlight the contextual impact on work performance would fall under Metacognitive skills to evaluate contexts and assumptions. More specifically, a contextual issue could be unhealthy competition within an organisation that contributes to a lack of cooperation and low productivity. Hence, more than providing additional training to get workers to work faster, team-bonding activities to close gaps in working relationships may be a more effective way to make the organisation healthy again.

Chapter 28

For the error and the task design to be refined to match the specified outcomes, the designer has to know the impact the learning activities are making on the learners. For example, is there a continuity of application, after the initial excitement from the learners who may be highly motivated after training? If the activity does not sufficiently meet learner's needs, then it may be necessary to analyse the data about the learner's needs again.

- **Checking for Competence**

There is a third consideration when learning activities do not seem to bring about the desired change. It has to do with the measurement of competence or observation of the desired behaviour. If the measurement process or indicators are not valid, meaning they measure behaviours which have nothing to do with the desired endpoint, then naturally, the learning activity will not produce those behaviours being measured. For example, if the DELETE learning activity is to produce staff with a clear idea of what the organisational customer service culture is but the measurement is on the staff's understanding of the organisational mission and vision, then the results will naturally not be positive since the staff may not have been inducted into the mission and vision of the organisation. In this case, the measurement indicators are not aligned with the outcomes of the learning activity and will need refinement and alignment.

How to Refine the DELETE Approach

I have always preferred the Rapid Prototyping approach to get learning activities off the ground and to utilise trials as a means to check effectiveness. However, this approach also means that the designers are going into the activity 'blind' with little information to support or contradict the design. Hence, the seven-step DELETE Design process will guide designers to specifically design error-based activities for better learning with the refinement coming in at the end of the entire process. Notably, most of the refinement should centre round the following three areas (see Fig. 32):

Refining Errors

Fig. 32.   Error Analysis, Error Design and Task Design

If the first step is not conducted properly with poor analyses and inaccurate findings, the design process will naturally become of little consequence since the data generated and findings will not be relevant or worse still, misdirect the design process. Hence, refinement of the DELETE approach will include a review of the data collection process along with the analysis of errors. You may find that a mistake in the analysis of errors may result in the wrong difficult concepts being identified, resulting in learners picking up concepts which may be easy or not so relevant.

Hence, the second step in designing the error requires the designer to be clear about the difficult concepts. Which are the difficult steps in the process? Knowing the difficult concepts allows the designer to target the specific areas when crafting the DELETE learning outcomes. Sometimes, it may be tough to decide since there may be different difficult concepts in one workflow or topic. Hence, the designer's own instructional design expertise here will play a determining role in deciding which topics or concepts will require more expertise.

Thirdly, the engagement task should be aligned with the learning outcomes. Whatever the learning outcomes, the task set should reflect what the learners need to do in relation to the error and context. If there is a mistake made and the learner when carrying out the task does not seemed to conduct what is truly needed to achieve the learning outcomes, then it will be a waste of valuable time and efforts on the part of the learner and for the educational institution or training provider. More critically, it could be an expensive lesson if the learners perform poorly or wrongly at work, resulting in serious consequences for themselves or others. They

> From a study on how medical students viewed medical errors, Fischer et al. (2006, p. 420) found that most respondents would learn better from actual errors than near misses. One student commented, 'You would still learn but it wouldn't be as complete learning as knowing about an error that has happened and what exactly the consequences were'.
>
> Other students noted they would learn best from errors that caused severe harm. This seemed to be based on the personal and emotional impact of such events. 'If it has a poor outcome, it's more likely to stick in my head because you feel, obviously, horrible for causing harm to the patient and causing a poor outcome, versus if there's no poor outcome, then you may be less likely to keep it in your mind'.

may choose to take legal action against the training organisation. Hence, during the trial, it is important to determine if the task is pitched at the right level and addresses the learning outcomes set.

Conclusion

As part of the continuous improvement process, error refinement is an important part of the overall DELETE approach. What should also be in the minds of DELETE designers is the alignment with the overall learning outcomes and job competence. Hence, the case should address the key competencies that the worker or the student needs to acquire eventually, to perform the job correctly.

Refining the DELETE process includes making modifications to:

- The error process which includes pre-error, error and the post-error stages depending on the outcomes to be achieved
- The learning process that includes the design task, reflection and experimentation

- Once ready, the modified learning design will be trialled and evaluated again to ensure validity and reliability in relation to the context and outcomes expected

There are other areas of refinement but those listed earlier are the critical are ones for consideration if the original DELETE design does not lead to the achievement of the learning outcomes.

The important thing in science is not so much to obtain new facts as to discover new ways of thinking about them.

Sir William Bragg

In summary, the list of learning outcomes described in this chapter from the metacognitive, cognitive, affective, sociality and psychomotor domains is meant to be illustrative of the impact of the DELETE approach and they are not comprehensive. There are other possible outcomes that could be achieved by varying the context, workflow, error presentation, rectification and consequences. Through the various permutations of these parameters, one can develop the pre-error and error skillsets such as metacognition, value-based decision-making skills and reflexive responses. The post-error skills would include decision-making to minimise the impact of the errors.

Through careful design of the **Error-Making** and **Learning** processes to achieve the learning outcomes, the teacher/trainer can target specific capabilities of the learner, for further development, beyond the usual problem-solving capability in an experiential manner. This is what the DELETE approach is about, designing errors for learning and teaching so that the learner becomes not just competent but achieves mastery by exploring boundaries and questioning assumptions, among other tasks.

In the next few chapters, we will look at several worked examples designed for students and adult learners so that you will have a better understanding of how DELETE activities can be designed.

Part 7

Worked Examples for Students and Adult Learners

Chapter 29
Designing Errors for Students: Examples

For students who are acquiring knowledge in new fields of study, the DELETE approach presents a means of short-circuiting the learning process by highlighting key mistakes that people generally make. It is not uncommon that students taking high-stakes examinations such as the 'Ordinary Levels' or 'Advanced Levels' examinations often resort to completing questions in 'Ten-Year Series' replete with model answers. Some students memorise the answers rather than attempt to answer the questions themselves. Over time, these students get decent grades at the examination, but may not have acquired strong problem-solving and critical thinking skillsets. They probably did get a better memory though, with this extremely painful method of rote learning.

What this points to is the general aversion of the current system and our educators to errors. Marks are awarded for getting the right answers rather than understanding how to tackle errors, which is what happens very often in real life anyway. Error avoidance and conducting a flawless performance are attributes that our educational system rewards. It is unclear if this is desirable all the time. Understandably, getting the right answers is important. This is akin to knowing where the centre-lane markings are, as our analogy goes, but knowing where the left and right boundaries of the road lie, is also critical so as not to go off road. This idea of not going off the road is especially important when it

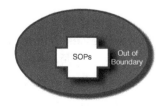

comes to novel problems and issues. Often, the centre-lane markings (SOPs) become blurred and knowing where the side boundaries are will be crucial to ensure learners stay focused and empowered to solve the problems. The errors that they know about and have tackled before will act as guides as to where the learners should NOT go. With this out-of-bounds area defined, learners will have greater confidence to solve the problem within the boundaries of the issues.

Why Use the DELETE Approach for Students?

There are compelling reasons to design errors to help students to learn more effectively due to the nature of students as novice learners in the respective topics. Due to their lack of real-world experience, students tend to navigate the various subjects with little background information, relying heavily on their cognitive ability to pick up the concepts and skills and move on to the next subject quickly. For students who cannot cope with the heavy workload, the level of motivation will vary drastically, depending on their passion and interest in the subject. In general, students who can manage the topics will tend to like the subject and the converse is also generally true.

Hence, DELETE comes in useful here to:

- personalise the learning process for the students by selecting the *skillsets* which the students have problems with. For example, some students have issues with carelessness so specific mistakes involving transfer errors or simple computation errors could be implanted into the solution for these students to detect and correct. By using these transfer errors as the targets, students address their specific weaknesses to improve on them intentionally.
- *increase motivation* through adaptive testing so that students who have problems solving the difficult questions (e.g. statistics) can now solve the easier ones before moving on to the more complex questions.

Designing Errors for Students: Examples

With early success, students tend to have confidence and motivation to press on.

- address *critical gaps* in performance for strengthening. For example, some students have difficulties in answering the latter part of a multi-step problem and often, it takes these students a long time (up to 10 minutes) just to finish the first segment of the sum and by the time they arrive at the segment they find difficulties with, they are already tired or lost interest in the question. Hence, by working out the solution and planting errors in the critical segment, the students can focus on strengthening their conceptual grasp of these critical skill sets without having to solve the earlier parts of the problem which they are already familiar, thereby saving the students, precious time and energy.

- *promote adaptive behaviour* such as responding to challenges rapidly with 'creatical' solutions. It may not be obvious now but possessing adaptive behaviour is a critical skill when changes in the 'rules of the game' occur constantly and being mindful of these changes becomes part of one's mindset at work or in school. Going back to the diagram analogy, it could be that with time, the new SOPs may actually be those which were not allowed in the past and those which were accepted are now forbidden.

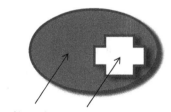

Out of boundary   New SOPs

For example, we were told in the 1980s that margarine was healthier than butter and so parents spent a little more money to buy tubs of margarine and ignored butter for health reasons especially to ensure their children grew up healthy. In the 2000s, experts informed us that margarine was even unhealthier than butter and was responsible for clogging up our arteries! Now, families purchase butter instead. What a difference 20 years can make. More importantly, how do we cope when research findings and environments change? We have to adapt accordingly. In similar fashion, as technology-enabled learning becomes more intuitive and learning effective, students and teachers may have to abandon conventional ways of learning and teaching to adopt new approaches to use their time and resources more effectively. By using errors, students and teachers can use errors as learning incidents to trigger their reflection and follow-up action.

- facilitate error identification and assumption checking. This is going to be a critical skill with AI generating images and texts which may not be entirely true. Going on the basis of partial falsehood means that readers need to put on a lens of always being wary of untruths embedded within texts or assumptions which need to be further tested to ensure the logic is sound. Checking for errors and wrong assumptions will likely be the way forward for learning and work.

The next segment demonstrates the different functions of the DELETE approach in detail, according to the needs of the students. We will start with focusing on preparing students for unexpected outcomes and environments in the volatile, uncertain, complex and ambiguous (VUCA) world.

Utilising the DELETE Approach for Students

While students in many Asian countries are well versed with completing assessment books and past examination questions to prepare for their examinations, they can be unprepared when new types of questions appear in the examination, leading to undue stress and pressure. The reason is clear. The students prefer to work on questions that they have already attempted or those they are familiar with. However, we note that in life, there are not many challenges which we are fully prepared for or know way in advance.

Hence, through the DELETE approach, we can provide opportunities and examples to prepare them for how they will work in school and at work in the future. The following illustrations will follow the order of metacognition, cognition, emotion, psychomotor skills, sociality and capability development for students. As cognitive development is a critical area for student learning given our highly competitive school system, this area will be emphasised accordingly.

Notably, helping students manage examinations and assessments will be foremost for most teachers and that is also the stance taken in this chapter.

Metacognition

i. To Hone Metacognitive and Predictive Ability

Example 1: Composition Passage — Loch Ness Monster

To be presented in a dynamic manner (i.e. teacher to show the passage in parts)

Task: Students are to predict the way the passage should eventually pan out. To do so, they are to state possible sentences following the sentences being presented and how the erroneous statements change the passage in a negative manner.

Show Slide 1

In the beautiful highlands of Scotland, there is a lake called the Loch Ness. In these peaceful surroundings, a sea monster known as the Loch Ness monster is said to be living in the lake. This creature known affectionately as Nessie ...

> **Question**
> What information should appear next? Why?

Show Slide 2

In the beautiful highlands of Scotland, there is a lake called the Loch Ness. In these peaceful surroundings, a sea monster known as the Loch Ness monster

Chapter 29

is said to be living in the lake. This creature known affectionately as Nessie is apparently a hideous looking monster from the dinosaur age, capable of eating dogs and small mammals and possibly having a hand in some of the persons missing around the Loch Ness since the early 1900s. Nessie is not so nice after all.

Questions (Show 1 at a time)
- Is the new sentence in accordance to what you expected? Why?
- How would you write the new sentence?

Show Slide 3 (with the erroneous sentence being highlighted)

In the beautiful highlands of Scotland, there is a lake called the Loch Ness. In these peaceful surroundings, a sea monster known as the Loch Ness monster is said to be living in the lake. This creature known affectionately as Nessie is *apparently a hideous looking monster from the dinosaur age, capable of eating dogs and small mammals and possibly having a hand in some of the persons missing around the Loch Ness since the early 1900s. Nessie is not so nice after all.*

Why is the highlighted sentence termed as an error in relation to the earlier part of the passage? *(changes the tone of the passage to become less formal e.g. 'not so nice after all')*

Show Slide 4 (with the actual sentence)

In the beautiful highlands of Scotland, there is a lake called the Loch Ness. In these peaceful surroundings, a sea monster known as the Loch Ness monster is said to be living in the lake. This creature

- What is likely to be included in the next paragraph?
- What would constitute an error in the next paragraph?

Designing Errors for Students: Examples

known affectionately as Nessie has been reported to be seen by many people around the lake. According to these reports/people, Nessie looked like a creature from the dinosaur age. It had a huge body, a small reptilian head and a long neck.

Show Slide 5

Does the Loch Ness monster really exist? According to my mother, the Loch Ness exists... only in people's dreams. She is adamant that there is no monster and that people are just out to milk tourists of their money. She also tells me to focus on my studies instead of thinking about monsters and money! Talk about being a dream destroyer!

Questions (Show 1 at a time)
- Is the new paragraph in accordance to what you expected? Why?
- How would you write the new paragraph?

Show Slide 6 (with the erroneous sentence being highlighted)

Does the Loch Ness monster really exist? According to my mother, the Loch Ness exists... only in people's dreams. She is adamant that there is no monster and that people are just out to milk tourists of their money. *She also tells me to focus on my studies instead of thinking about monsters and money! Talk about being a dream destroyer!*

Why is the highlighted sentence termed as an error in relation to the earlier part of the passage? *(changes the tone and direction of the passage again to content that distracts the reader from the topic)*

Show Slide 7 (with the actual sentence)

Does the Loch Ness monster really exist? No one can tell for sure. Ever since the sighting of the monster, many people have been keeping watch at the lake, hoping to catch a glimpse of Nessie. In 1934, a doctor, Colonel Robert Wilson, even managed to photograph the creature. The picture revealed a creature with a long neck sticking out of the water.

- Is this a better ending? Why?
- What rule did the errors break in the past few slides? *(rules of continuity and tonality in formal writing)*

Debrief

The purpose of the DELETE approach in the above example focused on developed metacognitive skills which essentially empowers the learners to predict and analyse the errors based on their earlier prediction. The impact is to have learners to take a proactive approach to reading passages and to evaluate when certain passages are written in ways which *run counter* to the way the story is developing. The errors provide useful focal points for evaluation and justification.

ii. **To Develop Ability to Evaluate Contexts and Assumptions**
   — to identify contextual cues so as to prevent applying the wrong approach to a similar context

Example 2: Composition-Writing — Drowning
Title of Composition: The Day I Nearly Drowned
   It was a beautiful day. My family of four, including my parents, my brother and I decided to head to the beach for a lazy afternoon dip in the cool waters off East Coast Beach. Being an avid swimmer, I was game for some water sports and a dose of swimming to work off the holiday fat

that I had accumulated as a result of all the bingeing from the end-of-year parties with classmates and friends.

Grabbing my swimming costume and a pair of goggles, I jumped into our small family sedan and sped off to our favourite spot on the beach...

Reflection

- How is the composition shaping up to be?
- What are possible areas that the writer can go wrong in?

It was amazing how a small area can hold so many people. When we reached the beach, it was as if the entire population in the vicinity had decided to take the afternoon off to cool themselves here. It was so packed that we had only standing space left. We could barely move after we managed to find a spot near the car park. There was not much of the sandy beach left for us and we had to wade carefully through the crowd to avoid stepping on any sunbathing bodies. It was so crowded that I was basically pushing people out of the way just to get wet in the waters! Once in the water, I found myself carried along by others. There wasn't any swimming to speak of and I could only 'float' in the water even though I wasn't using any float. I was utterly disgusted when I could not even get my head into the water because of the tight squeeze. There were uncles, aunties and kids who could barely paddle all jousting for an inch of the precious real estate in the sea! It was utterly unbelievable.

Finally, I managed to push myself out towards the open sea, just to get some breathing and swimming space...

Reflection

- How is the composition shaping up to be as it reaches the climax?
- Suggest how the writer can go wrong at this point.
- One student proposed having the lifeguard to save the author and end the story accordingly. What do you think?

Chapter 29

With my head bobbing up and down in the open waters, I can barely make out where my parents and brother were on the beach. They seemed to be waving to me at one point and I simply waved back. I decided to try to swim and make the most of the remaining time to get some exercise done. As I got into position, a huge wave hit me in the chest and disorientated me. I was stunned momentarily. On impulse, I took a deep breath, forgetting that my head was still in the water. With that, I gulped down a mouthful of water. Unfortunately, the salty water made its way into my oesophagus and I could not breathe. I tried surfacing for air. It was futile as I could not figure out which way was up! At that point in time, I thought I was about to drown. Fortunately, a steady hand caught hold of me as I tried to kick my way through the water. With a firm grip, he pushed me up to the surface and I could take my first breath after what seemed like eternity. I sputtered and coughed and nearly passed out. Then, without warning, the same hand which seemingly saved me, now started to push me down into the water! It caught me by surprise. I was about to lose consciousness.

Suddenly, a startlingly sound from behind me gave me a fright, 'Wake up! Wake up'! With that, I turned and found myself in cold sweat on my bed. Wow! That was a close shave. It was nothing but ... a nightmare. I was still alive.

Reflection

- What are some key errors that the writer made with this composition?
- How did these errors occur?
- What assumptions did the writer have to make these errors?

Debrief

The ending was unfortunate as it resulted in an 'out of point' decision from the marker. This meant that the writer wrote out of context when the title of the composition was 'The Day I Nearly Drowned'. By making this story to be a nightmare, the entire body of the composition, despite the very nice

Designing Errors for Students: Examples

buildup, became irrelevant. It was a waste that the ending did not match with what the title required. The possible causes include the writer having memorised the ending and trying to fit it into the passage as well as trying to give a twist to the story but forgetting what the title given was.

The other error was the exaggeration about the number of people at the beach. While it is possible to have to grapple with many people, it seemed that the writer went on and on about the tight squeeze and not being able to get 'wet'. It seemed a little overboard and uncalled for.

Finally, the proportion of text that dealt with the drowning seemed quite small compared to the buildup. It may not be a major point for contention, but there is a small risk that the focus is not quite there when required. The writer will do well to get right into the thick of the drowning and focus on that to maximise the climax and achieve a better result.

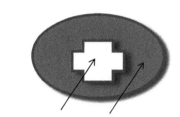

Adhere to given title

Do not end with a twist that makes the entire story irrelevant to the title

In short, the SOP is to adhere to the title given and the boundary is that the entire story, including the ending, must stay integral to the given title. Ending the story with a twist can be a useful technique to increase reader satisfaction but it can backfire spectacularly if students do not realise that there is an important boundary line which should not be crossed.

In addition, knowing what you do NOT want in a story is important (i.e. the boundaries you don't want to cross). For example, having the lifeguard save the author is dead boring and something you may want to avoid because 50 other students will be using that ending. What are the other boundaries that you don't want to cross? To ensure that the students do learn from the DELETE case, end off with the following questions:

a) What are other errors that you can make when you end a story?
b) Can you list other possible ways in which you can skew the story away from the title?

Chapter 29

Why is DELETE Useful to Learning Composition-Writing?

Firstly, not many students will think of a twist to a story such as *'The Day I Nearly Drowned'*. However, unlikely as it may be, there is still the danger that students will still make the mistake especially when trying to impress the marker during a high-stakes examination. As such, waiting for someone to make this mistake and to talk about it in class can be a useful incidental teaching moment but this opportunity may be few and far in between. Hence, it is still important to incorporate some of these errors into the curriculum to make explicit the SOPs and the boundary lines for students to understand and be clear about them.

Secondly, such uncommon mistakes can increase the metacognitive awareness of students to these and other possible mistakes. The principle of adhering to the title of the composition and not writing out of point is clearly illustrated in this DELETE case.

Cognition

i. **To Strengthen Conceptual Understanding and Skillsets in Targeted Problematic Areas**
    — To question why learners make certain Critical Errors
    — To blank out critical information in the question, with comments in the erroneous working/answer for the learners to arrive at their own conclusion at what the question was asking for

Example 3: English Cloze Passage
The following is a torn piece of paper extracted from part of the Secondary 3 English Paper II answer key used by teachers for marking. Only a portion of the cloze passage is visible. If you picked up the torn piece of paper, can you figure out what the earlier part of the passage looks like? Why do you think the answers indicated in the blanks are wrong?

Designing Errors for Students: Examples

A working copy of a marking key for an English Cloze Passage in the Secondary 3 Examination Paper with blotted out words

Passage

The honey bee is a very unusual kind of insert. Unlike other insects which live (1) _____, the honey bee lives as part of a community, also known as a colony.

> Only accept words that have the opposite connotations of together or community
> Errors: together, clustered

Heading the colony is the queen bee. She is larger than the rest of the bees. Her primary role in the colony is to lay eggs. Most of the other bees are the worker bees. These bees collect nectar and pollen from flowers. The nectar collected carried by the worker bees is deposited on the hive and then converted into honey. The worker bees also help (2) _____ the operations in the hive, which includes cleaning the hive of any debris and waste.

> Only accept the infinitive tense
> Errors:
> - 'runs' or 'ran'
> - 'keeps' or 'kept'

Reflection Questions

Blank 1:
1. The errors indicated in the first box include 'together' and 'clustered'. Suggest one reason for not accepting these answers.
2. If the correct answer is 'alone', what could be the word that is blotted out just before the word 'other'? Why do you say so?

Blank 2:
3. What do you notice about the errors indicated in the second box? Why are these errors just variations in tense?

4. What grammatical rule involves the infinitive (e.g. to run)?
5. If the blotted word is 'help', how does it bring in the rule about infinitive tense for the word 'run'?

Debrief

By getting the students to review how cloze passages are designed and what grammatical rules underpin the structure of the sentences, it will prepare students for conceptual complexities in how texts are constructed.

ii. To Develop Creatical Thinking Ability
— to add missing information to the problem for creative solutioning process

Example 4: Physics Question on Moment
James, a 15-year-old student, boards the crowded Mass Rapid Transit (MRT) train. He soon realises that he is surrounded by giggling secondary school girls who have just finished a sports event. Amidst the bantering among the girls standing around him, James steadies himself as the train speeds off to the next station. Without a grab pole or any handrail to hold onto, James soon finds himself swaying as the train checks itself due to a train fault. Suddenly, the train screeches to a stop and James flies through the air lands onto a petite girl next to him. The girl screams and pushes him away. Although James tries to pick himself up, but the jerky motion of the train doesn't make it easy.

Reflection
- What assumptions did James have when he was standing in the train? Why did he have those assumptions?

Designing Errors for Students: Examples

- If you were James with no room to move in the train, how would you have prevented yourself from falling over? (Use Physical laws and principles to suggest at least three possible answers.) You can add other details to the story to support your solution.
- If you are allowed to choose one of the following, which would you have chosen to stop yourself from falling? Most students chose belt with buckle. Why so? What about you?
  - Belt with buckle
  - Bag with books
  - Ball with cones
  - Sticky shoes
- What is the next mistake that James is likely to make? Why?

Part 2

In order to get away from the girl, he pushes himself against the jerking force of the train but without much success. The girls surrounding him are stunned. They try to pull him away from their friend. Gradually, with much difficulty, James gets to his feet. His face is as red as a tomato. With a soft apology, he quickly alights at the next stop amidst the glares from the girls in the compartment. What an embarrassing encounter!

- What should James have done to get away from the girl? How would that work?

Assuming that the same situation occurs to you and you carry a nearly empty backpack on your shoulder, with five textbooks in your hand. The train moves off and you fall on the girl next to you.

- What should you have done to steady yourself before the train moved off?
- What else could you have done?

Chapter 29

Part 3

With the same situation about to occur to you, but this time round, you are smarter. You remove the backpack on your shoulders and place the books into your bag. Holding the bag with your hands and keeping as low as possible, you maintain a low centre of gravity. You are 1.7 m tall and your centre of gravity is 0.7 m from your head. The train is moving at 50 km/h while your feet are 40 cm apart, facing the door of the train.

- How heavy must the books and backpack be?
- Alternatively, what else can you adjust besides the weight of the books?

If you do fall on someone, besides pushing against the braking force of the train, how else can you try to move?

Debrief

If we are remind ourselves that the purpose of this question is to develop *creatical* ability for effective solutioning, the focus is not on just solving the question but to allow students to be both creative (in coming up with new and better solutions) and critical (in analysing the issues and solve the problem).

Hence, getting students to constantly zoom in and out of the question, to take a step back and then to get in to try and solve the question is important. It is about trialling and testing possibilities and making prototypical solutions and dumping them if they don't quite work.

To end off, students may want to address the following questions, just see other relevant contexts that this question and the principles uncovered may also be relevant:

- How do this series of questions help you understand moment and gravity?

- What other Physical concepts have you thought about besides moment?
- In what real-life contexts would the earlier idea of holding a bag low enough to stabilise one be applicable too?

The solution for the series of questions above is likely to centre round moment and lowering the centre of gravity through the use of weights (books). This question encourages the student to consider the circumstances under which Physics is applicable, for the secondary school student. In addition, moving with the braking motion of the train may be easier, i.e. rolling forward rather than pushing back against the train.

Differentiation Strategies

At the curriculum level, differentiation can be easier said than done due to the need for the teacher or trainer to juggle several tasks or learning activities at the same time. Differentiation of materials based on ability can be challenging at best and a paper exercise at worst. The reason is that the teacher will find it extremely difficult to explain specific concepts without leaving either the highly able learners bored, or the weaker learners lost. Using the DELETE approach, the same problem can be tweaked with different errors so that the weaker learners will experience success when the attempt to resolve easier errors while the more able learners can attempt to take on higher order thinking skills such as questioning assumptions and recommending solutions.

For example,

The quadratic equation below needs to be solved:

$$4a + 3b = 10$$
$$3b - 2a = 4$$

The solutions with the embedded errors are:

easy	difficult
$4a + 3b = 10$ ... (1) $3b - 2a = 4$ ... (2) $(1) - (2)$ $4a - 2a = 6$ $2a- = 6$ $a = 3$ (substituting into (1)) $4(3) + 3b = 10$ $3b = -2$ $b = -2/3$	$4a + 3b = 10$ ... (1) $3b - 2a = 4$ ... (2) $(2) \times 2$ $6b - 4a = 8$ ... (3) $(3) - (1)$ $3b = -2$ $b = -2/3$ $b = -2/3$ (substituting into (1)) $4a + 3(-2/3) = 10$ $4a = 8$ $a = 2$

The easy DELETE error constitutes a matter of computational error, while the difficult DELETE error involves how the solver needs to be extra careful when multiplying operational signs (e.g. $+ \times + = -$) for these equations. The difficulty lies in the ability of the learner to find out proactively where the error is and how to question assumptions when designing this question. As a result, the learners need to investigate how solvers tend to make mistakes and in so doing, become aware themselves what they ought to be mindful and careful of.

iii. To Sharpen Cognitive Adaptability and Flexibility

Going forward, students are going into a *VUCA* world where careers are not going to be a straight-line trajectory but one involving numerous jobs across different sectors and industries. Being proactive and strategic to capitalise on trends and new developments will be critical to ensure one is in the driver's seat when it comes to taking on jobs which are productive and in demand. Many governments have adopted this pragmatic approach to ground students in character development and values inculcation so that they are equipped with the necessary resilience to manage change. The prospect of unexpected outcomes is real, and students should be prepared for it. Hence, using the DELETE approach to train students to manage their environments and lives is in line with the trend in education across developed countries today.

DELETE is useful to structure role plays and simulations for the students to build a psychological alertness for unexpected outcomes.

Example 5: Planning for Student Leadership Camp
The student leaders have been asked to plan a four-day programme for an upcoming camp within a one-week timeframe. The objectives of the camp are to expose 200 fellow 15-year-old students to outdoor camping and cooking, and to build resilience among the students. The student leaders are given three possible venues for their selection and are instructed to come up with a list of logistics and food items as part of the planning process.

At the point when there is only 1 hour remaining (from their one-week timeframe), the student leaders are asked to submit their draft plan. Based on the draft plan, teachers can select the following errors to highlight for the student leaders to respond to:

1) No plan in place to cater to students with special dietary needs (e.g. halal, vegetarian)
2) No alternative venue selected; the chosen venue is suddenly closed due to safety reasons
3) No wet weather programme nor provisions were made to address for wet weather issues

The student leaders are then given 1 hour to respond to the error/s pointed out. Based on the final plan submitted, the teacher takes the student leaders through a reflection process to evaluate how they responded to the error and what contexts and assumptions led to the oversight.

Chapter 29

After the reflection process, the teacher paints a scenario whereby the error was played out because it was not noticed, and the eventual consequence was that (in accordance to the error highlighted earlier):

1) About 15 students were left eating only biscuits throughout the four days because their dietary requirements were not considered. Some developed gastric problems and others complained of constant hunger as a result.
2) The 200 students were left stranded outside the closed campsite venue without transportation at 6 p.m. in the evening. The safety of the students was being compromised since there are wild animals in the vicinity.
3) It rained incessantly throughout the four days of camping and the majority of the tents were destroyed as a result. More than half of the students fell sick and were feverish by Day 3 of the camp.

The students are now asked to respond and adapt if the above scenario (select the relevant one) were to materialise. How would they react given that they are responsible for the camp programme and the safety of the 200 students in front of them? They have **15 minutes** to come up with a workable plan.

In the midst of the discussion, at the **10-minute point**, the student leaders are given the information that 1/3 of the students have telephoned their parents to ask them to come round to pick them up. What should the student leaders do now?

They have only **10 minutes** to respond before the students pack up to prepare to leave.

Debrief

At the end of the activity, the teacher needs to take the learners through a self-evaluation process by examining the following questions:

a) How would they rate themselves individually and as a committee on the level of responsiveness to the changes?
b) How did they process the information and their decision-making process?
c) Have they considered all perspectives before arriving at their decisions?
d) Was the decision a joint one made by the committee or one made by the most dominant student leader? Why?
e) What are the assumptions they had when making those decisions?

The focus of this DELETE approach is to develop cognitive flexibility and adaptability. Hence, by forcing the learners to make time-sensitive decisions with a situation that was spiralling out of control, it will be useful to determine how they cope under pressure. While this approach is similar to many situational tests and role plays, there is one fundamental difference — the careful design of the errors to bring out the critical skillsets being assessed and taught. The intentionality of the error design is important to ensure the learners experience sufficient pressure to respond quickly and correctly.

Emotion

i. **To Develop Values and Beliefs**
   — to design errors to trigger the self-evaluation process so as to develop new values and beliefs if the current ones are deemed as irrelevant or invalid

Example 6: Compassion towards Animals

True Story of Dewey, the Library Cat

Slide 1 (Error Presentation)

I admit it. I am guilty. I had no choice. Yes, it sounds like a lame excuse but as an 11-year-old, I did not know better. I was desperate and so I put him in the book return bin one cold January night in 1988. I didn't think my kitten might die from the cold.

Reflection Questions

- What was the author's error?
- What were his values? State at least two values evident from the above passage?

Designing Errors for Students: Examples

Slide 2

I only knew that if I kept my kitten in the house, my parents were likely to put it down as we already had four cats at home and having another one was out of the question. What could I have done? Thinking about it again, I was wrong to have abandoned my kitten especially when he was vulnerable and could have died. You see, my kitten had a story to tell.

Reflection Questions

- What would you have done if you were the author? Why?

Slide 3

When the library staff at Spencer Public Library found him in the bin, shivering and hungry the following morning, they decided to care for it. Subsequently, Dewey was declawed, neutered and given the proper vaccinations. People from as far away as New York donated money to buy food for Dewey. Not only that, they also visited the library just to see him. Dewey generated a lot of publicity for the library and was featured in the local newspapers, magazines and television programmes.

Reflection Questions

Now that you know Dewey's story, would you have changed your response to the earlier question on what you would have done if you were the author? Why? Do you need to reconsider your values towards pets?

Slide 4

Finally, on 29 November 2006, Dewey passed away due to a stomach tumour. He died in the arms of the library director after celebrating his

19th birthday. Although Dewey is gone, he is remembered by thousands of people whom he touched by simply being himself in the library. As for me, it is a sombre reminder how every animal, no matter how young, is precious. I didn't manage to keep a great cat but I am happy that the library and the public gained one as a result. Life does work itself out after a while, it seems. (Adapted from http://www.spencerlibrary.com/dewey.shtml)

Reflection Questions

- Does the end justify the author's decision to abandon his kitten? Why?
- Do you have similar or different values towards pets? Do you need to change? If so, what will your new values be? State them.

ii) To Strengthen Psychological Resilience for Unexpected Outcomes

Show the worst possible ending (see Fig. 33) and ask learners to choose the options at each conditional branching that WILL lead to the shown end state. The learner's task is to analyse the likelihood of such a scenario happening and what is the worst that can happen to the learner if the scenario really takes place. By adopting the worst-case scenario approach, learners become familiar with the bad decisions which characterise the downwards spiral that lead to the undesired end state. In doing so, learners become prepared both mentally and psychologically for the worst-case scenario, especially if the follow through activity on how to cope with such an end state is carried out effectively.

Given that a negative approach is taken here, it is important to prime and prepare the learners that while they are being taken on such a journey, the purpose is to 'inoculate' them against such outcomes in the future,

Fig. 33. Learning Process to Strengthen the Psychological Resilience of Learners

if they do occur. Learners are encouraged not to adopt such mindsets or attitudes to life.

Example 7: Cyber Blackmail
The video opens with a scene of a student crying with her head buried in her hands, sitting in front of a laptop, trying to access a social media platform. She realises she has been duped and is now panicking. What does she do? Her photos are now with her online 'boyfriend' who 'dumped' her immediately after she sent her photos over. These photos are not just ordinary ones but ones showing her in different states of undress and in compromising positions. How is she going to face her parents and her friends if they see those photos? Then, a message pops up on the screen. It states, '*If you do not want your photos to be circulated to your classmates, pay $10,000 tomorrow*'. At that point, the teenager collapses onto the floor. She realises her boyfriend was not who he claimed to be. At this point, the video stops and the viewer is prompted to return to the start.

Start Scenario

Valerie was introduced to the social media site by her good friend. Apparently, her good friend found some great online mates through the site. As Valerie surfs around, she realises that there are some really cute guys online, and they appear to be around her age. She also saw one whom she realises studies in a boys' school next to hers. At this point, she gets really excited and calls her friend to confirm whether the boy is someone they know.

Using Conditional Branching (through an e-resource) to elicit decision-making and analysis, students will go through several critical junctures (see Fig. 34). Their task is to reach the negative end state (i.e. Valerie receives the online blackmail). The effect is that the students should be alerted when such a scenario takes place and they can warn their friends or remind themselves of the possible consequences.

Chapter 29

Fig. 34. Branching Scenarios for Cyber Blackmail Example

Debrief

How do teenagers end up doing things online that they would not normally do in real life? This is an important question for the students to reflect on and respond, especially in relation to what Valerie experienced.

Designing Errors for Students: Examples

Reflection Questions
- Where were the critical junctures when Valerie made wrong decisions?
- What were some actions that 'Brian' did which led Valerie on?
- What would you do if you were Valerie?

To build the psychological resilience using conditional branching and in a manner that is productive, it is important for students to stop and reflect rather than to keep clicking through. Some additional sign-posts (such as 'Oh oh… this is a danger sign that Brian is not who he claims to be' and 'How do we know this person is harmless? What are his or her intentions?')

Psychomotor

ii. To Increase Reflexivity to Errors

Psychomotor skill training tends to focus on developing the consistency and accuracy of movements for the completion of tasks. Among students, these psychomotor training sessions centre round sports, art, technical skills (e.g. home economics and wood or metal work) and laboratory skills (e.g. pouring chemicals into test tube). Taking table tennis as an example, the use of DELETE to design errors can be applied to retrieving deceptive shots.

Example 8: Retrieving Deceptive Shots
It is a common trick of opponents playing fast shots changing the swing of the bat to put a spin to the table tennis ball, making it go near the net, instead of smashing it to the far end of the table. If the player retrieving the shot expects a long shot, he or she would have moved further back, thereby missing the net shot as the player needs to change direction to move forward towards the net.

In order to develop quick reflexivity to deceptive shots, training of your leg movements to adapt quickly to shots that have changed direction may help in both metacognitive and psychomotor training. You are to move away from the table in anticipation of the long shot and then shift forward quickly as the ball drops near the net. Practise the error rectification to reduce the reaction time. This is phase 1. When you are ready, the shot may also be long so as to vary the type of shot in order to reduce the familiarity effect. You should be ready to retrieve the ball regardless of whether it is a long or short ball.

In phase 2, you are to move forward to the net but the ball turns out to be long. In this case, you have to change direction and move backwards to retrieve the long ball. Again, vary the shot once you are familiar with the change in direction.

Finally, switching sides by moving your arm from left to retrieve a shot on the right and vice versa is important to rectify directional errors occurring sideways. This may involve twisting of the body to retrieve fast shots. Again, error-based training will prepare the player to retrieve shots *AFTER* the error has been made by increasing the reflexivity in the movements.

The above error-based training is only one example of how intentionally 'performing errors' and then rectifying them can be used to prepare sportspersons for actual performance during competitions. Besides table tennis, football, basketball and badminton are other examples of ball or racket games which can utilise directional change training methods.

Other examples of reflexivity training using error-based learning include:

- What should a runner do when a runner unintentionally steps on a stone or an object during a road race, which may result in a twisted ankle? What is the reflexive response to prevent injury?
- How should one react if a stray ball comes flying in your face? Should you duck, use your arm to block or turn away?
- What should a competitive swimmer do if the pair of goggles becomes dislodged midway through the 100 m freestyle race?
- How do you respond if you are holding a test-tube of concentrated sulphuric acid suddenly cracks and the liquid starts flowing onto the laboratory table?

- What should you do if the drill bit suddenly starts spinning before you can remove the metal piece with the partially drilled hole from the drilling platform?

At the more complicated levels, strategic changes can also be trained (e.g. when a particular planned strategy based on certain assumptions proved to be false) so that the coach or the captain in the game can now respond faster during the game to quickly  tweak the plan and meet the new challenges. Hopefully, the new strategy can also net them the game. However, training strategic thinking will likely be a cognitive approach more than a psychomotor skill training focus.

Sociality

i. To Develop Teamwork

There are several possibilities of using DELETE to design errors in order to build teamwork. One example is by using science experiments whereby a member picks up a wrong (harmless) chemical (because it is wrongly labelled) and they have to resolve why the results do not correspond with the theory. The example given below is from an outdoor trekking scenario. This is also usually the type of exercises used by teachers to build teamwork and leadership skills.

Example 9: Trekking

Using a trekking exercise (i.e. to read maps in order to reach several checkpoints) as the context, teams of five to seven members are tasked to complete the trek using the map given to them. The first team to complete gets additional points.

However, an error is designed into the map such that the teams will take a wrong turn at a critical point midway through the trekking exercise.

There is only one map and the team members are expected to rotate among themselves to read the map. Hence, at a certain point in time, the team will realise their 'error' and start to review their location in relation to the map. The members will need to maintain composure, regain their bearings, forgive the 'errant' map reader, unite and motivate everyone and decide on the next steps. All these sub-processes are part of the skills underpinning teamwork and are to be carried with minimal guidance or instruction from the facilitators or teachers. At the appropriate moment, when the issues are resolved or before the team dynamics degenerates beyond acceptance, they can be provided with the correct map and a brief review session can be conducted to extract key reflections and learning points from the members.

During this period of 'reorientation', several issues need to be resolved. For example, how does the team respond towards the member who 'made' the error? Does the team forgive the member and regroup to make up for lost time and resources or is there a certain level of blame and guilt? This psychological resilience to focus on the task at hand and not blame others is critical to leadership development and the building of teamwork. It will also more specifically cultivate collaborative skills among the members, to help out when a member is weak or unable to complete the task.

Debrief

Clear notes (or video recordings) on how the team resolves the problem with the erroneous map will be useful in assisting the members to identify and review their coping mechanisms when they were faced with uncertainty. At both the individual and team levels, take time to analyse how and why the members behaved or felt in a certain manner. This is especially important for members who exhibited negative emotions or behaviour, leading to a degeneration of team spirit and unity. Such negative blaming or pessimistic responses need to be arrested if the team is to grow.

Designing Errors for Students: Examples

In addition, by not letting the teams know about the error in advance, the designed error should provide opportunities for the teams to check themselves and to question assumptions. This builds mindfulness, beyond following instructions blindly. Hence, the facilitator's role, besides building teamwork, is also to build psychological resilience and mindfulness through the exercise and embedded error. Avoid giving the game away too early. Let the resentment simmer and allow the members to resolve the issue. This resolution process is part of one's learning journey towards maturity and should not be aborted but embraced.

ii. To Cultivate Collaborative Skills

Unlike teamwork, collaborative skills are more specific, comprising contributions of expertise and experiences, guiding others, negotiations and resolving conflicts. Collaboration is usually also more focused, to achieve a particular goal, whereas teamwork is about a collective effort and depends very much on how the members work with each other to build the team.

Example 10: Team Problem-Solving

Groups of three students are tasked to solve a difficult Mathematics problem. As there are three parts to the problem, each student is assigned to tackle one part and subsequently, put the solutions to the three parts together to solve the problem. The problem is designed with errors embedded it such that when the solutions to the three parts are put together, the final solution does not work out. The group members will have to collaborate with each other to trouble shoot each other's parts to resolve the issue. If necessary, the teacher can support by providing cues to the team after a period of time, to reflect if the question is correctly phrased and if it is solvable.

Again, it is important to craft the error around the difficult concept so that substantial learning for the students can take place, besides the development of collaborative learning skills.

Chapter 29

Holistic Development

iii. To Prepare the Individual for Future Skill Needs

It is difficult for most training programmes and educational products to promise capability development as the learning outcome because of the time and resources required. Here, we are talking about capability as beyond just being able to perform the tasks to carrying out a job within an authentic work environment. For students, this may or may not be relevant. Depending on how young the students are, there may not be a necessity to ensure job competence and capability yet, especially for primary school students. Still, it is never too early to develop job capability since it takes a long term for students to develop different domains of skills and competence in resilience, communication skills, problem-solving skills, creativity and other essential skills for work.

In that respect, students by the time they reach teenage years should be exposed to authentic work environments and be given some responsibilities to see a project through. Independent work behaviour and responsibility are examples of capabilities that a young person will need when he or she enters the workforce. Using the DELETE approach is one useful and effective way to build resilience and determination for future work capability, if there are concerted efforts to work with the students on these areas over a period of time.

Example 11: Encoding Institutional Knowledge Through Error Cards

Developing task cards to resolve 'An error a day' can be useful to primed students to review their assumptions and context for learning. By getting students to be mindful of the possible errors embedded into the problems and adopting an analytical stance to error-resolution on a daily basis, the habit of not taking things at face value is useful especially when many assumptions are made very often concerning learning and performance. These task cards can range from subject-specific (e.g. Science, Geography and Mathematics) to general subjects (e.g. logic, general knowledge and current affairs) and work issues (e.g. commenting on your boss' appearance

Designing Errors for Students: Examples

even if it is a compliment on your first day at work, insisting on your viewpoints when you are new to the team, try to operate the machines on your own even when you are stuck and unfamiliar with them).

The important point is not about identification and rectification of errors but to question why these errors were made in the first place and

The Ebola Threat

The Americans took scanty precaution to the spread of Ebola to the United States despite the rapidly increasing incidences in West Africa. After two to three months of observation and with the first case of Ebola landing on American shores on 4 October 2014 that the American immigration department finally took serious action to check passengers and possible infections of the Ebola virus.

- What were the assumptions made that led to such slow response rates?
- What is the cost to the United States if Ebola took root in the United States as compared with battling it in West Africa?
- How would have the experience with the Ebola virus prepared the healthcare authorities for the onslaught of COVID-19 pandemic?

Words of Perception

It is common for students to write the following sentence:

I felt the ground shook when the bull elephant approached me at the zoo.

The common rule is to use the past tense when describing an event in the past. However, this sentence comprises a word of perception (such as 'felt', 'see', 'hear' and 'feel') that the verb following the word of perception remains infinite (no past or perfect tense).

What is the other option if the author wants to keep the verb 'shook'? Can the words of perceptions be removed from the sentence? What would be the sentence?

what principles or assumptions need to be reviewed as part of the learning process. These reminders can bring about a level of mindfulness that pre-empt errors or to help learners resolve the errors quickly if they arise.

Debrief

Allowing students to attempt these DELETE questions either on their own or with their peers in a self-directed manner (with attached answers) can be one means of developing a metacognitive awareness of how they are learning difficult concepts and the assumptions they have towards them on a daily or weekly basis. However, do prepare the students sufficiently so that they have a good grasp of the concepts before they attempt these

---

Is Javier Overcharging?

Javier bought 35 football cards for $19.20 and is reselling 20 of them to you. He wants to earn 20% over his overall investment from the sale of just these 20 cards. Which is cheaper for you — to buy from him based on his computation below or should you teach him the correct approach?

Javier's Erroneous Working

Total cost of 35 cards = $19.20

80% – $19.20
1% – $0.24
100% – $24

He intends to resell the 20 cards for **$24**.

a) Would you buy from him based on this selling price? Is this price a better deal for you?
b) Would you tell him how to recalculate his selling price? Why or why not?

DELETE questions in order to not confuse them too early on in the learning process.

Developing capability in an incremental manner by focusing on students' mindfulness and eliciting their interest in daily affairs can be useful for subsequent work performance. Issues such as ethics and values are also part of the daily discussion. See the example below 'Is Javier Overcharging?' Beyond discussing Mathematical concepts, the error also contextualises the skill within a potential value issue and requires care in tackling as there are self-interests at stake.

Why Is DELETE Useful for Students?

In summary, not many people realise that the majority of the mistakes that students make are considered common mistakes with most of these mistakes made repeatedly by the same students (i.e. did not learn from their errors). Hence, teachers generally highlight these common errors as part of lessons in class to remind students to avoid making them. However, it is sometimes left to chance when students make these mistakes repeatedly and teachers pick out these errors to give special attention to. There are the less common mistakes which may not be highlighted and hence, left untaught. These uncommon mistakes can still be critical and may surface during examinations. The challenge then is to uncover some of the uncommon mistakes and make them clear to the students. By using DELETE, these specific uncommon errors can be also highlighted without waiting for students to make these mistakes.

Secondly, beyond training academic skillsets, DELETE addresses psychological, social and emotive capabilities (e.g. resilience, teamwork and mindfulness), which then to be left out during most class lessons. Hence, to build life-long learning, DELETE has a place to kickstart this awareness among students for capability development and not just building competency.

Chapter 29

How Does the DELETE Approach Work for Teachers?

It is useful to recap here that teachers can utilise the DELETE approach to reshape the learning experience for their students. Error-based learning incidents can make the lessons more interesting especially when interspersed between typical classroom instruction and presentations. Listed below are three reasons for the use of the DELETE approach in the classroom:

a. *To Focus on Key Skills and Concepts*

Depending on whether the students are already skilled in the topic or concepts, the appropriate DELETE error can be designed to take the students to the next level of competency and/or capability. What is important is to state upfront that the activity involves an error and the corresponding task should also be stated, to make clear the objectives of the learning activity. With that, the students will be aware where the errors are located in the process of learning and understanding. The errors are meant for them to pick up new concepts not to reinforce erroneous ways of doing things and that clarity is important, especially for the weaker students and the less proficient.

b. *To Design Differentiated Instruction*

In line with the Flipped Classroom approach, DELETE can now be used to deepen learning especially if the students are aware of the concepts based on the videos they have watched, and they are not starting from scratch. By designing errors into the practice (assignments done in school), students can move from basic questions to more complex ones involving 'creatical' abilities, metacognition and ones questioning assumptions especially for students who already understand the basic skills. In short, differentiated instruction is a real possibility with DELETE to vary the nature of the questions and assignments beyond just cognitively complex into other metacognitive skillsets.

c. *To Make Lessons More Interesting*
DELETE questions are generally more interesting to solve since there is the element of 'Can you spot the error'? as well as skipping the easy segments to focus on the complex elements based on the ability level of the students. If pitched at the appropriate level of difficulty, students will experience success and be motivated to attempt other related questions.

Conclusion

This chapter attempts to describe the application of the DELETE approach within the school context. Naturally, there are many different types of schools, educators, students and school environments. Hence, the DELETE approach may not work for all. However, it may still be a useful tool to diversify the learning approaches for students, especially when there is a need to focus on the difficult concepts or to facilitate psychological, emotive and social learning. The fitness for purpose mentality is important for educators to put on in order to ensure that the DELETE approach is utilised appropriately to maximise the benefits for the students.

Chapter 30: Designing Errors for Adult Learners

Wise men learn by other men's mistakes, fools by their own.

H. G. Bohn

I have specifically dedicated one chapter to adult learning examples since some of these cases will require a more context-heavy approach and these can be difficult to craft. The difficult concepts may also not be as evident. Usually, it will be up to the highly experienced practitioners or experts who will be able to identify difficult concepts quickly. They will be able to highlight what makes a task difficult and the errors associated with a particular critical task. Besides the designing of the error, designers need to be aware that the context should be set carefully for adult learners since misinterpretation can occur when the context is not well-designed, resulting in a lack of clarity for the readers. Again, the experts should inform this process of designing the context as well.

One of the key benefits of using DELETE for designing adult learning is the development of learner character and metacognitive capability to help him or her achieve job mastery. Beyond the focus on competencies, there is a further strengthening of learner mindfulness to identify job issues or anomalies before or when they occur. According to Dreyfus (2004), a certain level of intuitiveness and mindfulness is the hallmark of the expert when dealing with work issues. The expert simply 'knows' and is able to work

Chapter 30

through problems based on experience and an innate understanding of the issues at hand. However, while experience takes time and opportunities to accumulate, there is an additional element of constructive reflection and critical analysis of the experiences in order to turn them into useful reference points for future decision-making.

The following examples will illustrate the **process** of arriving at the errors and designing the appropriate DELETE cases for the designer of adult learning courses.

Examples

1. Medical doctor diagnosing the medical condition of a patient (cognitive domain)
2. Courseware developer applying instructional design theories (cognitive domain)
3. Sales assistant serving customer (social domain)
4. Soldier throwing a hand grenade (psychomotor domain)
5. Assessor making an assessment decision (cognitive/affective domain)
6. Facilitator managing a difficult learner (cognitive/social domain)

These cases are obviously not comprehensive but they serve to illustrate the flexibility of the DELETE approach as well as possible difficulties in designing good errors for learning. The technical competence of the DELETE designer cannot be understated here. It takes experience and some level of creativity to provide a twist, sometimes, to make an error authentic and interesting.

As you engage with the errors in these examples, bear in mind how learners will experience them and what could entail a positive and not so positive learning process for them. Being mindful about the user experience will be useful for your own reflection later.

Example 1: Medical Doctor Diagnosing the Medical Condition of a Patient (Metacognitive Domain)
Honing Metacognitive and Predictive Skill

— to predict whether a solution is forthcoming, or the solver is on the wrong track

In this case, imagine that you are a medical doctor diagnosing the medical condition of patients. The following case is adapted from a true story of a patient who was seeking professional opinion concerning an infection of the lymph nodes in the neck.

You will be asked to provide detailed descriptions on your thought processes throughout the case as it unfolds. The deeper you can articulate concerning your thoughts, the more helpful it will be subsequently when it comes to honing your metacognitive and predictive skill.

Card 1

Mr Nala is a patient from India. He flew into Jakarta this morning, having swollen lymph nodes. Apart from the pain in the neck area, Mr Nala suffered no other observable discomfort. His temperature was at a normal 37°C. The infectious disease specialist had already seen him and diagnosed him to be suffering from a bout of infection of the lymph nodes in the neck. Finally, when you had a chance to work with Mr Nala after your clinic had closed, it was past 6 p.m. and the patient appeared tired from the long wait and the lack of rest. The patient was surrounded by his three children and his wife. They appeared anxious to get a confirmation of the diagnosis from you. There was the possibility of cancer of the lymph nodes, which was a lot more serious than an infection, as you can imagine. You don't get a good feeling about the case and it would appear, based on your years of experience in working with patients with infection, that the patient was a little too well to be suffering from an infection. However, the family is not

Chapter 30

very well-to-do and it is unclear if putting Mr Nala through the positron emission tomography-magnetic resonance imaging (PET-MRI) scan will provide conclusive data about his condition. It could be a huge waste of resources.

1. What are you thinking about now? Why?

Card 2

As a result of your decision, Mr Nala underwent PET-MRI the following morning to study the soft tissues, nerves and blood vessels in the head and neck regions. Two hours later, after the scan was completed, the radiologists huddled together to determine which part of the diseased tissue is best suited for sample extraction based on the review of the scan. The good news is that there appeared to be some inflammatory cells, suggesting that Mr Nala could indeed be suffering from an infection of the lymph nodes. The family sighed with relief. With this piece of good news, they could avoid a huge outlay of resources and more importantly, their father/husband's life is assured. The team of specialists met up for a final team meeting. Everyone seemed to be satisfied with the results of the scan. The solution was to prescribe a bout of oral antibiotics to reduce the infection and strengthen Mr Nala's own immune system to fight the virus. Mr Nala could begin packing his bag for his flight home. It called for a celebration.

1. What are you thinking about now? Why?
2. Did you predict the outcome of the diagnosis stated above?
3. Now what, given that you are having those thoughts, are you going to do?

Card 3

However, the overall picture of an infection did not seem to fit. You spent the night reviewing the facts for the case. What went through your mind were firstly, the results of the tests associated with infection were all negative. This meant that somehow Mr Nala's body was not fighting the infection, which was very strange. Secondly, Mr Nala did not display the usual 'toxic' signs — such as having a fever, a flushed face, sweaty or oily skin and prolonged tiredness. While the symptoms associated with looking 'toxic' are difficult to define, it is something that experienced doctors observe, concerning patients with infection. This worrying over nothing is probably what others will term as intuition or sixth sense and probably comes with experience. You just know that something is not quite right.

The following morning, despite the reassuring preliminary results from the PET-MRI scan, you suggested that the patient stayed on at the hospital for further checks till the diagnosis is clear. By afternoon, the pathologist was not so convinced that the cells are inflamed. 'They look malignant', she pronounced. By then, the full battery of cancer tests was ordered for Mr Nala. The results came back — lymphoma or cancer of the lymph nodes.

1. What are you thinking about now? Why?
2. Do you switch out of thinking about an issue quickly? Do you get distracted easily?
3. Do you think through or deeply enough to consider all aspects of the situation?

The family was extremely anxious when they received the news. The teenage son became agitated since this news was contrary to the earlier diagnosis of infection. You assured them that lymphoma was very responsive to treatment and the patient has an excellent chance of cure. Truly, Mr Nala has since started on chemotherapy and his progress is remarkable. In hindsight, sometimes, it is useful to still rely on one's instinct and experience despite what the results of the tests show. Otherwise, Mr Nala may not have responded so well to treatment if his condition was not diagnosed correctly early enough.

Chapter 30

1. What do you think about the initial error in diagnosis?
2. Have you considered all aspects of the issue?
3. In what ways is your mode of thinking when approaching a problem a weakness or strength? Does your thinking hinder or facilitate performance?

Debrief

Now that you have studied and responded accordingly to the case, it is useful to take a step back to reflect on how you thought. Remember that the objective is to hone your metacognitive and predictive skill. It is also about maintaining calmness, despite the emotional outburst from the son. Managing the relatives of the patient would be an important social skill. As such, it is NOT important whether you knew enough about medicine and pathology to make the diagnosis but rather what and how you were thinking about the issue given the lack of details and background.

Some key questions you may want to ask yourself throughout the activity:

1. Did I employ a range of diverse thinking processes?
    - ☐ Utilise a problem-solving approach
    - ☐ Question assumptions
    - ☐ Check truthfulness or validity of facts
    - ☐ Reflect on my beliefs and values
    - ☐ Defer to alternative opinions from others in the team (including the facilitator)
2. Did I engage my emotions when thinking through the issues?
    - ☐ Note the emotions of the characters in the case
    - ☐ Identify with the characters and empathise appropriately
    - ☐ Experience a shifting of emotions as the story unfolds (from a sense of relief to anxiety and back to relief again)

3. Did I make references to my personal experience when thinking through the issues?
   - ☐ Visualise the story based on your understanding of the context and roles (e.g. doctors to wear white overcoats with stethoscope around their necks)
   - ☐ Make decisions based on what happened in the past

From the designer's point of view, it is important to determine if the learners had the opportunities to develop their metacognitive and predictive skill in order to fulfil the desired learning outcomes. Sufficient support and feedback to the learners should be given at appropriate moments to anchor the learning and to ensure the development of metacognitive capabilities. Getting the learners to articulate what they are thinking at different points in time is useful to check mental processes, values and belief so as to direct these learners to think more constructively for a more useful outcome.

Example 2: Sales Assistant Serving Customer (Metacognitive Domain)
Deriving the Context for Application
— to troubleshoot where and how the error occurred so as to prevent recurrence of error

In the case of a sale interaction that went wrong, the salesperson will have to examine carefully what occurred during the interaction that led to such unexpected consequences. On the surface, the customer was pleasant and unassuming. There were no outward signs of displeasure. However, a closer examination of the interaction revealed some interesting errors committed by the salesperson.

Read the following. There will be more information given to you as the case unfolds.

Chapter 30

Card 1

> Salesperson: Hello, how can I help you? This is our latest range of perfume products, most suitable for your loved ones.
> Customer: I am looking around.
> Salesperson: Are there any particular brands that you are looking for?
> Customer: Nothing in particular… maybe something suitable for my daughter.
> Salesperson: Sure. This is the latest product with a great fragrance, most suitable for women attending functions or just for office work.
> Customer: Hmm…
> Salesperson: Give it a try. Let me spray a little on your wrist… (proceeded to hold the customer's hand and started spraying the perfume). The perfume is not overwhelming and comes with a fruity fragrance (still holding customer's hand). Let me guess … Your daughter is a successful career woman … someone in her late 30s. This fragrance will fit her very …
> Customer: Erm … Thanks for the information … I will … think about it. (Walks away)

Now, how would you classify the above attempt by the salesperson to sell? Was there anything wrong or worth improving with the interaction? Reflect on the following points:

1. the salesperson's greeting of the customer
2. the manner in which the product was introduced
3. the content of the conversation
4. the other aspects of the interaction

Reflect on other possible contexts or factors involved in this interaction between the customer and the salesperson.

Task (Checking Assumptions)

What were some assumptions that the salesperson had when interacting with the customer?

1.
2.
3.

What about my own assumptions when I interact with customers? Do they affect my work performance?

Card 2

Take a look at the complaint letter.

> Dear General Manager,
>
> It pains me to write this letter about your staff during my visit to your store two weeks ago. I wanted to buy a bottle of perfume for my daughter and was served by your staff at the perfume counter. While the salesperson was courteous and professional at the start of the conversation, I was extremely offended when I was told that my daughter should be in her late 30! Did I look so old that I would have a 30-year-old daughter or was it because I was well dressed? Perhaps, your staff needs additional training to know what to say to customers in order not to offend them. For the record, I was buying the perfume for my daughter so that she can attend her secondary school prom night!
>
> Tan

Chapter 30

Task

Now that the complaint letter states clearly the reasons for the dissatisfaction, what were the errors made? How can the interaction be improved?

1.
2.
3.

Which part of the interaction with the customer would you consider to be the turning point in the sales process?

1.
2.

Card 3

Below is the letter from the General Manager to the customer.

Dear Ms Tan,

We sincerely apologise for the sincere mistake made by our staff. He has been advised and coached by our senior staff to be more sensitive to our customer's needs. I assure you that the mistake was not intentional and we hope you will forgive him. As a sign of goodwill, we would like to offer restitution. With this letter, you can go to any of our stores to pick up a bottle ladies' perfume for yourself or your daughter, with its value not exceeding $50.

   I hope, with this gesture, you will continue to consider patronising our store.

   Thank you and please come again.

Yours sincerely,

Mitch Lee (Mr.)
General Manager

Designing Errors for Adult Learners

Task

Based on the letter from the General Manager, are there other assumptions which you made that need to be addressed? How do these assumptions now change the context of the interaction?

1.
2.
3.

What do you think may also be underlying issues that the customer may have concerning the interaction?

1.
2.

Card 4

Below is the email reply from the customer to the General Manager.

Dear Mr Lee,
Thank you for your letter and kind gesture. I do appreciate your willingness to make restitution on behalf of your staff. I admit that he was a little over-zealous when trying to achieve the sales target. Perhaps a little sensitivity would have made the experience more pleasant for everyone. It was very uncomfortable to have him hold my hand for quite a few seconds.

Just to set the record straight. I am Mr. Tan, not Ms. Tan. Now, I know that you did not quite clarify the issue with your staff. Maybe you also need to work on your management style.

Thank you.

Yours sincerely,

Tan (Mr.)

Task

Based on the reply from the customer, do you think there are other more serious issues underpinning the organisation's work culture? What do you suggest?

1.
2.
3.

Taking a step back, how have your own assumptions and thoughts changed compared to at the start of the discussion?

1.
2.
3.

What have you picked up from this activity concerning assumptions and questioning contexts?

1.
2.

Debrief

1. What were the factors that contributed to the error/s?
2. How did the assumptions contribute to the errors?
3. Were the assumptions the key reasons for the errors?

_____

Critical Concepts in Managing Customers

What assumptions and contexts are involved in the customer's and salesperson's perception of:

- Cultural norms — age, gender and physical touch
- Sales interaction — degree of aggression versus passivity

Often, general Standard Operating Procedures (SOPs) can be very wrong when interpreted in a different context, for example, the salesperson holding the hand of the customer. The SOP was unlikely to have been intended for a male salesperson since most perfume salespersons are female and most customers are also female. Hence, holding the female customer's hand by the female salesperson is not seen as appropriate but useful to establish bonding with the customer. However, a male salesperson holding the hand of the male customer does not seem to be appropriate. Hence, the SOP needs to state the context, i.e. only applies to female salespersons with female customers.

When training salespersons and retail staff, it is critical to ascertain what perceptions and assumptions they have towards the customers and the sales process.

In addition, staff also may:

- face problems at home or at work
- need to undertake further training and assessment to address skills gaps
- be lost or confused when the situation turns unpredictable unfamiliar
- not be able to propose novel or innovative solutions to overcome the problem and may need more help

As such, supervisors will need to set up systems to provide just-in-time guidance to support frontline salespersons. This systemic approach to supporting salespersons can be a lifeline when customers become nasty or unreasonable.

Issues to Consider When Using the DELETE Approach

Considerations when using DELETE approach to question assumptions and contexts, and in so doing, further develop critical analytical thinking skills:

- The gradual unveiling of the case to reveal more intricacies and details of the context.
- By revealing the details in bite-sized chunks, the learning experience may be better structured and controlled for deeper reflection.
- It can be technically challenging for designers to work out the cases for this approach if the designer is not a subject matter expert.
- The difficult concepts have to be carefully identified to craft the learning design.

Example 3: Soldier Following SOP in Throwing Hand Grenade (Holistic (Metacognitive with Psychomotor) Domain)

Deriving the Context for Application

— to identify contextual cues so as to prevent applying the wrong approach to a similar context

The DELETE approach used here is to strengthen the learner's ability to identify contextual cues so as to reduce the likelihood of wrong application in a different context, e.g. the male salesperson holding the male customer's hand. In this particular case, the ability to differentiate context is developed by getting the learners to practise crafting the possible wrong contexts which resulted in the error committed.

Video Case

The video shows the soldier taking the necessary precautions to check the grenade, check the ground ahead to ensure there are no friendly forces, remove safety pin, let the catch go and count to three before pulling hand back to release the hand grenade. The corporal seemed to have observed all the correct steps that he has been taught in throwing the hand grenade. However, the result was a disaster which resulted in his death. Despite all the correct training and safety precautions, the dead soldier could not foresee such an outcome. It devastated the entire platoon, and the commanders were summarily arrested on the count of negligence.

Reflection

- Which could have happened?
- Was it the soldier's fault? If not, whose fault is it?
- What were his assumptions?

Task

Fill in the context for this case to show how under different contexts, the correct procedure in throwing the hand grenade can be a frightfully wrong process.

Add or amend the current procedure to address the possible context you have created above.

Are there other possible contexts that soldiers need to consider under real war conditions?

Referencing

Conduct your own study on how soldiers are killed by their own hand grenades. What are common causes of these deaths?

Re-experimentation

Based on one of the contexts that you suggested, can you now counter propose a new SOP for arming and releasing the hand grenade to make the procedure safer and more effective in war time?

Example 4: Assessor Making an Assessment Decision (Cognitive Domain)
Developing Creatical Ability

— to fill in the information gaps with possible scenarios for a creative solutioning process

Case: *(Learners are to creatively and critically decide what the context and actions were which resulted in possible errors), e.g. special needs, missing out key evidence, not giving learners opportunities to cover gaps, accepting evidence that is not valid, using a different method to cover gaps (OQ to cover PP)*

The candidate, Julie, sat nervously outside the assessment room, waiting for her turn to take the assessment on visual merchandising. Her job as a retail assistant involves making product displays to encourage shoppers to enter the store and purchase the products. Her assessor beckoned her in as the previous candidate left the room. He gave her a smile, just to reassure her and started the assessment process. The assessment proceeded quickly. Julie demonstrated what she knew about visual merchandising. There were some parts which she wasn't very confident about, but the assessor guided her through. She also had to answer some questions at certain points when she became confused about the procedure. The assessor was very patient with her and gave her a lot of time and guided her to answer the questions correctly. Following the performance segment, she sat down to explain to the assessor certain organisational SOPs in relation to product display. After about an hour, the assessor ushered her out with the assurance that she managed to complete the assessment. However, Julie wasn't convinced that she was fully competent.

In any case, she was given the 'competent' result and she was relieved to have completed the assessment.

The same assessment was observed by an external auditor in the next room who raised the alarm about the validity of the assessment. The auditor was adamant that the assessment did not satisfy the key criteria of a competency-based assessment. What do you think happened? Suggest possible activities or actions taken by the assessor and/or the candidate to warrant such a reaction from the external auditor.

Reflection

- Which actually happened?
- Was it the candidate's fault? If not, whose fault is it?
- What were the assumptions behind the assessor's and candidate's actions?

Task

1. Insert the details for the context with regards for this case to show how under different contexts, the stated procedure in assessment was wrong.
2. Add or amend the current procedure to address the possible context you have created above.
3. Are there other possible contexts that assessors need to consider under assessment conditions?

Referencing
Conduct a search on how candidates deemed competent can be assessed incorrectly. Provide details of how assessments can be conducted wrongly.

Re-experimentation
Following the audit, another candidate, when assessed, correctly placed the merchandise in the right position. However, the assessor took longer than usual to arrive at the assessment decision. Even after the assessment, the assessor ushered the candidate out of the assessment room without giving the assessment decision. What do you think could be the issue now? Justify your answer.

Example 5: Facilitator Managing a Difficult Learner (Cognitive and Sociality Domains)
Sharpening Cognitive Adaptability and Flexibility
— to cope with a constantly changing wicked problem and error

Changing conditions as the problem evolves ... learners guess and predict issues and then are presented with new issues to solve ... to target continuous problem solving and authentic workplace condition

Part 1
You are the facilitator in a class when you are confronted with a difficult question by a persistent learner... putting down learner etc. ... learner trying to gain sympathy and support from other learners during break time ... continues to pose questions which tend to be sarcastic rather than meaningful ... refuses to participate in group discussion after a while ... threatens to write to management for fee refund ...

Task

- How will you respond?
- What do you think of the learner's actions?
- Are your thoughts at this point in time appropriate? Why?

Part 2

Learner was absent on Day 2 ... found out that he is a cancer victim and needs therapy every few weeks ... drugs also make him more volatile in his temper ...

Task

- How will you respond now?
- What do you think of the learner's actions?
- What has changed?
- Do you think your thoughts on Day 1 are still appropriate?

Part 3

The learner returned to class for the next three days and continued to pose difficult questions and make demands such as asking you to give him personal tuition at 9 p.m. at night via skype. He also asked you to vet his assignment and rewrite certain parts which he was not so confident about. On the last day of the training, he verbally abused a fellow classmate and ridiculed him for being stupid, in not picking up the concepts fast enough.

Task

- How will you respond now? Why will you respond in such manner?
- State whether your responses are similar or different from those on Day 1?

- *Which values are you demonstrating when you make the earlier decisions?*

Part 4

About one week after the conclusion of the workshop and with all the learners, including the difficult learner with cancer, clearing the assessment, you heard a disturbing piece of news. After which, you regretted helping the difficult learner and wished you stuck to your original stance on Day 1.

Task

- *What disturbing piece of news will result in you regretting your actions?*
- *Which value/s are you demonstrating here?*
- *Overall, what are the key values and mindset that you bring along to the classroom when working with learners?*

Part 5

The disturbing piece of news was that the learner did have an illness but it was not as serious as cancer. It wasn't life-threatening and he was on medication which causes some drowsiness.

Task

- *How does this case change the way you view difficult learners?*
- *Will you accept underlying causes behind certain behaviours as acceptable even at the expense of other learners? Why?*

Besides the error and the task, the referencing and active re-experimentation will have to take place to complete the learning cycle for the learners. Structuring the referencing process with targeted clear notes will be necessary for the learners to 'try again' in the active re-experimentation stage. The crux of the entire E^3 process still depends largely on the quality and accuracy of the error designed. If the design of the error is based on an accurate analysis of the difficult concept and is pitched at the right level of difficulty (Bloom's Taxonomy), the setting of the task based on the outcomes will follow suit with the rest of the DELETE process (Referencing and Re-experimentation) completing the loop. From the instructional design point of view, the use of errors for learning is not new. What is new in DELETE is the careful and intentional design of errors to facilitate learning under different contexts so as to surface assumptions and address the 'correct' mentality when in a chaotic and complex world, 'correct' is always based on context. Once the context changes, the solution which may be correct for a long time is no longer correct and can be extremely wrong. Hence, increasing the metacognitive awareness is crucial to alert workers to possible errors especially when processes are automatised and no one is checking on these processes anymore. It will be these processes which will generate the most unimaginable errors.

Addressing the Emotional Aspect of Human Development: Teaching Values Through DELETE

Besides training cognitive abilities, DELETE approach can also develop the appropriate values needed for the organisation. Described below are short examples of how cases can be written to promote the development of values within organisational, religious and family contexts. These examples are to provide samples of how DELETE cases can provide a different slant to the design and the subsequent learning experienced.

Example 6: Courseware Developer Applying Instructional Design Theory (Emotive Domain)
Developing Appropriate Values and Beliefs
— to emphasise the importance of values and beliefs under different contexts

Chapter 30

Jeff was a senior courseware developer at a retail company and he was keen to apply some instructional design theories to structure the learning process for those in the front line customer service Parts. Given that the service staff are primarily cosmetics salesgirls who needed to be updated on product information and on competitors' products on a regular basis, Jeff decided to utilise Knowles' Self-Directed Learning Theory to structure the lesson. He used the following structure based on the 5 characteristics of adult learners:

Table 39. Lesson Plan for the Programme for Salespersons

Duration	Activity	Andragogical Characteristics	Remarks
10 min	Explain difficulties in managing customers and how knowing customers will facilitate better work performance	Relevance to work	
30 min	Present the five key concepts related to managing customers	Readiness	
10 min	Get salespersons to assess themselves based on their ability to remember the concepts	Motivation	Written test
20 min	Get salespersons to role play difficult customers and critique their performance	Problem-focused (Orientation)	
20 min	Elicit prior knowledge of salespersons concerning customer types	Adult learner's experience	
15 min	Salespersons determine if they need to undertake the same paper assessment again	Self-concept	Written test
15 min	Conclude with a recap of the key concepts in managing customers and product sales		

Jeff submitted the above lesson plan to the organisation's facilitator but received adverse comments. Bearing in mind that the workshop was supposed to equip the salespersons with skillsets to manage customers, why was Jeff ridiculed for being unrealistic and presumptuous of the salespersons' motivation to learn on their own?

Designing Errors for Adult Learners

Task

Imagine that you are a learner participating in Jeff's programme as depicted above. What comments will you give to Jeff? What are the beliefs and values you possess about instructional design when you made those comments to Jeff?

Reference Sources

- Differences between learning theories and instructional design theories
- Can Knowles' andragogical characteristics be used as an instructional design theory?

Debrief

Ultimately, it is not whether Jeff made the right call in this particular case but more importantly, why Jeff was ridiculed and how you as the evaluator critique Jeff's instructional design. There are many different perspectives to instructional designs and underpinning the critique are our own beliefs about what constitutes good design and how instructional design theories are used to anchor the learning. For example, some learning designers are constructivist in nature and believe that good designs require the learners to build their own understanding of the concept through an experiential approach (e.g. role plays or workplace engagement). Other designers are more cognitivist and believe that learners should learn systematically through carefully crafted lectures or content downloading sessions with just in time questions answered.

Depending on one's professional beliefs, the perspectives taken could be very different. The DELETE case allows learning designers to mull over the 'error' and make their own decisions pertaining to the error. In this regard, making the professional beliefs evident is important to drive future behaviours, whether intentional or unintentional.

Chapter 30

Example 7: Officer Cadets Playing With Their Swords of Honour One Day Before the Passing Out Parade

In order to impress on new army graduates from an officer course the importance of carrying themselves well as new officers, this DELETE case based on a true story is used to drive home the message that they are to live up to the authority the army has given to them. New officers are expected to maintain decorum and observe dignity accorded to their officer rank.

Setup of DELETE Case

- Issue — Army cadets awaiting their passing out parade, with some time on their hands.
- Solution — Read a book or practise their drill.
- Error — Cadets playing with their Swords of Honour by engaging in sword play in their own bunk, resulting in the cadets involved being demoted to sergeant and not receiving their officer rank even though the graduation ceremony was only one day away. Despite their sincere pleas, the Commanders maintain their final decision which was to give the sergeant rank to the two cadets involved in the sword play.
- Task — List the values that underpin the punitive measure meted out by the Commanders. Do you agree with the decision made?

By giving this DELETE case to the cadets, there is a message that the Army will be able to send out which is to impress on the cadets the importance of maturity and decorum as future officers. The severity of the punishment along with the standards expected of graduating cadets will make a strong impact on them, following which, it is unlikely any cadet will engage in play with the ceremonial swords again.

Example 8: A Man With His Umbrella

A man left his home with an umbrella and a haversack. He was going to see his wife. Not long after, while walking along the road, it started to drizzle. When the rain drops first fell on the man, he looked up at the sky but he did not open the umbrella. The rain was too light. He hurried on. Then, the rain drops increased in numbers and pelted him but yet, he did not open the umbrella. He glanced at the umbrella in his hand, but he hid it in his jacket with a sigh as if it needed protection from the rain. Then a tear fell, and another one. Soon, he was weeping as he hurried along in the torrential rain. He was getting drenched. His hair flattened as the rain washed out his hair gel. His shoes swished with water and yet, he refused to open his umbrella.

Why?

- The umbrella wasn't his. It was his wife's.
  What's wrong here?
- His wife had just passed away after 40 years of marriage. He was on his way to visit her in the columbarium.

  What values are we talking about here?
  What do you think he wanted to do with the umbrella?

- He wanted to place the umbrella with his wife so that she can be reminded of their first date which occurred in the rain.

Setup of DELETE Case

- Issue — rain
- Solution — open the umbrella

- Error — no umbrella that he could have used
- Task — examine the contextual cues and possible reasons/values behind the 'error' i.e. not using the umbrella with him

Some errors are intentionally committed based on values — the man rather get drenched than devalue the umbrella for his wife, by getting it wet. This DELETE case is interesting in the manner which the story unfolds. The values uncovered are gradual and are deeper compared to the earlier ones (e.g. not getting wet vs. remembering his wife).

Conclusion

Over the eight use cases, you can probably arrive at your own impression of how a case study adopting the DELETE approach (whether dynamic or static/partial or full presentations of context, task, error, consequences and rectifications) can be designed to achieve different outcomes. Your understanding of the learners' work affordances would be a determining factor when crafting the case study in terms of the authenticity of the workflow and outcomes.

Validating the case studies and other DELETE activities with the targeted learners to fine-tune the engagement experience will be useful. It is a critical step to achieve the desired learning outcomes.

Chapter 31

Designing Errors Based on Real Life Examples for Purposive Learning

In this chapter, we examine how real-life examples of incidents gone wrong can be redesigned for learning instances with clear implications for planning and development for authorities and planners. All of these incidents can help us uncover first principles and release insights for future behaviour, in view of possible similar occurrences.

Example 1: King Solomon, Two Women and Two Babies

We started with the sayings of King Solomon and we will end with one of his famous acts of wisdom. When he was called upon to judge between two women (1 Kings 3:16–28) who brought two babies — one dead and one alive — to him, to decide whose baby belonged to which mother, given that both gave birth to the babies at the same time. He asked for a sword and at the moment when he decided to dissect the living baby to give one half to each mother, the actual mother screamed and asked the baby to be given to the other mother instead while the other woman claimed that it was a fair decision.

With that, King Solomon adjudged that the mother of the living baby was the one who screamed and told the servants to hand the living baby to the woman. Now, in hindsight, this test was designed based on DELETE principles because… the value of fairness is ingrained in legal judgments as justice so halving the two babies, to be shared between the two women would have been 'fair and just' but obviously, it would have been the 'wrong' context compared to other inanimate objects such as property and finances. More importantly, the assumption that the mother would love the baby and would not want the baby to be killed was a universal value that guided this DELETE example.

Error Design

- Issue — Who is the actual mother of the baby who is alive?
- Solution — Sharing of the baby physically (i.e. cutting him into two halves) would be fair to both mothers
- Error — Killing the baby to make it fair to both mothers would be unfair to the baby and the actual mother
- Task — What made this 'solution' by King Solomon a seemingly 'DELETE' approach? Discuss. What would be a similar situation where leveraging on a universal value (e.g. altruism, kindness, hope) can cause someone to behave in a sacrificial manner?

The underlying concept here is the contextual boundaries linked to the rule of fairness. In this case, the contextual boundaries of fairness are breached when King Solomon proposed killing the baby based on the rule of fairness to the two mothers. You would likely agree that it would be an 'error' if the ruling was carried out. The rectification and the consequence were presented in full (i.e. to dissect the baby and both mothers would have part of the baby which was fair).

By leveraging this 'error', King Solomon triggered the sacrificial love of the mother for her child as she gave up her right to the child in order to let the child live. Who are the learners in this case then? What was the learning outcome? Based on this case, the audience (and the readers of this case, including future judges and lawyers) would be the learners and the learning outcome is to trust in human universal principles (e.g. maternal love) to drive human behaviour. It is about developing values, under the Emotion domain.

Example 2: Penalty and Free Kicks in Soccer

It was a common practice that when penalty kicks are taken, the ball should go to either the top or the bottom corners of the goal post. These were the most difficult to reach spots for the goalkeeper and most likely would yield the goal.

However, in recent years, penalty takers have added a third option, lifting the ball down the middle where the goalkeeper would have been standing before diving to the left or right. Now, this is interesting as if the goalkeeper did not take any action, the ball would have hit the goalkeeper and it would be the easiest of all saves.

The kick was executed in anticipation that the goalkeeper would most likely make the error of diving to the right or to the left, resulting in the likely goal if the ball was shot down the middle. With this anticipation of how the goalkeeper would act, then the resulting action by the penalty taker becomes obvious — down the middle is actually the safest approach. The irony was that once the middle approach becomes the norm, the goalkeeper will choose to remain still and catch the ball floating towards him. The second guessing of the goalkeeper's actions is part of DELETE because the rule of saving the penalty by stopping the ball from getting into the goal remains, but the context has expanded to include the addition of the third option of shooting down the middle where the goalkeeper stands.

Error Design

- Issue — Guessing the direction that the goalkeeper will dive in and kicking the ball in the other direction
- Solution — Creating more options for the penalty taker to take the kick
- Error — Tricking the goalkeeper to dive in the wrong direction
- Task — Discuss the potential errors that the goalkeeper will make and how to increase the rate of errors by the goalkeeper

Similarly, when players taking the free kick near the goal post have always attempted to hit the overhead shot above the wall of opposing players standing between the ball and the goal. In recent years, players have added another option of kicking the ball *under* the wall as the wall of players typically jump to stop the overhead ball from flying into the goal. Again, once the context is expanded to include this option of shooting under the wall, the opposing team puts in a player lying on the ground to stop any ground balls.

The review of contexts is useful to provide new ways of playing to the rules, especially when others have yet to grasp the opportunities and will need time to respond, during which you have the advantage of being the first mover.

Example 3: Ukraine and Russia — Deception by Showcasing the Wrong 'Rules' or 'Action Plans'

In the war between Ukraine and Russia, in the late 2022, Ukraine shared plans openly to attack the south of Ukraine where Russian forces were amassed. These open plans resulted in Russia redeploying troops from the east to the south of Ukraine. Eventually, once the mobilisation of Russian troops took place, Ukraine attacked eastern Ukraine, leading to the routing of the Russian troops and the rapid assault and capture of these towns in Eastern Ukraine.

The rewriting of rules (e.g. using drone technology, including low-cost commercial drones) in the war has led to warfare experts running back to the drawing board to re-evaluate their understanding of how war ought to be conducted and prevented in the future. With possible drone swarms becoming a reality in the near future, it is questionable if large acquisitions of prohibitively expensive war planes and ships are a good return on investment, in view that these war machines are not easily hidden from satellites and can be targeted by drones for a quick kill.

Designing Errors Based on Real Life Examples for Purposive Learning

With artificial intelligence, the possibility of robotic soldiers can increase destructive power with less endangerment to human lives (for the attacking force). Sending in 100,000 robotic soldiers may be an easier button to press than conscripting human civilians and pressing them into war. Does this make war more likely since the cost to human lives could be lower? Obviously, this is an oversimplification of the issues at stake but what is clear is that the rules of warfare, with the corresponding contexts are being changed at a very rapid pace and our militaries will need to take stock and not be caught unaware.

Designing errors into the training to force intentional and careful rethinking of the rules and contexts would be of paramount importance — a matter of life and death, in this case.

"Common sense is not so common after all."
Unknown

Error Design

- Issue — Using strategic planning and deception in warfare
- Solution — Increase second guessing by external stakeholders so as to complicate decision-making for the enemy
- Error — 'errors' for the enemy to pick up so as to mislead the enemy in making wrong decisions
- Task — Designing errors to mislead the enemy forces

In this DELETE exercise, the focus is to create misleading 'errors' for the enemy to make. It would focus on building metacognitive skills where understanding one's assumptions and those of the enemy's is critical for this approach to work. Again, the contextual boundaries (e.g. attacking civilian infrastructure and the surroundings of the nuclear plants) may be revisited and redrawn when the enemy changes the approach. Being prepared by being unpredictable is an important attribute of warfare.

Chapter 31

Example 4: The Itaewon Crush in Seoul on 29 October 2022 and the Indonesian Soccer Crush on 1 October 2022

On 29 October 2022, at Itaewon, a famous clubbing district in Seoul, revellers were found enjoying Halloween parties with crowds moving along streets. As the young people emerged from the underground train station and another crowd moved in the opposite direction in the area, the two streams of the crowd collided along a narrow street and at that juncture along the street, the revellers were caught in a crush resulting in more than 150 young people died.

Associated Contexts: Indonesian Soccer Crush Leading to at Least 125 Deaths on 1 October 2022

With the Indonesian soccer crowd crush, there had been concerns in the lead-up to the game between Arema FC and long-time rivals, Persebaya Surabaya, as there had been incidents of violence between the fervent fans from the two clubs.

On the evening of 1 October 2022, after the final whistle, Arema fans moved onto the pitch, where the team's footballers were gathered in the middle. Police had already escorted Persebaya to their changing rooms. Many of those streaming onto the field had appeared to come to 'show support, not attack'. At some point, police began to fire tear gas into the thousands-strong crowd, volleys aimed at dispersing them. One eyewitness reported that police fired tear gas rounds 'continuously and fast'. Some witnesses said that the police were unnecessarily brutal — and that along with the clouds of stinging gas, officers were beating fans with batons. As such, the fans resorted to pushing their way through the crowd via the narrow passageways in the stadium.

Error Design

- Issue — people management procedure when there is a sudden increase in crowd size in an enclosed or small space
- Solution — identifying physically tight spaces (e.g. passageways in football stadium) and situations (e.g. street celebration) and drawing up a crowd management plan for these occasions and locations
- Error — Conduct error-based learning in three phases with the error being revealed gradually as the crowd gathers. Add triggers such as a bomb blast or a fire started by a short circuit during a New Year celebration at a crowded square to create panic and crowd crush.
- Task — Identify locations where crowd management is needed and conduct strategic planning of crowd control measures for these locations. Discuss how the two incidents are similar? What contextual boundaries are similar and what boundaries are different? Explain.

Example 5: Collapse of Pedestrian Bridge in India in end-Oct 2022

A colonial-era pedestrian bridge packed with revellers collapsed, resulting in at least 132 people dead, many as a result of falling into the river below, police say. Authorities said nearly 500 people were celebrating the last day of the Diwali festival on and around the nearly 150-year-old suspension bridge in Morbi when supporting cables snapped after dark on Sunday.

CCTV footage showed the bridge structure swaying — with a few people apparently deliberately rocking it — before it suddenly gave way. The walkway and one fence crashed into the river, leaving the other side dangling in mid-air and hundreds of people in the water. It was a disaster with families with multiple deaths and injuries.

Chapter 31

Associated Incident: Collapse of the Basse-Chaîne Bridge Spanning the Maine River, France, in 1850

The collapse of bridges is not unprecedented. On 16 April 1850, a battalion of nearly 500 French soldiers struggled to stay upright during a thunderstorm as them marched across the Basse-Chaîne Bridge spanning the Maine river. The high winds, combined with the force of the soldiers' rhythmic steps, caused the 335-foot-long suspension bridge to sway severely, snapping its wire cables. One of the 11-year-old structure's cast-iron towers collapsed on the soldiers, and the deck plummeted into the river below. The accident, which killed 226 people, was due to multiple factors, including the storm, the corrosion of the bridge's anchors and the soldiers' synchronous stepping. The disaster also highlighted the importance of 'breaking step' to avoid achieving resonance when crossing bridges.

Error Design

- Issue — Strength of the supporting structures for bridges
- Solution — Computing the strength needed to support the weight of people using the bridges
- Error — Providing only the strength of the structure
- Task — Finding the other issues involved in computing bridge construction and structure (i.e. frequency of steps or swaying caused by pedestrians and reducing resonance accordingly).

The DELETE approach is to provide the context and issues without giving the final reason (which has to do with resonance formation due to the coordinated force exerted) for the collapse of the bridges. The presentation of the cases should be phased so that the students evaluate the issues for themselves before stumbling upon the primary cause of the disaster (resonance).

Conclusion

Going forward, what does DELETE mean to the typical teacher or trainer in the classroom? How can any designer utilise DELETE to make learning happen? What are some of the key elements to look out for in DELETE which are essential to the learning process?

Quite simply, DELETE as a concept is to utilise common or critical errors as points of engagement for the learner so that there are kinks in the learning process for the learner to identify and issues to solve. This creates disequilibrium which is useful for learners to increase their attention and concentration level (just like in the case of someone driving on a long and straight highway for hours when suddenly there is a series of turns in the road). The motivation level goes up as learners attempt to solve something that someone else could not. More importantly, the challenge is there to identify issues and make good something that is wrong. Research has shown that it is easier for learners to correct or modify something that is already present than to create something from scratch. On this note, weak students may be more motivated to learn through the DELETE approach than to want to try solving a problem from the start. Often, these students do not know how to start and do not want to try. As such, they have already given up even before giving the question a decent attempt.

DELETE does not solve all learning problems. It is hoped that DELETE provides an alternative to the current plethora of solutions and learning processes for learners so that a more targeted and possibly less resource- and time-consuming approach can alleviate the current 'chore' that many of our students perceive learning to be.

Chapter 32 How the DELETE Approach Differs from Other Instructional Designs

It is a good question when we ask why we are doing the things that we do and how different it is from what we use to do. Listed below are some areas which the DELETE approach differs from other instructional designs.

Intentional Error Design

Besides looking at what to do (according to the SOP), DELETE approach requires learners to remediate those errors crafted into the experience. These errors need to be strategic and intentional to drive the uncovering of first principles. This approach differs from general situational tests where the actions of the learners drive the situational development. With the DELETE approach, the errors (either by the learners or other parties) are intentionally crafted into situation, for the learners to respond to.

Focus on Learning BOTH Rules and Contextual Boundaries

Throughout this book, the discussion is on BOTH rules (or SOPs) and contextual boundaries as errors occur when the rules are different and hence, will be broken, and/or when the contextual boundaries shift.

For example, what happens if the assumption held by global players that the Taiwan–China and the North–South Korea conflicts are separate and should be dealt with on different platforms is an error? Can the DELETE approach be used to design an error where the military planners look at the development of the war situation with *both* conflicts occurring *simultaneously* despite planning for the occurrence of only one conflict? How is the remediation to be conducted if such an error in assumption and planning were to occur? In this case, the contextual boundary (of only one conflict happening) is breached and needs to be expanded to include simultaneous conflicts in North-East Asia.

The Development of Metacognition and Emotion

Unlike most instructional designs, the DELETE approach includes metacognitive and emotion development in a natural manner. Getting the learners to reflect upon one's current thinking and assumptions intermittently is part of the DELETE experience and is meant to develop metacognition. Likewise, emotions and values are also evaluated regularly to enhance the resilience of the learners by pushing the contextual boundaries especially when the unexpected occurs and learners are put in a compromising and emotively charged situation.

Time-Based Injections

Almost without apology, the DELETE approach does stop the learning experience to intermittently inject new situations, contexts and errors for learners to uncover the first principles and assumptions that they could be holding. The cognitive dissonance projected by the time-based changing circumstances and contexts can lead to learner disorientation and challenge even the most proficient learner to review their current understanding of the concepts and expand their repertoire of expected behaviour, leading to expertise.

Going Beyond Competency, Driving Expertise

Unlike most instructional designs, the DELETE approach is about going beyond the typical learning outcomes, into outcomes which may be less measurable or observable but likely to be residing in the expert skill domains. In this regard, the DELETE approach is most suited to developing learners for the 21st century where artificial intelligence (AI) and automation will likely take on the skillsets in the 'competent' category. Here, outcomes are measurable and observable as this space allows for 'objective' feedback to be given to the AI and automaton for rapid correction and improvement. Moving human practitioners to the realm of expert skills, becomes a natural progression. However, the development of expert skills takes many years, of which error-based learning may help expedite the process, by driving development beyond competencies (performing tasks) into capability and expertise (handling job roles).

Conclusion

The DELETE approach leverages the constructivist learning experience, with the errors providing stimulus for the learners to rethink and reflect their own understanding of the issue and context. The key is not about disrupting pedagogical theories but to strengthen the approach to drive the learning outcomes to achieve higher levels of the Bloom's Taxonomy and beyond. What is unique about DELETE is the exploration of the boundaries which are often ignored in most learning activities.

Most designers may adopt the DELETE approach in specific segments of the learning process, to achieve outcomes which go beyond competencies. We may not always use DELETE throughout the training programme because that is not necessarily the best approach for the learners.

Chapter 33
Working with AI and Next Steps

You might have heard of ChatGPT, the generative artificial intelligence (AI), and a language model developed by OpenAI. It is able to generate natural language responses, which allows it to be utilised in a wide range of applications, from data analysis to content creation. We wonder what the impact of ChatGPT and other Generative AI have on work, as well as its limitations and potential future implications.

In other words, is Generative AI our new teacher at school or a new colleague at work?

Text-Based and Graphics Work and Jobs

Due to its ability to generate high-quality text quickly, tasks such as report writing, content development, literature research, note-taking and images are completed within a fraction of the time taken by a human. While the output may not be perfect, the output is usually sufficient for the professional to make quick edits for submission. This has led to an increase in productivity for professionals in a variety of fields, including marketing, journalism and academia.

Similarly, ChatGPT is able to parse large amounts of textual data and images quickly and effectively, making it useful for tasks such as data churning and analysis. For example, identifying precedents by poring over past legal cases or reviewing numerous journal articles on a specific topic are tasks of the past. These tasks can now be taken over by ChatGPT and professionals in fields such as finance, law and healthcare will now only need to review the outputs to ensure accuracy, edit the text and send it to their recipients. What used to take hours or days to painstakingly perform will now take minutes.

Education

If you are an educator or a student, practitioners in the industry have raised concerns that ChatGPT may promote plagiarism. Students will find it highly useful to generate first drafts of reports and essays quickly, but academic integrity and authenticity of the assessment evidence will be questionable. The question of responsibility for aiding plagiarism may not be answered but ultimately the student needs to decide if his work reflects his or her true ability, and the institution will need to put out guidelines and rules to clarify the boundaries to the use of ChatGPT.

Assessing Students in Spite of AI

What ChatGPT will mean for students and adult learners is that leveraging ChatGPT to work more efficiently will be the norm going forward. It will also mean that skills such as report-writing and data churning may become less valued and the ability to think responsively and work in teams will be valued more. Being able to evaluate ChatGPT's outputs to ensure accuracy and relevance is a critical competency that the workforce will need to have.

Error-Based Learning is one of the approaches that can drive the development of responsive thinking and social skills. It is also typically phased (i.e. dynamic inputs) which meant that learners often need to adapt to ever changing parameters, reflecting a level of authenticity found in our working environment. Being able to evaluate ChatGPT's outputs for errors and omission is exactly what the DELETE approach is designed to do, in training learners to identify errors.

The Road Ahead

Looking to the future, ChatGPT will have an outsized impact on the way people learn and work. Its ability to generate natural language responses make it a versatile tool to perform a wide range of tasks. As it is, the technology impacts numerous areas such as education, marketing, management, accounting, healthcare, engineering and law and with this impact, the nature of work has changed for many of the professionals operating in these fields. We need to review how to transit these professionals into tasks which require higher order skills (e.g. metacognition, research and innovation) and correspondingly, the type of training our young are receiving. Certain tedious tasks (e.g. interpreting data, graphs, report-writing and literature searches) may become less relevant at work and so, will need to be downplayed or reduced as part of academic training.

It was 9 March 2016 on the sixth floor of the Four Seasons hotel in Seoul. Sitting opposite a Go board and a fierce competitor in the deep blue room, one of the best human Go players on the planet was up against the AI algorithm AlphaGo.

Before the board game started, everyone had expected the human player to win, and until the 37th move, this was indeed the case. But then AlphaGo did something unexpected — it played a move so out-of-your-mind weird, its opponent thought it was a mistake. Nevertheless, from that moment the human player's luck turned, and AlphaGo won the game, and the rest is history.

In the future, AI may also be able to generate unforeseen responses, which may lead to human errors (see story in textbox). When training with AI, these unpredictable moves leading to human errors can be useful to prepare humans for contexts and workflows, which may not be familiar or are outside the boundaries. Evaluating the outputs from the AI will be an important competency for all workers.

Chapter 33

AI such as ChatGPT is only at the start of its journey. We as individuals and the organisations that we work in will do well to leverage and master the technology for productive work. This will maintain our competitiveness in a world with an uneven playing field, where ChatGPT and its like, will separate the sheep from the goats.

Final Word

The advent of advanced AI and the transforming job landscape will pose challenges to the learning and development space. One of the key areas that educators need to be mindful of is that as work changes, the training programmes will also need to change accordingly. Beyond writing reports or creating new images, workers will need to evaluate work outputs by AI and edit to fit their work needs. This capability to identify issues (or errors) and edit them will be a key skill going forward, for all workers. Designing Errors for Learning and Teaching (DELETE) will be one approach that practitioners and experts can fast track the learning process of novices and beginners in the field so that they can level up quickly and take on higher order competences for effective work performance in the AI-infused work environments. We have to work fast so that we can right-level the learning for our learners. Let's push on together.

Before God we are equally wise and equally foolish.

Albert Einstein

References

Ackerman, C. E. (2018). *Learned Helplessness: Seligman's Theory of Depression*. PositivePsychology.com. Retrieved 22 May 2023, from https://positivepsychology.com/learned-helplessness-seligman-theory-depression-cure/.

Bandura, A. (1986). *Social Foundations of Thought and Action: A Social Cognitive Theory*. Upper Saddle River, NJ: Prentice Hall.

Barrero, J. M., Bloom, N., & Davis, S. J. (Dec 2021). Why working from home will stick. *National Bureau of Economic Research Working Paper 28731* … Retrieved on 26 Dec 2022 from: https://wfhresearch.com/wp-content/uploads/2021/12/WFHResearch_updates_December2021.pdf

Bedny, G., & Meister, D. (1999). Theory of activity and situation awareness. *International Journal of Cognitive Ergonomics, 3*(1), 63–72.

Billett, S. (2001). Learning through work: Workplace affordances and individual engagement. *Journal of Workplace Learning, 13*(5), 209–214.

Billett, S. (2004). Workplace participatory practices: Conceptualising workplaces as learning environments. *Journal of Workplace Learning, 16*(6), 312–324. Retrieved on 28 Jan 2013 from: http://www98.griffith.edu.au/dspace/bitstream/handle/10072/5128/BostonconfernceJWL.pdf?sequence=1

Brookfield, S. (1995). *Becoming a Critically Reflective Teacher*. San Francisco, CA: Jossey-Bass.

Carayon P. (2012). Emerging Role of Human Factors and Ergonomics in Healthcare Delivery — A New Field of Application and Influence for the IEA. Work, *41*(01), 5037–40. doi: 10.3233/WOR-2012-0096-5037.

Choy, M. (Dec 2002). Learning to learn. *Harvest Times*, CHC, Singapore.

References

Choy, M., Ong, R., Alliangan, M., & Lui, T. (2021). Designing nano learning™ loops within chatbot conversations for effective learning. *UNESCO APAC Conference Proceedings Paper*, 22 Sept 2021.

Dave, R. H. (1970). Psychomotor Levels. In Robert J. Armstrong (Ed.), *Developing and Writing Behavioral Objectives*. Tucson AZ: Educational Innovators Press.

Deloitte (2014). *Global Human Capital Trends 2014*. Retrieved on 20 May 2023 from: https://www2.deloitte.com/us/en/insights/focus/human-capital-trends/2014.html.

Dreyfus, S. E. (2004). The five-stage model of adult skill acquisition. *Bulletin of Science Technology & Society, 24*, 177. Retrieved on 21 Oct 2014 from: http://www.bumc.bu.edu/facdev-medicine/files/2012/03/Dreyfus-skill-level.pdf

Dweck, C. S. (1975). The role of expectations and attributions in the alleviation of learned helplessness. *Journal of Personality and Social Psychology, 31*(4), 674.

Dweck, C. S. (2006). *Mindset: The New Psychology of Success.* New York: Random House Publishing Group.

Endsley, M. (1988). Design and evaluation for situational awareness enhancement. *Proceedings of the Human Factors Society 32nd Annual Meeting* (pp. 97–101). Santa Monica, CA: HFES.

Endsley, M. R., & Kiris, E. O. (1995). The out of the loop performance problem and level of control in automation. *Human Factors, 37*(2), 381–394.

Feltovitch, P. J., Prietula, M. J., & Ericsson, K. A. (2006). Studies of expertise from psychological perspectives. In K. A. Ericsson, N. Charness, R. R. Hoffman, & P. J. Feltovitch (Eds.), *Cambridge Handbook of Expertise and Expert Performance* (pp. 41–68). Cambridge: Cambridge University Press.

Fischer, M. A., Mazor, K. M., Baril, J., Alper, E., DeMarco, D., & Pugnaire, M. (2006). Learning from mistakes: Factors that influence how students and residents learn from medical errors. *Journal of General Internal Medicine, 21*, 419–423.

Flavell, J. H. (1979). Metacognition and cognitive monitoring: A new area of cognitive-developmental inquiry. *American Psychologist, 34,* 906–911.

Flavell, J. H. (1987). Speculations about the nature and development of metacognition. In F. E. Weinert & R. H. Kluwe (Eds.), *Metacognition, Motivation and Understanding* (pp. 21–29). Hillside, NJ: Lawrence Erlbaum Associates.

References

Fox, K. C. R., & Christoff, K. (2014). Metacognitive facilitation of spontaneous thought processes: When metacognition helps the wandering mind find its way. In S. M. Fleming & C. D. Frith (Eds.), *The Cognitive Neuroscience of Metacognition* (pp. 293–319). Springer-Verlag Berlin Heidelberg. Retrieved on 15 Mar 2015 from: http://link.springer.com/chapter/10.1007/978-3-642-45190-4_13

Frese, M., & Altmann, A. (1989). The treatment of errors. In L. Bainbridge & S. A. Quintanilla (Eds.), *Developing Skills with Information Technology* (pp. 65–86). Chichester, UK: Wiley & Sons.

Gaba D. M. (2000). Anaesthesiology as a model for patient safety in health care. *BMJ, 320*(7237), 785–788.

Gaba, D. M., Howard, S. K., & Small, S. D. (1995). Situation awareness in anaesthesiology. *Human Factors, 37*(1), 20–31.

Gharajedaghi, J. (2011). *Systems Thinking: Managing Chaos and Complexity, A Platform for Designing Business Architecture*, Third Edition. Elsevier, Morgan Kaufman.

Hart, A. (1986). *Knowledge Acquisition for Expert Systems.* New York: McGraw-Hill.

HR News (Feb 2022). The 5 trends in learning and development. Retrieved on 2022 Dec 26 from: https://hrnews.co.uk/learning-and-development-trends-in-2022/

Institute of Medicine (1999). *To err is human: Building a safer health system.* Retrieved on 21 May 2023 from: https://nap.nationalacademies.org/resource/9728/To-Err-is-Human-1999--report-brief.pdf

Illeris, K. (2002). *The three dimensions of learning: Contemporary learning theory in the tension field between the cognitive, the emotional and the social.* Leicester: NIACE. Malabar: Krieger.

Illeris, K. (2008). *Learning, work and competence development.* Retrieved on 30 Jun 2009 from: http://www.saqa.org.za/docs/events/illeris_paper08.pdf

Jørgensen, P. S. (1999). Hvad er Kompetence? *Uddannelse, 9*, 4–13. [What Is Competence?].

Kanki, B., Helmreich, R., & Anca, J. (2010). *Crew Resource Management.* San Diego, CA: Academic.

Keith, N., & Frese, M. (2008). Effectiveness of error management training: A meta-analysis. *Journal of Applied Psychology, 93*(1), 59–69.

Kellenberg, F., Schmidt, J., & Werner, C. (2017). The adult learner: Self-determined, self-regulated, and reflective. *Signum Temporis, 9*(1), 23–29.

Krathwohl, D. R., Bloom, B. S., & Masia, B. B. (1964). *Taxonomy of Educational Objectives: The Classification of Educational Goals. Handbook II: Affective Domain.* New York: David McKay Company University of Mississippi School of Education.

Land, R., Cousin, G., Meyer, J. H. F., & Davies, P. (2005). Threshold concepts and troublesome knowledge (3): Implications for course design and evaluation. In C. Rust (Ed.), *Improving Student Learning — Equality and Diversity.* Oxford: OCSLD.

Lave, J., & Wenger, E. (1991). *Situated Learning: Legitimate Peripheral Participation.* New York: Cambridge University Press. https://doi.org/10.1017/CBO9780511815355

Livingston, L. (u.d.). *Metacognition: An overview.* Retrieved on 7 Apr 2015 from: http://gse.buffalo.edu/fas/shuell/cep564/metacog.htm

Manser T. (2009). Teamwork and patient safety in dynamic domains of healthcare: A review of the literature. *Acta Anaesthesiologica Scandinavica, 53*(2): 143–51.

Marr, B. (2022). *The five biggest education and training technology trends in 2022.* Retrieved on 26 Dec 2022 from: https://www.forbes.com/sites/bernardmarr/2022/02/18/the-five-biggest-education-and-training-technology-trends-in-2022/?sh=2d790b4a2f4d

Martin, T. A., Keating, J. G., Goodkin, H. P., Bastian, A. J., & Thach, W. T. (1996). Throwing while looking through prisms: I. Focal olivocerebellar lesions impair adaptation. *Brain, 119,* 1183–1198.

Meadows, D. (2008). *Thinking in Systems: A Primer.* White River Junction, VT: Chelsea Green Publishing.

Meyer, J. H. F., & Land, R. (2006). *Overcoming Barriers to Student Understanding: Threshold Concepts and Troublesome Knowledge.* London and New York: Routledge.

OwlLabs (Sept 2021). *State of remote work.* Retrieved on 3 Jan 2023 from: https://owllabs.com/state-of-remote-work/2021/

Ownsworth, T., Fleming, J., Tate, R., Shum, D., Griffin, J., Schmidt, J., Lane-Brown, A., Kendall, M., & Chevignard, M. (2013). Comparison of error-based and errorless learning for people with severe traumatic brain injury: Study protocol for a randomized control trial. *Trials, 14,* 369. Retrieved on 28 Jun 2014 from: http://www.trialsjournal.com/content/14/1/369.

Piaget, J. (1959). *The Language and Thought of the Child (Vol. 5)*. London & New York: Psychology Press.

Pedersen, S. A. (1988). Modelling the background of knowledge and belief In L. P. Goodstein, H. B. Andersen, & S. E. Olsen (Eds.), *Tasks, Errors and Mental Models.* London: Taylor & Francis.

Reason, J. (1990). *Human Error.* New York: Cambridge University Press.

Richland, L., Kornell, N., & Kao, L. (2009). The pretesting effect: Do unsuccessful retrieval attempts enhance learning? *Journal of Experimental Psychology: Applied, 15*(3), 243–257.

Salant, Y., & Spenkuch, J. L. (2022). *Complexity and choice.* Retrieved on 20 Dec 2022 from: https://ssrn.com/abstract=3878469 or http://dx.doi.org/10.2139/ssrn.3878469

Salas, E., Tannenbaum, S. I., Kraiger, K., & Smith-Jentsch, K. A. (2012). The science of training and development in organizations: What matters in practice. *Psychological Science in the Public Interest, 13*(2), 74–101.

Salomon, G., & Perkins, D. N. (1998). Individual and Social Aspects of Learning. *Review of Research in Education, 23,* 1–24.

Schoenfeld, A. H. (1992). Learning to think mathematically: Problem solving, metacognition, and sense making in mathematics. In D. A. Grouws (Ed.), *Handbook of research on mathematics teaching and learning: A project of the National Council of Teachers of Mathematics* (pp. 334–370). Macmillan Publishing Co, Inc.

Seligman, M. E. (1972). Learned helplessness. *Annual Review of Medicine, 23*(1), 407–412.

Sennet, R. (2008). *The Craftsman.* London: Yale University Press.

Skinner, B. F. (1953). *Science and Human Behavior.* New York: Macmillan.

Smith, K., & Hancock, P. A. (1995). Situation awareness is adaptive, externally directed consciousness. *Human Factors, 37*(1), 137–148.

Stanton, N. A., Chambers, P. R. G., & Piggott, J. (2001). Situational awareness and safety. *Safety Science, 39,* 189–204.

ten Berge, T., & van Hezewijk, R. (1999). Procedural and declarative knowledge: An evolutionary perspective. *Theory & Psychology, 9*(5), 605–624. https://doi.org/10.1177/0959354399095002

Tetlock, P. E. (2005). *Expert Political Judgment: How Good Is It? How Can We Know?* Princeton, NJ: Princeton University Press.

Tobler, P. N., O'Doherty, J. P., Dolan, R. J., & Schultz, W. (2006). Human neural learning depends on reward prediction errors in the blocking paradigm. *Journal of Neurophysiology, 95*(1), 301–310.

Vygotsky, L. S. (1978). *Mind in Society: The Development of Higher Psychological Processes*. Cambridge, MA: Harvard University Press.

Wilson, D., Perkins, D. N., Bonnet, D., Miani, C., & Unger, C. (2005). *Learning at Work: Research Lessons on Leading Learning in the Workplace*. Cambridge, MA: Presidents and Fellows of Harvard College.

Zimmerman, M. A. (1990). Toward a theory of learned hopefulness: A structural model analysis of participation and empowerment. *Journal of Research in Personality, 24*(1), 71–86.

Annex A
Lesson Design Template for the DELETE Approach

Learner Profile
- *Cognitive*
- *Emotion*
- *Sociality*

Content Characteristics
- *Cognitive*
- *Affective*
- *Psychomotor*
- *Social*

Delivery Mode
- *Classroom*
- *Workplace*
- *Online*
- *Blended*

Annex A

DELETE Stage	Parameter	Remarks
1. ERROR ANALYSIS		
Key Skill/Knowledge		
Difficult Concepts		
Procedural/Declarative*		
Procedural/Declarative*		
Procedural/Declarative*		
Are the Errors Made by Learners		
Common/Critical/Clear*		
Common/Critical/Clear*		
Common/Critical/Clear*		
These Errors are Errors of		
Commission/Omission*		
Commission/Omission*		
Commission/Omission*		
2. ERROR DESIGN		
Domain/Level		
Cognitive		
Psychomotor		
Affective		
Social		
Metacognitive		
3. ERROR REFINEMENT		
Domain		
Level		
	TASK	
4. TASK DESIGN		
Domain		
Level		

Lesson Design Template for the DELETE Approach

DELETE Stage	Parameter	Remarks
Expected Metacognitive Processes		
Task (State Question/Activity)		
	PROCESS	
5. ENGAGEMENT PROCESS		
• Error Presentation	Complete Partially — Dynamic or Static Fully — Dynamic or Static Absent	
• Peer Reflection and Planning		
• Task Engagement (e.g. DELETE E^3 Learning Cycle)		
• Theorisation and Re-Feeding		
• Re-experimentation		
	SUPPORT	
6. SUPPORT		
• Social		
• Instructional (e.g. hint)		
• Feedback		
• Resources		

Annex B
Notes and Models

A) **The DELETE Approach: Four Parameters**

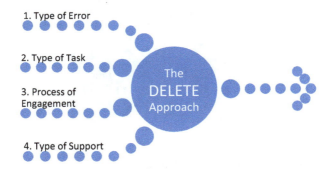

B) **The Engagement and Learning Process**

Annex B

C) The DELETE E³ Learning Cycle

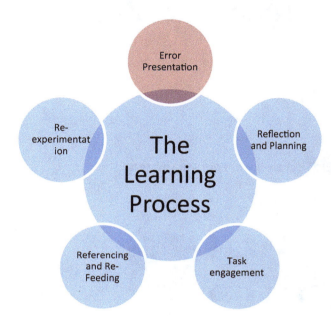

Process of Designing Errors for Learning
The DELETE Design

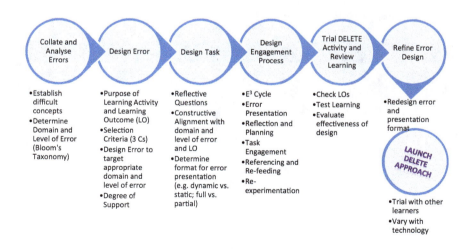

Index

21st-century competencies, 278

activity approach, 23
adaptability, 210, 300, 322, 358, 396
adaptive, 54, 342
adaptive behaviour, 343
adaptive thinking, 277
ADDIE, 331
Advanced Beginner, 25, 30
affective, 89, 190, 279, 283, 311
affordances, 54, 55, 107, 218
agency, 79
ambiguity, 59, 62
ambiguous, 302
artificial intelligence (AI), 46, 141, 219, 248, 321, 327, 344, 409, 417, 419, 420, 422
assessment, 77, 79
assumption, 26, 56, 57, 76, 77, 79, 108, 109, 127, 131, 140, 143, 147, 150, 160, 161, 171, 219, 239, 293, 319, 348, 371, 374, 390, 415, 416
assumption checking, 344
atmosphere, 36, 38, 49, 88
attention levels, 14
Augmented Reality (AR), 46
automation, 46

benchmark, 5
Bloom's Taxonomy, 101, 102, 117, 118, 171, 182, 205, 399
boundaries, xv, 6, 21, 29, 30, 64, 65, 80, 302, 325, 341, 352
Boundary-Crossing Errors, 9
Brookfield, Stephen, 109

ChatGPT, 42, 46, 419, 420
Choy, 35, 46
Clarity of error, 172, 195
Cognition, 40, 49, 205, 206, 223, 229, 283, 297, 332
cognitive, 19, 20, 76, 119, 150, 177, 186, 212, 219, 223, 235, 249, 254, 257, 259, 311, 394, 396
cognitive assimilation, 15
cognitive dissonance, 20
cognitive impairment, 19
collaborative, 38, 267
Commission, 182, 193
Commonness of error, 172, 196
compensate, 16
competence, 54, 56, 180, 205, 228, 277, 334, 380
competency, 132, 248
competent, 26, 29, 30, 62, 261

435

Index

complex, 52, 302
complexity, xiv, 62
consequence, 4, 7, 97, 288, 292, 300, 303, 326, 336
constructive alignment, 73
constructivist, 71, 77
context, 6, 7, 9, 65, 67–69, 265, 288, 293, 297, 306, 325, 335, 348, 393
contextual boundaries, 64–68, 77, 79, 415, 416
contiguity, 97
contingencies, 30
control, 19
Coursera, 45
creatical, 139, 156, 159, 230, 232, 233, 277, 301, 343, 354, 356, 394
critical gaps, 343
Criticality, Clarity and Commonness, 193
Criticality of error, 172, 194
critical reflection, xv
curriculum design, 73–75, 83
curriculum model, 74, 76

declarative, 64, 101, 193, 224
Declarative errors, 182
declarative knowledge, 167, 171, 183, 185
Degree of Support, 107
desirability, 4
deviation, 4, 17
diagnose skill gaps, 283, 324, 333
Differentiated curriculum, 81
difficult concept, 167–169, 224, 226
disposition, 55
Dreyfus, 25, 26, 54, 57, 379
Dweck, Carol, 5, 18
dynamic, 136, 288, 289, 295, 298, 306, 312, 315, 317, 325
dynamism, 289, 291, 301, 313, 327

E^3 Approach, 105
E^3 experiential approach, 105
ecological approach, 23
EdX, 45
Emotion, 40, 49, 205, 206, 249, 333, 416
emotional, 279, 305, 384, 399
emotional quotient, 278
Endsley, 24
Engagement and Experimentation cycle, 145
Engagement and Experimentation (E^3) Learning Cycle, 134
Engagement Process, 103, 144
error analysis, 224
error correction, 115
Error Engagement and Experimentation (3Es) Cycle, 104, 328, 330
Error Engagement and Experimentation (E^3) Learning Cycle, 141, 257
error-free, xiv
error identification, 330, 344
errorless, 19, 21, 23, 26
errorless learning, 21
Error-Making and Learning Processes, 93, 118
error phase, 90
error presentation, 104, 134, 139, 141, 144, 148, 149, 154, 157, 285, 337
Error Presentation, Engagement and Experimentation (E^3) Learning Cycle, 147
Error Presentation Process, 135
Error Refinement, 331
error scenarios, xv
Errors of Commission, 191, 192

Index

errors of omission, 191, 192
error task, 163
expectation, 3–5, 7
experience, 10
Experiential Learning Cycle, 104
Experiential Learning Model, 97
experimentation, 283
expert, 25–27, 30, 57, 62, 80, 178, 204, 379
expertise, 20, 24, 29, 49, 53, 59, 61, 72
exploratory trial and error, xv

feedback, 178, 267, 269
First Follower effect, 161
first followers, 162
first principles, vi, xv, 11, 69, 77, 78, 80, 81, 282, 415, 416

Gagne's nine Events of Instruction, 97, 105, 177
Game Theory, 155
global perspective-taking, 302
graduate profile, 77
Group think, 160
growth mindset, 5

holistic, 275, 277, 278, 284, 321, 323, 333, 372, 392
Holistic Development, 205, 206

identification, 373
Illeris, 33, 40, 54
Innovates, 30
innovation, 61
Institutional Knowledge, 372
instructional design, 54, 55, 73–76, 80, 97, 163, 335, 399, 401
instructivist, 55

integrate, 283
Integrate Skillsets, 321
intended action, 7
intention, 4
Intentional Error Design, 415
intentionality, 361
interjections of errors, 93
Interpersonal, 267

Knowles, Malcolm, 401
Knowles' Self-Directed Learning Theory, 400
Kolb, David, 104
Kolb's experiential learning cycle, 264
Kolb's Experiential Learning Theory, 176

lapses, 4, 63
learned helplessness, 17, 18
learned hopefulness, 18
learner agency, 14, 48
Learner-Centric Design, 332
learner support, 137
Learning, 49
Learning, Atmosphere, Mind and Production model (LAMP), 33–36, 39, 48, 49
learning design, 55, 62
learning designers, 31
learning pipes, 35, 38, 89
long-term memory, 214

Massive Open Online Courses, 45
mastery, 6, 96
mental algorithm, 22
metacognition, 11, 21, 27, 69, 88, 107, 205, 206, 210, 219, 279, 284, 291, 293, 332, 345, 416

Index

metacognitive, 65, 89, 95, 96, 115, 119, 156, 159, 180, 187, 207, 209, 212, 216, 229, 232, 248, 260–263, 277, 282, 311, 376, 379, 381, 385, 392, 409
metacognitive awareness, 27, 76
metacognitive capability, 20, 80
metacognitive knowledge, 209
metacognitive regulation, 209, 211, 263
Mind, 49, 88
mindful, 91, 213, 214, 228, 229, 271
mindfulness, 52, 62, 212, 215, 216, 218, 219, 269, 293, 371, 379
mistakes, 4, 63
motivated, 413
motivation, 132, 176, 254, 273, 317, 342, 343

Nano-learning, 46, 48
nano-learning cycle, 33, 46, 103
Nano Learning™ Loop, 47
negative transfer, 65, 66, 143
non-performance, 8
Not-To-Do rule, 64, 65
novice, 20, 24–27, 29, 30, 56–58, 261, 262
novice-expert, 63

Omission, 193
Omission errors, 182
Ownsworth, 26

partial, 312
pattern, 17
pedagogical beliefs, 78
Pedersen, 24
personalise, 342
perspective-taking, 239, 302, 303

Piaget, 34
point of intervention, 92
Points of Interjection, 92
post-error, 89, 92, 95, 133, 336
post-error phase, 90, 283, 322
Praxis, 75
predictability, xv
pre-error, 89, 95, 133, 322, 336
pre-error phase, 90, 92
Presentation of Errors, 241
procedural, 64, 171, 182, 193, 224
Procedural Knowledge, 167, 184, 185
Process, 75
product, 75, 76
production, 36
production pipes, 35, 38
professional beliefs, 83
professional identity, 78
proficient, 29, 30
psychomotor, 124, 188, 205, 206, 259, 260, 263, 277, 283, 311, 314, 333, 369, 392
punishment, xiv
Purpose-Driven Error Design, 332
Purposive Learning, 405

Reason, 62, 63, 131
rectification, 140, 149, 243, 263, 288, 292, 300, 306, 315, 318, 326, 330, 337, 373
rectification of errors, 92
rectify, 4
re-experimentation, 151, 155, 159, 394, 399
re-feeding, 145
reference point, 5
referencing, 394, 398
Referencing and Re-feeding, 144, 151, 155, 158

Index

reflection, 65, 263, 282, 287, 318, 327, 336, 360
Reflection and Planning, 154, 157
reflective, 77
reflective practice, 218, 219
reflexivity, 259, 298, 313, 367, 368
reinforcement, 20
relearning, 68, 69
resilience, 76, 106, 107, 248, 249, 253–255, 278, 307, 364
Romiskowski's Psychomotor Theory, 105
rules, 69

satisficing, 28, 29
scaffolded, 30
Schoenfeld, Alan, 27
self-determination, 44
self-internalise, 22
self-regulation, 44
Sennet, Richard, 58, 59, 321
situational awareness, 22–24
skillset integration, 277
skillsets, 283
slips, xiv, 4, 63
social, 267, 274
social interactional process, 40
sociality, 40, 41, 49, 125, 159, 205, 206, 267, 283, 315, 317, 327, 333, 369, 396
Standard Operating Procedures (SOPs), 16, 52, 57, 64, 153, 220, 264, 288, 293, 342, 351, 352, 391, 415
static, 288, 295, 297, 325

Syllabus, 75
systems thinking, 239

task engagement, 143, 150, 154, 158, 330
Three Dimensions of Learning model (TDLM), 33, 39–41, 48, 49
threshold concepts, 168
Tobler, 58
To-Do rules, 64, 65
trial and error approaches, 63
trial-and-error learning, 19
Type of Errors, 100
Type of Support, 106, 177
Type of Tasks, 102
Types of Support, 162

Udemy, 45
uncertain, 302
uncommon, 352
uncommon mistakes, 375
unpredictability, 57, 58, 61, 62, 138
unpredictable, 52, 239

variability, 8, 62
virtual reality (VR), 46, 324
Visibility, 289, 291, 327
Visual–Tactile producers, 35
volatile, vi, 25, 302
VUCA, 15, 16, 41, 44, 48, 53, 65, 250, 284, 344, 358
Vygotsky, 34

workflow, 288, 297, 298, 306, 317, 325, 337

Printed in the USA
CPSIA information can be obtained
at www.ICGtesting.com
JSHW052318021023
49296JS00014B/5